FINAN...... ...G
C......

• •

Paper 9
Management Accounting Techniques

CIMA

Revision Pack

Stage 3

Published December 1993 by the Financial Training Company
136–142 Bramley Road, London W10 6SR

Copyright © 1993 The Financial Training Company Limited

ISBN 1 85179 592 8

Printed in England by Communications In Print plc, Basildon, Essex.

37653

Contents

* * * * *

Introduction

THE FINANCIAL TRAINING COMPANY

The Financial Training Company is one of the UK's leading providers of training for those employed in the financial and accountancy sectors, legal profession, the City, commerce and industry. It is a subsidiary of a very successful Dutch publishing company, Wolters Kluwer. Financial Training was established in 1958 and has been involved in providing training for the CIMA exams for over ten years.

As well as running *open learning* programmes, the Financial Training Company also supplies study materials such as this Revision Pack for use on other courses.

QUALITY PUBLICATIONS

At the Financial Training Company, we invest considerable resources in our publishing activities. All our CIMA texts are tailored specifically towards the CIMA syllabus. Our Revision Packs are prepared and edited by our own tutors and in-house authors, all of whom are highly skilled professionals who are either qualified accountants or specialists in their field. Between them they have a wide range of experience of working in accounting practice, industry and commerce. In addition, we have large editorial and production departments dedicated to producing quality publications.

New style, new contents

As well as introducing a new logo and cover design, we have also changed the style of our texts. You will notice improvements in both (i) the layouts and (ii) the charts and diagrams.

Constantly changing

As you know, the business world is moving faster and faster each year. To keep you up to date with changes, we publish our Revision Packs annually.

THE REVISION PACK

This Revision Pack will provide you with sufficient question practice to ensure confidence in the exam. The aim is to cover all areas of the syllabus and give a balanced range of questions, most of which are taken from recent exam papers.

Questions

Attempt questions without reference to your notes and time yourself strictly.

Answers

The model answers are there to help you; learn from their structure and content and check your answers against them carefully.

Mock exam

You should complete your revision programme by attempting the mock exam *under exam conditions*. This should provide you with an excellent opportunity to practise your exam technique.

STUDENTS ENROLLING ON REVISION COURSES

This Revision Pack provides the material for the revision course.
Students enrolling on these courses should not use the questions in
this Revision Pack before attending the course.

Syllabus

AIMS

To test the candidate's ability to:

(a)   use management accounting, statistical and quantitative techniques at an advanced level;

(b)   apply these to the production and presentation of management information for planning, decision-making and control;

(c)   understand the strengths and limitations of any technique used.

KNOWLEDGE LEVELS

In the syllabus each topic has been given a number from 1 to 4 to indicate the level of ability required of the candidate.

Ranking for syllabus topics

Appreciation

To understand a knowledge area at an early stage of learning, or outside the core of management accounting, at a level which enables the accountant to communicate and work with other members of the management team.

1

Knowledge

To advise on such matters as laws, standards, facts and techniques at a level of detail appropriate to a management accounting specialist.

2

Skill

To apply theoretical knowledge, concepts and techniques to the solution of problems where it is clear what technique has to be used and the information needed is clearly indicated.

3

Application

To apply knowledge and skills where candidates have to determine from a number of techniques which is the most appropriate and select the information required from a fairly wide range of data, some of which might not be relevant; to exercise professional judgement and to communicate and work with members of the management team and other recipients of financial reports.

4

STUDY WEIGHTINGS

A percentage weighting is shown against each topic in the syllabus; this is intended as a *guide* to the amount of study time each topic requires.

All topics in a syllabus must be studied, as a question may examine more than one topic or carry a higher proportion of marks than the percentage study time suggested.

The weightings *do not* specify the number of marks which will be allocated to topics in the examination.

CONTENT

* * * * *

Note: All questions in this Revision Pack have been cross referenced to the relevant section of the syllabus. If there is a section of the syllabus without a specific question or questions allocated to it, you should assume that the examiner is unlikely to set a question *solely* on that particular area, although the topic may be tested as background knowledge in parts of other questions.

* * * * *

		Ability required	*Question reference*
1	**Information systems** (Weighting 10%)		
	Information flows for accounting purposes; feedback, feed-forward control systems; financial modelling and simulation	4	5.12
	Use of computers and data processing; non-accounting systems; derivation of financial information	4	11.1
2	**Quantitative applications** (Weighting 35%)		
	Budgeting using probability	3	5.5, 5.6, 5.8
	Project planning using network analysis	3	7.1-7.4
	Decision-making with decision trees	3	5.4, 5.9
	Ascertaining relationships between variables using simple and multiple regression and correlation	3	2.1, 2.2
	Significance testing: meaning and use of results of t-test, F-test and chi-squared test	3	8.1-8.4
	Business modelling using a linear programming including understanding simplex tableaux sensitivity	3	6.1-6.3

GUIDANCE NOTES

The following guidelines have been drafted by the chief examiner for this subject. They are intended to inform students about the scope of the syllabus, the emphasis to be placed on certain topics and the approach examination questions will adopt.

In addition to the aims mentioned in the syllabus, this subject is intended to build upon the knowledge gained in earlier stages, especially from Quantitative Methods and Cost Accounting, in preparation for the four Management Accounting papers in Stage 4. The integration of quantitative methods and management accounting in the one syllabus seeks to break down any artificial barriers which may be thought to exist between the subjects. In this way it is hoped that, in practice, the management accountant will be better able to draw upon the most appropriate technique or concept from whatever its source and thus produce more relevant management information.

In accordance with the aims in the syllabus and those above, the paper will:

(i)   require students to have detailed knowledge of the various techniques and concepts and to be able to apply them to practical problems, especially those concerning planning, decision-making and control;

(ii)   require students to comment on, criticise, and analyse the information obtained using conventional techniques – students will be expected to know the limitations of, and difficulties associated with, the implementations of any technique they use;

(iii)   include questions combining topics from several areas of the syllabus. For example, the use of probability, statistical concepts, sensitivity analysis and other such topics could occur in questions that are predominantly accounting in nature. Similarly, management accounting principles could be found in predominantly operational research questions. As a consequence of this a sound understanding of principles is vital.

1 Information systems (weighting 10%)

The emphasis in this section will be on the use and application of computers and packages, not on the design of computer systems. In particular, students will be expected to know when and how to use computers and software to improve the quality of management information. Students will be expected to be able to interpret computer-produced results and to be aware of the problems associated with the use of particularly relevant packages, eg. spreadsheets, modelling packages, linear programming, network analysis and so on.

No questions will be asked on computer hardware but it will be assumed that students have the level of knowledge specified in the syllabus for Information Technology Management at Stage 2.

2 Quantitative applications (weighting 35%)

Students are reminded that this section develops the knowledge gained in the Stage 1 paper Quantitative Methods and assumes that students are able to use the basic statistical and mathematical principles covered in that paper. This means that questions could cover topics included in Quantitative Methods but not specifically mentioned in the MAT syllabus. A sound knowledge of foundation statistical principles is required, including the properties and applications of the main distributions, ie. Normal, binomial, Poisson, chi-squared and so on.

The following is an expansion of the brief statements contained in the syllabus.

(a) **Budgeting and probability**

Detailed knowledge of the application of continuous and discrete probabilities to budgets is required. This includes expected values, joint and conditional probabilities and the use of appropriate statistical distributions and measures.

(b) **Project planning using network analysis**

This includes critical path planning, least cost scheduling, the treatment of uncertainty using probabilistic and statistical analysis, the calculation of various floats and the use of computers for network analysis.

(c) **Decision-making with decision trees**

This includes the treatment of probabilities including expected value and Bayesian, the drawing and evaluation of decision trees, discounting, pay-off tables, decision rules such as maximin, maximax, etc, the value of perfect and imperfect information.

(d) **Ascertaining relationships between variables using simple and multiple regression and correlation**

This includes the calculation and interpretation of the coefficients of correlation and determination, a simple regression using various methods including least squares, assessing the accuracy of the regression line, understanding and interpreting multiple regression. Students will not be required to calculate multiple regression coefficients.

(e) **Significance testing: meaning and use of results of t-test, F-test and chi-squared test**

This includes the use and meaning of significance testing, type I and II errors, one and two-tailed tests, using the common distributions (Normal, t, chi-squared, F, etc), choice of significance levels, the use of significance testing in decision-making.

(f) **Business modelling using linear programming including understanding simplex tableaux and sensitivity**

This section includes the principles of mathematical modelling, the formulation, solution and interpretation of LP models using graphical and simplex methods, the calculation and interpretation of shadow prices, sensitivity analysis, dual formations. Integer and dynamic programming is not included.

(g) **Business modelling using simulation**

This section requires a knowledge of the role and purpose of simulation, typical application areas, the ability to formulate, manipulate and interpret a simple simulation, the treatment of uncertainty, the role of computers in simulation.

(h) **Determining service levels using queuing theory**

This section includes the relationship of queuing theory to service costs and decision-making, the characteristics of simple queues, single and multi-channel systems, the problems in applying queuing theory. Students will not be expected to memorise the formulae for multi-channel systems.

Note: The emphasis in the examination paper will be on the use of the above techniques in accounting problems, concentrating on how these techniques improve planning, decision-making and control as well as on the ability to carry out calculations. Mark allocation will reflect this.

3 Marginal costing (weighting 15%)

This section requires a detailed knowledge of all aspects of marginal costing and breakeven analysis especially in relation to planning and decision-making. The relationship to economic theory must be understood especially with regard to cost, demand and other influences on pricing. A knowledge of differential calculus is required but not partial differentiation.

Thorough understanding of learning curve theory is required, including the calculation of the learning coefficient and how to apply learning curve theory in standard costing, budgeting and decision-making.

A detailed knowledge is required of common costs including identification, methods of sharing, problems of control, use in decision-making and performance appraisal.

4 Standard costing (weighting 15%)

A thorough understanding is required of all aspects of standard costing, including a knowledge of all types of standard, the calculation and interpretation of all variances, dealing with inflation and uncertainty, planning and operational variances, behavioural aspects, the use of standards for planning and control, bookkeeping for standard costing, the significance of variances and control charts, benefits and deficiencies of standard costing and so on.

5 Budgets and budgetary control (weighting 10%)

Again, a thorough understanding of budgetary planning and budgetary control is required, including the budgeting process and organisation, budget relationships, all types of budgets including cash and working capital, appropriate forecasting methods both short and longer term (eg. regression analysis, moving averages, time series analysis, exponential smoothing, etc.), fixed and flexible budgets, behavioural influences, calculation and interpretation of budget variances, rolling, incremental and zero base budgets, the treatment of inflation and uncertainty.

In addition, an outline knowledge is required of the scope and methods of profit improvement, cost reduction and value analysis. Detailed questions on specific techniques such as work study, and organisation and methods will not be asked, although students are expected to understand the purpose of such techniques.

6 Capital investment appraisal (weighting 15%)

This section includes two areas – investment centres and performance appraisal, and project appraisal using DCF and other methods.

Students will be expected to have a good understanding of the meaning of investment centres, their relationship to cost and profit centres, the measures used for performance appraisal including return on capital employed and residual income, the effect of the various performance measures, and the relationship of performance appraisal and budgeting.

Under the DCF and project appraisal section the emphasis will be on the use and meaning of the main DCF methods (eg. NPV, IRR, NTV, annualised equivalents), comparison with traditional methods such as payback and accounting rate of return, the treatment of inflation and uncertainty (including the use of statistical concepts), the sensitivity of results, capital rationing, simulation and project appraisal.

Note: The cost of capital will always be supplied and there will be no questions on project or company financing, the capital asset pricing model or taxation.

Finally, the student is required to understand the principles of life-cycle costing and its relationship with project appraisal.

The examination

FORMAT OF THE EXAMINATION

The examination is 3 hours long.

Candidates will be required to answer *five* questions out of *eight*. Each question is worth 20 marks.

EXAMINATION TECHNIQUE

Helpful hints

Exam questions may involve interpretation and analysis rather than just 'jumping in at the deep end' and the following should be considered.

(a)   Read the whole question and the requirements very carefully. There may well be a large amount of data, both relevant and irrelevant, to sort out.

(b)   If there are any ambiguities, it is important that you state any assumptions that you make. The examiner has indicated that different interpretations of some questions are both possible and acceptable.

(c)   Present your answer neatly and logically, ensuring that you explain exactly what you are doing.

(d)   Questions may well present you with stylised business environments, so ensure that you relate your answer to the specific problem set. Avoid the common mistake of writing down all you know about a topic when much of it may not be relevant.

(e)   Answer the question in the format it requests. If a report to management is requested, specific marks will be awarded for presenting your answer as a report.

(f)   Make sure that you do not go over the allocated time on any question.

(g)   The examiner's commentary on past examinations shows that he is disappointed with students' ability to think in practical terms. Much credit will be gained by making common-sense points relevant to the question, rather than a great deal of theoretical discussion.

(h)   Remember it is quality not quantity that counts – do not be afraid to think before you write. It is time well spent, not wasted.

ANALYSIS OF RECENT PAPERS

	1991		1992		1993
	May	*Nov*	*May*	*Nov*	*May*
Regression and correlation				•	
Budgetary control					
Cost behaviour	•			•	•
Cash budgets					
Cost control					
Behavioural considerations		•			
Performance measures			•	•	
Standard costing/variances					
Operating statement				•	
Planning/operational		•			
Overheads					
Learning effects					•
Marginal costing/decision making					
General	•		•	•	••
Joint products					
Risk and uncertainty	•	•			
Sensitivity analysis		•			
Pricing		•			
Linear programming					
Graphical method	•				
Network analysis			•		•
Significance testing	•				•
Capital investment appraisal/ discounted cashflow (DCF)	•	•			

| | 1991 | | 1992 | | 1993 |
	May	Nov	May	Nov	May
Information technology					
Data collection		•			
Models and simulation			•		
Stock control				•	

Note: Each dot represents a question or significant part of a question in the exam paper.

Revision topics

1 Cost ascertainment and behaviour

(a) The nature of cost accounting.

(b) The concepts of cost centres, cost units and traceable costs.

(c) Direct and indirect costs.

(d) Fixed and variable costs.

(e) The elements of cost, material costing, labour costing and product costing.

(f) Allocation, apportionment and absorption of overheads.

(g) Marginal and absorption costing.

(h) The relationship between cost and financial accounting.

(i) Assumptions of linearity and break even.

(j) Learning curve theory

    (i) use of formula $y = ax^{-b}$
    (ii) conditions for learning
    (iii) applications for

2 Regression and correlation

(a) The nature of simple and multiple regression.

(b) Basic linear regression using scatter diagrams.

(c) Calculation and interpretation of the coefficients of both correlation and regression.

(d) The use of regression to forecast values of the dependent variable, given values of the independent variable.

(e) Use of standard errors to calculate confidence intervals for regression estimates.

(f) The statistical aids used for forecasting.

(g) The use of market research and time series analysis.

3 Budgetary control and profit improvement

(a) The CIMA definition of budgetary control.
(b) The administration of budgetary control.
(c) Limiting factors.
(d) Budgeting for sales.
(e) Mechanics of budget preparation.

(f) Budgeting for change.

(g) Budget periods and revisions.

(h) Budgets for control including flexible budgets.

(i) Human aspects of budgetary control.

(j) Traditional approaches contrasted with zero-based budgeting (ZBB).

(k) Implementing ZBB.

(l) Profit improvement plans (PIPs).

(m) The role of cost reduction.

(n) Application of value analysis.

4   Standard costing and variance analysis

(a) Setting cost standards.

(b) The use of learning curves for cost estimation.

(c) Standard costs for budget preparation.

(d) Standard costing and overhead recovery.

(e) Variance analysis including:

(i) sales variances;
(ii) material cost variances;
(iii) direct labour variances;
(iv) variable production overhead variances;
(v) fixed production overhead variances.

(f) Operating statements.

(g) Bookkeeping in a standard costing system.

(h) Marginal costing variances.

(i) Planning and operational variances.

(j) The significance and investigation of variances.

(k) Mix and yield variances including the revenue method for sales.

5   Marginal costing and decision-making

(a) The role of the accountant in decision-making.

(b) The limitations of absorption costing.

(c) Applications of marginal costing.

(d) Cost evaluation and the limitations of traditional assumptions of cost behaviour:

(i) relevant costs for decision-making;
(ii) the concept of opportunity cost;
(iii) the need for cashflow information.

(e) Breakeven analysis, applications, profit-volume graphs.

(f)   Cost evaluation in different situations in order to maximise contribution:

      (i)   the use of limited capacity;
      (ii)   second shift working;
      (iii)   adding new products;
      (iv)   joint products – sell or process further;
      (v)   shutdown of capacity;
      (vi)   techniques of production;
      (vii)   the 'make or buy' situation.

(g)   Pricing decisions:

      (i)   the importance of pricing decisions and determination of pricing policy;
      (ii)   elasticity of demand and maximising profits;
      (iii)   cost plus pricing models;
      (iv)   other pricing methods and pricing in practice;
      (v)   use of relevant costs to determine minimum contract price.

(h)   Decision making under uncertainty:

      (i)   the use of decision trees;
      (ii)   value of perfect information.

6   Linear programming

(a)   Formulation of a linear programming problem.

This is particularly important and you must be absolutely certain you are comfortable in this area. Easy marks are available and good work will provide a foundation for the remainder of the work on the question.

(b)   The graphical method of solving maximisation and minimisation problems where only two decision variables exist (eg. products competing for scarce resources). Remember to scale your graph so that it is large enough to read off a reasonably accurate answer.

(c)   The simplex method of solving a problem and, in particular, you must be able to solve a primal (maximisation) problem and its (minimisation) dual by the following steps:

      (i)   set up the initial tableau;
      (ii)   iterate from one tableau to the next;
      (iii)   derive a final tableau;
      (iv)   interpret the final tableau in respect of both primal and dual problems.

7   Network analysis

(a)   Activity on arrow networks.

(b)   Activity on node networks.

(c)   Critical path and project duration.

(d) Crashing of activity times to determine:

    (i)   minimum time and associated cost, or
    (ii)   minimum cost and associated time.

(e) Allocation of resources by bar and Gantt charts.

(f) The incorporation of uncertainty and the probability of completion within stated times.

8 Significance testing

(a) Small sampling theory and Students 't' distribution.

(b) The use of the chi-squared test as:

    (i)   a test of association between two sets of variables (contingency table);
    (ii)   a test of good fit between a set of observations and a known probability distribution (normal, binomial or Poisson).

(c) The general rules regarding degrees of freedom:

    (i)   Goodness of fit

n classes (totals forced)	$v = n-1$
Binomial/Poisson distribution (totals and means forced)	$v = n-2$
Normal distribution (totals, means and standard deviations forced)	$v = n-3$

    (ii)   Tests of association – contingency tables.
$$v = (r-1)(c-1)$$

    (iii) Remember that where data is discrete and $v = 1$ Yates correction should be applied (subtract 0.5 from the absolute value).

(d) The use of one-tailed and two-tailed tests.

9 Queuing theory

(a) The assumptions underlying the simple single channel queue and, in particular, the conditions necessary to allow its use.

(b) The steady state solution of the M/M/I model.

(c) Multiple-channel queues.

(d) Revise the method to be applied in performing a simulation and be sure that you get the allocation of random numbers correct. Questions may apply this method to stock or queuing situations although the method is not confined to these areas.

10   **Capital investment appraisal**

  (a)   The principles, merits and demerits of ROCE, payback, NPV and IRR.
  (b)   The arithmetic of discounting.
  (c)   Multiple yields.
  (d)   Mutually exclusive investments.
  (e)   Sensitivity analysis.
  (f)   Inflation in capital project appraisal.
  (g)   Non-annual time periods, life cycle determination.

11   **Information technology**

  (a)   The concept of the information centre.

  (b)   The electronic office.

  (c)   The facilities associated with (a).

  (d)   The business organisation and managerial information.

  (e)   Systems theory and the concepts of:

      (i)   adaptive systems;
      (ii)   open- and closed-loop systems;
      (iii) positive and negative feedback.

  (f)   Reporting to management.

  (g)   Models and simulation including problem-solving techniques.

  (h)   Stock control (not specifically mentioned in the syllabus but deemed knowledge).

Guide to questions and answers

PUBLISHER'S NOTE

Financial Training study materials are distributed in the UK and overseas by Stanley Thornes (Publishers) Limited. They are another company within the Wolters Kluwer group. They can be contacted at Stanley Thornes, Ellenborough House, Wellington Street, Cheltenham GL50 1YD Telephone (0242) 228888. Fax: (0242) 221914.

We are always open to suggestions for improvements to our publications, including notification of any errors. Please send them directly to the Publishing Division, Financial Training Company, at the address below.

Your chances of success in the CIMA exams will be greatly improved by additional tuition, either at one of Financial Training's centres or by home study. For details of our open learning programmes please contact us at:

Open Learning Department
The Financial Training Company
136–142 Bramley Road
London W10 6SR

Tel: 081 960 4421
Fax: 081 960 9374

Questions

1 COST ASCERTAINMENT AND COST BEHAVIOUR

1.1 Maneller Ltd

Maneller Ltd is a large, multidivision company. One of Maneller's divisions, the Tolly Division, manufactures aircraft. The division is currently developing a new type of aircraft that will determine the success of the division for the next few years.

Tolly has already spent £200 million on developing and testing the new technology that the aircraft will utilise. It is also constructing a new £20 million specialised production facility, which will become totally obsolete after production of the planes is completed. The engineering department has predicted that an additional £20 million will have to be spent on further development and testing before the aircraft is ready for production. Maneller's accounting policy was to capitalise all development and equipment costs until production actually started.

The division is currently attempting to determine a price for the aircraft and orders will be made on the basis of this established price, even though deliveries will not be made for one or two years.

The marketing department has forecast that demand for the aircraft will range between 240 and 360 units. The actual demand will be determined by both the ultimate aircraft characteristics and, more important, the aircraft price.

The division has made detailed predictions of the aircraft's production costs. Tolly has already contracted for parts for 240 aircraft, which will cost £3 million per aircraft. These contracts have a provision for parts for an additional 120 aircraft at a 10% decrease in cost per aircraft.

Direct labour is the most significant element of the production costs.

Labour costs are substantial in an absolute sense, but large reductions are possible because of the 'learning curve' that affects the labour costs during the production period. The learning curve applicable to the new aircraft is 80%, based on 30-unit production lots, the first lot having total labour costs of £300 million.

Combined applicable general, administrative and indirect production costs are estimated at £50 million annually. Historically, these costs have been applied on the basis of direct labour hours.

It has been decided that the fixed costs applicable to the project that must be recovered included £240 million previously mentioned plus whatever indirect production costs and general administration costs were incurred. Their prediction of the latter was £100 million if 240 units were produced and sold (2 years @ £50 million) and £150 million if 360 units were produced and sold (3 years @ £50 million).

Required

(a)   Calculate the price which must be set to break even, assuming

        (i)   240 units are sold; and

        (ii)   360 units are sold.   (10 marks)

(b)   A price of £9 million has been set, resulting in orders for 280 planes. The marketing department now reports that a potential new customer will purchase 50 planes, but only if the price is £8.6 million or less. This price reduction would have to be made retrospective and applied to all customers. Should Tolly accept the order? (State and comment on any assumptions made.)   (5 marks)

You are reminded that the learning curve formula is:

$$y = ax^{-b}$$

where

y =   cumulative average time per batch
a =   time taken for first batch
x =   cumulative units produced, expressed as a number of batches
$-b$ = $\dfrac{\text{log of learning \%}}{\log 2}$

(Total 15 marks)

1.2   Cost behaviour (M91)

Conventionally it is often assumed that costs can be easily separated into fixed and variable elements and that the variable element behaves linearly and is affected only by changes in the level of activity, yet cost behaviour in practice is much more complex than this simple model suggests.

Required

(a)   Explain the above statement.   (10 marks)

(b)   Describe other possible approaches to the problem of analysing cost behaviour.
                                                (7 marks)
(Total 17 marks)

1.3   New environment (M92)

The new manufacturing environment is characterised by more flexibility, a readiness to meet customers' requirements, smaller batches, continuous improvements and an emphasis on quality. In such circumstances, traditional management accounting performance measures are, at best, irrelevant and, at worst, misleading.

Required

(a)   Discuss the above statement, citing specific examples to support or refute the views expressed.   (10 marks)

(b)   Explain in what ways management accountants can adapt the services they provide to the new environment.   (7 marks)
(Total 17 marks)

2 REGRESSION AND CORRELATION

2.1 Coefficient of determination (M88)

(a) A management accountant is analysing data relating to retail sales on behalf of marketing colleagues. The marketing staff believe that the most important influence upon sales is local advertising undertaken by the retail store. The company also advertises by using regional television areas. The company owns more than 100 retail outlets and the data below relates to a sample of 10 representative outlets.

Outlet number	Monthly sales	Local advertising by the retail store	Regional advertising by the company
	£'000 y	£'000 per month x_1	£'000 per month x_2
1	220	6	4
2	230	8	6
3	240	12	10
4	340	12	16
5	420	2	18
6	460	8	20
7	520	16	26
8	600	15	30
9	720	14	36
10	800	20	46

The data has been partly analysed and the intermediate results are available below:

$\Sigma y = 4{,}550$ $\Sigma y^2 = 2{,}451{,}300$ $\Sigma x_1 y = 58{,}040$

$\Sigma x_1 = 113$ $\Sigma x_1{}^2 = 1{,}533$ $\Sigma x_2 y = 121{,}100$

$\Sigma x_2 = 212$ $\Sigma x_2{}^2 = 6{,}120$ $\Sigma x_1 x_2 = 2{,}780$

Required

Examine closely, using coefficients of determination, the assertion that the level of sales varies more with movements in the level of local advertising than with changes in the level of regional company advertising. (8 marks)

(b) Further analysis of the raw data reveals a coefficient of multiple correlation of 0.99 and hence a coefficient of multiple determination of 0.98. Using the least squares multiple regression equation, a sales forecast for an outlet in the same areas as outlet 8 in the original data has been prepared for a planned level of £12,000 of local advertising. This produces a sales forecast of £597,333 for the next month.

Required

Interpret the above information for the marketing manager and explain the value and limitations of regression analysis in sales forecasting. What other factors should be taken into account when preparing a sales forecast? (12 marks)

Note: The coefficient of determination for y and x_1 may be calculated from:

$$r^2 = \frac{(n\Sigma x_1 y - \Sigma x_1 \Sigma y)^2}{\left(n\Sigma x_1{}^2 - (\Sigma x_1)^2\right) \times \left(n\Sigma y^2 - (\Sigma y)^2\right)}$$

(Total 20 marks)

2.2   Cecil Beaton plc (M89)

Cecil Beaton plc produces a wide range of electronic components including its best-selling item, the laser switch. The company is preparing the budgets for 19X9 and knows that the key element in the master budget is the contribution expected from the laser switch. The records for this component for the past four years are summarised below, with the costs and revenues adjusted to 19X9 values.

Sales	*19X5*	*19X6*	*19X7*	*19X8*
(units)	150,000	180,000	200,000	230,000
	£	£	£	£
Sales revenue	292,820	346,060	363,000	448,800
Variable costs	131,080	161,706	178,604	201,160
Contribution	161,740	184,354	184,396	247,640

It has been estimated that sales in 19X9 will be 260,000 units.

Required

(a)   As a starting point for forecasting 19X9 contribution, project the trend, using linear regression.
(10 marks)

(b)   Calculate the 95% confidence interval of the individual forecast for 19X9 if the standard error of the forecast is £14,500 and the appropriate t value is 4.303, and interpret the value calculated.
(3 marks)

(c)   Comment on the advantages of using linear regression for forecasting and the limitations of the technique.
(7 marks)
(Total 20 marks)

3   BUDGETARY CONTROL AND PROFIT IMPROVEMENT

3.1   Processors Ltd

Processors Ltd, a manufacturing company in a process industry, prepares an annual budget which it updates after the first six months of each financial year. You are given the following information from which the latest budget will be prepared.

Manufacturing costs

Variable (according to quantity produced)
Materials: 23,000 kg @ £10.00 per kg
Labour: 360,000 hours @ £0.80 per hour
Power: 2,400,000 units @ £0.01 per unit

Fixed
Works overheads: 12 months @ £20,000 per month

Distribution costs

Variable (according to quantity sold)
Carriage: 20,000 kg @ £2.40 per kg

Fixed
Transport office: 12 months @ £1,000 per month

Selling costs

Fixed
12 months @ £7,500 per month

Administration costs

Fixed
12 months @ £14,000 per month

Output and sales

20,000 kg

The selling price is calculated to show a 20% profit margin on total budgeted costs.

The financial year commences on 1 January. During the course of the year to which the above figures relate, prices rise rapidly. It is decided to re-budget for the year on the assumption that as from 1 July all variable costs are increased by 5% and all fixed costs by 1%.

During the first half of the year the volume of output and sales is 2.5% above budget and it is estimated that this higher rate will be maintained for the rest of the year if there is no change in selling price. However, if the selling price is raised, it is anticipated that every £0.20 increase in price per kg will result in a decrease of 20.5 kg in the quantity sold in the half-year. It is decided to increase price from 1 July by £2.40 per kg.

Required

(a)   Calculate the initial selling price at 1 January.
(b)   Produce a statement showing the revised budgeted profit for the year.   **(15 marks)**

3.2   **Sizer**

(a)   'Budgetary control is one of the most useful accounting tools for planning, co-ordinating and controlling the activities of a business.'

An Insight into Management Accounting (Sizer)

(i)   Outline the aims of budgetary control and the advantages of such a system.

(6 marks)

(ii)   List *five* of the main budgets used in a system of budgetary control and outline the contents of each budget and the relationship that exists between them.

(5 marks)

(b) 'Zero-base budgeting is a powerful management tool in controlling costs.'

Set out the nature of zero-base budgeting indicating, in particular, the steps involved in its application, its advantages and disadvantages and the areas where it is especially effective.
(9 marks)
(Total 20 marks)

3.3 LMN Co (M90)

The LMN Co is preparing budgets for the first quarter of 19X1. The company has a single product, the details of which are:

	£
Budgeted variable costs per unit	
Materials	12
Labour (4 hours at £6)	24
Production overhead	8
Selling price per unit	90

Administration overhead is £23,000 per month and the fixed production overhead is £15,000 per month, including £3,500 depreciation.

The factory has a normal capacity of 1,500 units per month. Finished goods stocks are valued at full production cost and the budgeted opening stock at 1 January 19X1 is 1,200 units valued at £66,500. It is company policy to keep finished stocks at a constant ratio to the budgeted unit sales of the following month. Extra production over 1,500 units per month can be achieved by working overtime which means paying labour double time for the overtime.

Expected sales	Units
December 19X0	1,300
January 19X1	1,000
February 19X1	1,400
March 19X1	1,600
April 19X1	1,800
May 19X1	1,550

Materials are paid for in the month following delivery and enough stock is kept to cover the next month's budgeted production. Sales are on credit with 30% of debts collected in the month of sale and 67% in the following month, the balance being bad debts. All other costs are paid for in the month they are incurred and no capital expenditure is expected.

Required

(a) Prepare a singled budgeted profit and loss account for the quarter (January, February, March).
(8 marks)

(b) Prepare cash budgets for each month of the quarter.
(9 marks)

(c) Reconcile the net cash movement for the quarter to the budgeted profit.
(5 marks)
(Total 22 marks)

3.4   Japanese companies (M90)

Thomas Sheridan, writing in *Management Accounting* in February 1989, pointed out that Japanese companies have a different approach to cost information with 'the emphasis based on physical measures', and 'the use of non-financial indices, particularly at shop floor level'. He argues that their approach is much more relevant to modern conditions than traditional cost and management accounting practices.

Required

(a)   Explain what is meant by 'physical measures' and 'non-financial indices'.   (3 marks)

(b)   Give *three* examples of non-financial indices that might be prepared, with a brief note of what information each index would provide.   (5 marks)

(c)   Outline the existing cost and management accounting practices you consider inappropriate in modern conditions.   (9 marks)
(Total 17 marks)

3.5   B Ltd (M92)

Extracts from the budgets of B Ltd are given below.

	Period 1	Period 2	Period 3	Period 4	Period 5
Sales and stock budgets (units)					
Opening stock	4,000	2,500	3,300	2,500	3,000
Sales	15,000	20,000	16,500	21,000	18,000
Cost budgets (£'000)					
Direct labour	270.0	444.0	314.0		
Direct materials	108.0	166.4	125.6		
Production overhead (excluding depreciation)	117.5	154.0	128.5		
Depreciation	40.0	40.0	40.0		
Administration overhead	92.0	106.6	96.4		
Selling overhead	60.0	65.0	61.5		

The following information is also available.

(1)   Production above 18,000 units incurs a bonus in addition to normal wage rates.

(2)   Any variable costs contained in selling overhead are assumed to vary with sales. All other variable costs are assumed to vary with production.

Required

(a)   Calculate the budgeted production for periods 1 to 4.   (3 marks)

(b)   Prepare a suitable cost budget for period 4.   (10 marks)

In period 4 the stock and sales budgets were achieved and the following actual costs recorded.

	£'000
Direct labour	458
Direct material	176
Production overhead	181
Depreciation	40
Administration overhead	128
Selling overhead	62
	1,045

Required

(c)   Show the budget variances from actual.   (3 marks)

(d)   Criticise the assumptions on which the cost budgets have been prepared.   (6 marks)
(Total 22 marks)

3.6   Flexible budgets (M93)

It is common practice to flex a budget linearly according to the volume of production, using labour or machine hours as a proxy, yet this often results in a budget which is inaccurate and is thus less useful for control purposes.

Required

(a)   Explain why inaccuracies may result from the procedures commonly used to flex a budget.   (7 marks)

(b)   Explain how these inaccuracies detract from effective control.   (4 marks)

(c)   Discuss alternative ways of budgeting which might improve both accuracy and control.   (6 marks)
(Total 17 marks)

4   STANDARD COSTING AND VARIANCE ANALYSIS

4.1   AC/DC Co

The AC/DC Co manufactures special electrical equipment in Kowloon. The management has established standard costs for many of its operations and uses a flexible budget. Overhead is applied on a basis of standard labour-hours. The rectifier assembly department operates at the following standard rates:

One multiplex rectifier TR–906

Materials

4 sheets soft iron, 9 × 16 in.	@	£1.12 each
2 spools copper wire	@	£2.39 each
Direct labour rate		£2.50 per hour
Combined overhead rate		£2.10 per direct-labour hour

The flexible budget indicates that total overhead would amount to £4,489 and £4,989 at production levels of 500 and 600 units, respectively. The production budget for the past month called for 2,340 direct-labour hours, £2,925 variable-overhead costs, and £1,989 fixed-overhead costs. Only 550 rectifiers were produced, at the costs listed below:

Materials purchased	Direct labour
3,000 sheets soft iron, £3,300	2,113 hours, £5,409.28
1,500 spools copper wire, £3,600	

Materials used	Overhead
2,215 sheets soft iron	Variable costs, £2,769
1,106 spools copper wire	Fixed costs, £2,110

Required

Calculate the following:

(a)   the standard time for assembling a rectifier;
(b)   the standard unit cost;
(c)   the material price variance during the past month;
(d)   the material usage variance;
(e)   the direct-labour price variance;
(f)   the direct-labour efficiency variance;
(g)   variable-overhead spending variance;
(h)   variable-overhead efficiency variance;
(i)   fixed-overhead budget variance;
(j)   fixed-overhead volume variance.   **(15 marks)**

4.2   Ruggerball Ltd

(a)   Ruggerball Ltd does nothing but manufacture rugby balls. As each ball is completed it is booked out to a subsidiary company Try Ltd   Ruggerball's budget for the seventh four-weekly control period of its financial year was as follows.

	£	£
Sales (6,000 units @ £8 each)		48,000
Variable costs:		
Bladders (6,000 @ 50p each)	3,000	
Leather (200 ten hide bales @ £76 each)	15,200	
Sundry and packaging materials	1,300	
Direct labour (5,000 hours @ 90p per hour)	4,500	
	24,000	
Fixed costs:		
Administrative and establishment expenses	4,239	
Staff and directors' salaries	8,261	
		36,500
Budgeted net profit		11,500

During power shortages during the 'three-day week', Ruggerball was only able to manufacture during 60% of the budgeted production hours and was unable to sanction any overtime. Despite this the direct labour force was paid in full for the budgeted hours. Various other differences from budget occurred and the following are the actual figures for the period:

	£	£
Sales (4,000 units @ £9 each)		36,000
Variable costs:		
Bladders (4,000 @ 70p each)	2,800	
Leather (100 ten hide bales @ £133.33 each)	13,333	
Sundry and packaging materials	867	
Direct labour (5,000 hours @ £1 per hour)	5,000	
	22,000	
Fixed costs:		
Administrative and establishment expenses	4,385	
Staff and director's salaries	8,315	
		34,700
Actual net profit		1,300

Required

(i)   Prepare a statement reconciling the budgeted contribution with the actual contribution, stating the variances in the way which you think will be most helpful to management. Present your calculations as schedules with references to the main statement.   (13 marks)

(ii)   Comment briefly on any apparent inter-relationships between the variances.
(3 marks)

(b)   In the next period, there was an adverse leather usage variance of £650, and a decision needs to be made as to whether to investigate the process to determine whether it is out of control.

On the basis of past experience, the cost of an investigation is estimated at £160 and the cost of correction if the process is out of control is estimated at £350. The probability of it being out of control is estimated at 0.4.

Required

Show calculations to support your decision as to whether or not to investigate the variance.
(4 marks)
(Total 20 marks)

4.3   Learning effects (M93)

A firm has developed a product for which the following standard cost estimates have been made for the first batch to be manufactured in Month 1.

Standard costs for the batch	£
500 labour hours @ £8 per hour	4,000
55 units of direct materials @ £100 per unit	5,500
Variable overhead 500 hours @ £15 per hour	7,500
	17,000

From experience the firm knows that labour will benefit from a learning effect and labour times will be reduced. This is expected to approximate to an 80% learning curve and to follow the general function

$$y = ax^b$$

where y = average labour hours per batch

         a = number of labour hours for the first batch

         x = cumulative number of batches

and b = learning coefficient.

(The learning coefficient is found as follows:

$$b = \frac{\text{Log } (1 - \text{proportionate decrease})}{\text{Log } 2}$$

The coefficient for an 80% learning curve is $b = -0.322$)

In addition, the growing expertise of labour is expected to improve the efficiency with which materials are used. The usage of materials is expected to approximate to a 95% learning curve to follow the general function.

$$y = ax^b$$

where y = average units of material per batch

         a = number of units for the first batch

and x and b are as explained previously

The actual production for the first six months was as follows:

Month 1	20 batches
Month 2	30 batches
Month 3	25 batches
Month 4	24 batches
Month 5	33 batches
Month 6	28 batches

160

During Month 6 the following results were recorded for the last batch made:

Actual results of last batch	
Labour hours	115
Direct wages	£978
Direct materials (41 units)	£3,977
Variable overhead	£1,685

Required

(a)   Calculate the learning coefficient for materials.   (3 marks)
(b)   Derive the standard cost of the last batch in Month 6.   (8 marks)
(c)   Calculate what variances have arisen in connection with the last batch.   (8 marks)
(d)   Explain what information the variances provide for management.   (3 marks)

(Total 22 marks)

4.4   Mix variances

(a)   Sales variances

	Products		
	X	*Y*	*Z*
Budget			
Unit sales	100	200	200
Price	£10	£15	£20
Standard unit cost	£8	£12	£15
Actual			
Unit sales	100	120	180
Price	£10	£16	£19
Actual unit cost	£7.50	£13.25	£15

Required

Analyse the difference between budgeted and actual sales into price, mix and quantity elements.   What assumption are you inherently making about the products being sold?

(b)   Materials variances

Product Q is manufactured by mixing L, M and N.

The standard cost card is as follows:

	kg		£
L	25	@ £2 per kg	50
M	75	@ £1 per kg	75
N	50	@ £4 per kg	200
	150		325
Normal loss	50		–
	100		325

Actual results:

Output of Q was 19,000 kg and the inputs were as follows:

	kg	£
L	5,000	11,000
M	14,000	14,000
N	11,000	37,400

Required

Compare budgeted and actual cost in as much detail as possible.

4.5   **Conan**

Conan Office Equipment manufacture and distribute three products: copiers, personal computers and word processors. They transfer finished goods to distribution centres at the following prices:

Copiers	£2,000
Personal computers	£5,000
Word processors	£1,000

Distribution centres sell goods via a number of salesmen who get commission as follows:

Copiers	20% of distribution centre profit (revenue-transfer cost)
Personal computers	5% of selling price
Word processors	£50 per unit

For the year 19X8 Conan decide to experiment with a new sales policy. In region A, they decide to increase spending on advertising and increase sales price to test the market. In a similar region, B, they propose to continue with the current policy in order to compare the two.

Actual results

Region A (new policy)

		Copiers	Personal computers	Word processors
Units sold 1,000		320	1,200	
Unit selling price		£2,400	£6,000	£1,200
Advertising cost		£100,000	£200,000	£50,000
Total distribution costs	£155,000			

Region B (old policy)

		Copiers	Personal computers	Word processors
Units sold		1,200	100	1,500
Unit selling price		£2,300	£5,800	£1,100
Total advertising costs	£Nil			
Total distribution costs	£180,000			

Conan wishes to analyse the difference in profits between the two regions using the following variances:

(1)   sales price, mix and quantity;

(2)   commission price, mix and quantity;

(3)   advertising expenditure; and

(4)   distribution expenditure and volume, (considered to be useful as all products when packaged are of similar weight and volume).

Required

(a)   Calculate the distribution centre profit of each region.

(b)   Reconcile the two figures using the analysis described.   **(15 marks)**

4.6   Thorpe Ltd

The management team of Thorpe Ltd feel that standard costing and variance analysis have little to offer in the reporting of some of the activities of their firm. 'Although we produce a range of fairly standardised products', states the accountant of Thorpe Ltd, 'prices of many of our raw materials are apt to change suddenly and comparison of actual prices with a pre-determined, and often unrealistic, standard price is of little use. For some of our products we can utilise the raw material which will, in our opinion, lead to the cheapest total production costs. However, we are frequently caught out by price changes and the material actually used often proves, after the event, to have been more expensive than the alternative which was originally rejected.'

'For example, consider the experience over the last accounting period of two of our products, Alpha and Beta. To produce a unit of Alpha we can use either 5 kg of gamma or 5 kg of delta. We planned to use gamma as it appeared it would be the cheaper of the two and our plans were based on a cost of gamma of £3 per kg. Due to market movements the actual prices changed and if we had purchased efficiently the costs would have been

gamma	£4.50 per kg
delta	£4.00 per kg

Production of Alpha was 2,000 units and usage of gamma amounted to 10,800 kg at a total cost of £51,840.'

'Product Beta uses only one raw material, epsilon, but again the price of this can change rapidly. It was thought that epsilon would cost £30 per tonne but in fact we only paid £25 per tonne and if we had purchased correctly the cost would have been less as it was freely available at only £23 per tonne. It usually takes 1.5 tonnes of epsilon to produce 1 tonne of Beta but our production of 500 tonnes of Beta used only 700 tonnes of epsilon.'

'So you can see that with our particular circumstances the traditional approach to variance analysis is of little use and we don't use it for materials although we do use it for reporting on labour and variable overhead costs.'

Required

Analyse the material variances for both Alpha and Beta utilising

(a)   traditional variance analysis;

(b)   an approach which distinguishes between planning and operational variances.

      (15 marks)

4.7 POV Ltd (M92)

POV Ltd uses a standard costing system to control and report upon the production of its single product.

An abstract from the original standard cost card of the product is as follows.

	£	£
Selling price per unit		200
Less: 4 kg materials @ £20 per kg	80	
6 hours labour @ £7 per hour	42	
		122
Contribution per unit		78

For period 3, 2,500 units were budgeted to be produced and sold but the actual production and sales were 2,850 units.

The following information was also available.

(1)   At the commencement of period 3 the normal material became unobtainable and it was necessary to use an alternative.   Unfortunately, 0.5 kg per unit extra was required as it was thought that the material would be more difficult to work with. The price of the alternative was expected to be £16.50 per kg.   In the event, actual usage was 12,450 kg at £18 per kg.

(2)   Weather conditions unexpectedly improved for the period with the result that a 50p per hour bad weather bonus, which had been allowed for in the original standard, did not have to be paid.   Because of the difficulties expected with the alternative material, management agreed to pay the workers £8 per hour for period 3 only. During the period 18,800 hours were paid for, but only 18,400 were worked.

After using conventional variances for some time, POV Ltd is contemplating extending its system to include planning and operational variances.

Required

(a)   Prepare a statement reconciling budgeted contribution for the period with actual contribution, using conventional material and labour variances.   (4 marks)

(b)   Prepare a similar reconciliation statement using planning and operational variances.   (14 marks)

(c)   Explain the meaning of the variances shown in statement (b).   (4 marks)
          (Total 22 marks)

4.8 County Preserves (M88)

County Preserves produce jams, marmalade and preserves. All products are produced in a similar fashion; the fruits are low temperature cooked in a vacuum process and then blended with glucose syrup with added citric acid and pectin to help setting.

Margins are tight and the firm operates a system of standard costing for each batch of jam.

The *standard cost* data for a batch of raspberry jam:

Fruit extract	400 kg	@ £0.16 per kg
Glucose syrup	700 kg	@ £0.10 per kg
Pectin	99 kg	@ £0.332 per kg
Citric acid	1 kg	@ £2.00 per kg
Labour	18 hrs	@ £3.25 per hour
Standard processing loss	3%	

The summer of 19X7 proved disastrous for the raspberry crop with a late frost and cool, cloudy conditions at the ripening period, resulting in a low national yield. As a consequence, normal prices in the trade were £0.19 per kg for fruit extract although good buying could achieve some savings. The impact of exchange rates on imports of sugar has caused the price of syrup to increase by 20%.

The *actual results* for the batch:

Fruit extract	428 kg	@ £0.18 per kg
Glucose syrup	742 kg	@ £0.12 per kg
Pectin	125 kg	@ £0.328 per kg
Citric acid	1 kg	@ £0.95 per kg
Labour	20 hrs	@ £3.00 per hour

Actual output was 1,164 kg of raspberry jam.

Required

(a) Calculate the ingredients planning variances that are deemed uncontrollable. (4 marks)

(b) Calculate the ingredients operating variances that are deemed controllable.   (4 marks)

(c) Comment on the advantages and disadvantages of variance analysis using planning and operating variances.   (4 marks)

(d) Calculate the mixture and yield variances.   (5 marks)

(e) Calculate the total variance for the batch.   (3 marks)
(Total 20 marks)

5   MARGINAL COSTING AND DECISION-MAKING

5.1   Types of cost (M92)

For decision-making, it is claimed that the relevant cost to use is *opportunity cost*. In practice, management accountants frequently consider costs such as *marginal costs*, *imputed costs* and *differential costs* as the relevant costs.

Required

(a) Explain the terms in *italics* and give an example of each.   (6 marks)

(b) Reconcile the apparent contradiction in the statement.   (6 marks)

(c)   Explain in what circumstances, if any, fixed costs may be relevant for decision-making.
(5 marks)
(Total 17 marks)

5.2   Letters (M89)

AB plc makes two products, Alpha and Beta. The company made a £500,000 profit last year and proposes an identical plan for the coming year. The relevant data for last year are summarised in Table 1.

Table 1: Actuals for last year

	Product Alpha	Product Beta
Actual product and sales (units)		
Total production and sales (units)	20,000	40,000
Total costs per unit	£20	£40
Selling prices per unit (25% on cost)	£25	£50
Machining time per unit (hours)	2	1
Potential demand at above selling prices (units)	30,000	50,000

Fixed costs were £48,000 for the year, absorbed on machining hours which were fully utilised for the production achieved.

A new managing director has been appointed and he is somewhat sceptical about the plan being proposed. Furthermore, he thinks that additional machining capacity should be installed to remove any production bottlenecks and wonders whether a more flexible pricing policy should be adopted.

Table 2 summarises the changes in costs involved for the extra capacity and gives price/demand data, supplied by the marketing department, applicable to the conditions expected in the next period.

Table 2

Costs
Extra machining capacity would increase fixed costs by 10% in total. Variable costs and machining times per unit would remain unchanged.

	Product Alpha	Product Beta
Price demand data		
Price range (per unit)	£20 – 30	£45 – 55
Expected demand (000 units)	45 – 15	70 – 30

Required

(a)   Calculate the plan to maximise profits for the coming year based on the data and selling prices in Table 1.
(7 marks)

(b)   Comment on the pricing system for the existing plan used in Table 1.
(3 marks)

(c)   Calculate the best selling prices and production plan based on the data in Table 2.
(7 marks)

(d)   Comment on the methods you have used in part (c) to find the optimum prices and production levels.   (3 marks)

Any assumptions made must be clearly stated.   **(Total 20 marks)**

5.3   EX Ltd (M93)

EX Ltd is an established supplier of precision parts to a major aircraft manufacturer. It has been offered the choice of making either Part A or Part B for the next period, but not both.

Both parts use the same metal, a titanium alloy, of which 13,000 kg only are available, at £12.50 per kg. The parts are made by passing each one through two fully-automatic computer-controlled machine lines (S and T) whose capacities are limited. Target prices have been set and the following data are available for the period:

Part details:

	Part A	Part B
Maximum call-off (units)	7,000	9,000
Target price	£145 per unit	£115 per unit
Alloy usage	1.6 kilos	1.6 kilos
Machine times		
Line S	0.6 hours	0.25 hours
Line T	0.5 hours	0.55 hours

Machine details:

	Line S	Line T
Hours available	4,000	4,500
Variable overhead per machine hour	£80	£100

Required

(a)   Calculate which part should be made during the next period to maximise contribution.   (9 marks)

(b)   Calculate the contribution which EX Ltd will earn and whether the company will be able to meet the maximum call-off   (3 marks)

As an alternative to the target prices shown above, the aircraft manufacturer has offered the following alternative arrangement:

Target prices less 10% plus £60 per hour for each unused machine hour.

(c)   Decide whether your recommendation in (a) above will be altered and, if so, calculate the new contribution.   (10 marks)
                                                                             (Total 22 marks)

5.4 Lecture example – Decision theory

Demand (units)	Probability
150	0.3
250	0.2
350	0.3
450	0.2

Must order before demand is known.
Unsold units are worthless and no disposal costs are incurred.
No stockout costs exist.

Possible order quantities: 200, 300, 400, 500

Selling price	£40
Cost	£25

Required

(a)   Calculate:

  (i)   the expected profit and related order quantity;
  (ii)   the order quantity using the maximin criterion;
  (iii)   the order quantity using the maximax criterion;
  (iv)   the order quantity using the minimax regret criterion.

(b)   How much would you be prepared to pay for perfect knowledge of demand before ordering?

A company has developed a new product and is considering whether to go ahead with production. Expected demand is as follows:

Year 1		Year 2		Year 3	
Probability	*Units*	*Probability*	*Units*	*Probability*	*Units*
		0.7	12,000	1.0	12,000
0.4	10,000	0.3	8,000	0.8	8,000
				0.2	4,000
		0.4	6,000	1.0	6,000
0.6	6,000	0.6	3,000	0.6	3,000
				0.4	1,000

Selling price	£20 per unit
Variable cost	£16 per unit
Fixed costs	£20,000 per annum
Machine cost	£30,000

		£
Scrap value after	1 year	13,000
	2 years	5,000
	3 years	Nil

(i)   Should the company proceed?

(ii)   How sensitive is the decision to the probability of high sales in year 2 given high sales in year 1?

5.5   Standard and deluxe (M90)

A manufacturer is considering a new product which could be produced in one of two qualities – standard and deluxe. The following estimates have been made:

	Standard £	Deluxe £
Unit labour cost	2.00	2.50
Unit material cost	1.50	2.00
Unit packaging cost	1.00	2.00
Proposed selling price per unit	7.00	10.00

Budgeted fixed costs per period:

0 – 99,999 units	200,000	250,000
100,000 and above	350,000	400,000

At the proposed selling prices, market research indicates the following demand:

Standard

Quantity	Probability
172,000	0.1
160,000	0.7
148,000	0.2

Deluxe

Quantity	Probability
195,500	0.3
156,500	0.5
109,500	0.2

Required

(a)   Draw separate breakeven charts for *each* quality, showing the breakeven points.
(7 marks)

(b)   Comment on the position shown by the charts and what guidance they provide for management.
(3 marks)

(c)   Calculate, for *each* quality, the expected unit sales, expected profits and the margin of safety.
(3 marks)

(d)   Using an appropriate measure of risk, advise management which quality should be launched.
(9 marks)
(Total 22 marks)

5.6   XYZ plc (M91)

The managing director of XYZ plc has devolved some decision-making to the operating divisions of the firm. He is anxious to extend this process but first wishes to be assured that decisions are being taken properly in accordance with group policy.

As a check on existing practice he has asked for an investigation to be made into a recent decision to increase the price of the sole product of Z division to £14.50 per unit due to rising costs.

The following information and estimates were available for the management of Z division.

Last year 75,000 units were sold at £12 each with a total unit cost of £9 of which £6 were variable costs.

For the year ahead the following cost and demand estimates have been made.

Unit variable costs

Pessimistic	Probability	0.15	£7.00 per unit
Most likely	Probability	0.65	£6.50 per unit
Optimistic	Probability	0.20	£6.20 per unit

Total fixed costs

Pessimistic	Probability	0.3	Increase by 50%
Most likely	Probability	0.5	Increase by 25%
Optimistic	Probability	0.2	Increase by 10%

Demand estimates at various prices (units)

			Price per unit	
			£13.50	*£14.50*
Pessimistic	Probability	0.3	45,000	35,000
Most likely	Probability	0.5	60,000	55,000
Optimistic	Probability	0.2	70,000	68,000

(Unit variable costs, fixed costs and demand estimates are statistically independent.)

For this type of decision the group has decided that the option should be chosen which has the highest expected outcome with at least an 80% chance of breaking even.

Required

(a)   Assess whether the decision was made in accordance with group guidelines.

(14 marks)

(b)   Comment on the estimates for the decision and describe what other factors might have been considered.

(4 marks)

(c)   Explain what is the group attitude to risk as evidenced by the guidelines.   (4 marks)

(Total 22 marks)

5.7   Z Ltd (M88)

Z Ltd is considering various product pricing and material purchasing options with regard to a new product it has developed. Estimates of demand and costs are as follows.

If selling price per unit is		£15 per unit	£20 per unit
Forecasts	*Probability*	Sales volume ('000 units)	Sales volume ('000 units)
Optimistic	0.3	36	28
Most likely	0.5	28	23
Pessimistic	0.2	18	13
Variable manufacturing costs (excluding materials) per unit		£3	£3
Advertising and selling costs		£25,000	£96,000
General fixed costs		£40,000	£40,000

Each unit requires 3 kg of material and because of storage problems any unused material must be sold at £1 per kg. The sole suppliers of the material offer three purchase options, which must be decided at the outset, as follows:

(1)   any quantity at £3 per kg; or
(2)   a price of £2.75 per kg for a minimum quantity of 50,000 kg; or
(3)   a price of £2.50 per kg for a minimum quantity of 70,000 kg.

Required

Assuming that the company is risk neutral:

(a)   prepare calculations to show what pricing and purchasing decisions the company should make, clearly indicating the recommended decisions;   (15 marks)

(b)   calculate the maximum price you would pay for perfect information as to whether the demand would be optimistic or most likely or pessimistic.   (5 marks)
                                                                                 (Total 20 marks)

5.8   Homeworker (M87)

Homeworker Ltd is a small company that manufactures a lathe attachment for the DIY market called the 'Homelathe'.

The data for manufacturing each batch of 10 Homelathes is as follows.

Components	A	B	C	D	E	Total
Machine hours	10	14	12			36
Labour hours				2	1	3
	£	£	£	£	£	£
Variable cost	32	54	58	12	4	160
Fixed cost (apportioned)	48	102	116	24	26	316
Total component costs	80	156	174	36	30	476

Assembly costs (all variable)		£40 per 10
Selling price		£600 per 10

General-purpose machinery is used to make components A, B and C and is already working to the maximum capability of 4,752 hours and there is no possibility of increasing the machine capacity in the next period. There is labour available for making components D and E and for assembling the product.

The marketing department advises that there will be a 50% increase in demand next period so the company has decided to buy *one* of the machine-made components from an outside supplier in order to release production capacity and thus help to satisfy demand.

A quotation has been received from General Machines Ltd for the components, but because this company has not made the components before, it has not been able to give single figure prices. Its quotation is as follows:

Component	Pessimistic		Most likely		Optimistic	
	Price	Probability	Price	Probability	Price	Probability
	£		£		£	
A	96	0.25	85	0.5	54	0.25
B	176	0.25	158	0.5	148	0.25
C	149	0.25	127	0.5	97	0.25

It has been agreed between the two companies that audited figures would be used to determine which one of the three prices would be charged for whatever component is bought out.

As management accountant of Homeworker Ltd, it is your responsibility to analyse the financial and production capacity effects of the proposed component purchase.

Required

(a) Show in percentage form the maximum increased production availability from the three alternatives, ie., buying A or B or C.   (4 marks)

(b) Analyse the financial implications of the purchase and, assuming a risk neutral attitude, recommend which component to buy out, noting that the production availability will be limited to a 50% increase.   (6 marks)

(c)   Prepare a profit statement for the period assuming that the component chosen in (b) is bought out and that the extra production is made and sold (show your workings).

(6 marks)

(d)   State *three* other factors you would consider if you were advised that management had decided to avoid risk as much as possible when buying out a component. (Calculations are not required for this section.)

(4 marks)

(Total 20 marks)

5.9   Ices

The managers of a dairy are planning to launch a new range of real cream ices and the marketing department has produced the following information.

Project horizon: six years

Annual total contribution of new range (undiscounted) and estimated probabilities

	Years 1–3	Years 4–6	Probabilities
If demand is high	£40,000	£30,000	0.75
If demand is low	£15,000	£10,000	0.25

If the present range of ice creams is continued and the new range is not introduced it is expected that sales will decline and the present contribution of £30,000 per annum will reduce by 5% per annum, meaning that contribution in year 1 is expected to be £28,500.

It is possible to commission a market research survey, at a cost of £12,000 to assess likely demand.   The market research company has been used before and its reliability can be summarised as follows.

Outcome of survey	Subsequent sales performance	
	High	Low
'High' forecast	70%*	20%
'Low' forecast	30%	80%

* This means that when sales were high, the survey had forecast this 70% of the time.

It has been decided that if the survey predicts high demand for the new range then £15,000 will be invested in new equipment and there will be increased marketing effort which it is estimated will increase contributions by £20,000 per annum if demand is high and by £10,000 per annum if demand is low.   However if the survey predicts low demand then it has been decided that the company will continue with the old range of ice creams.   The dairy has a cost of capital of 20% per annum.

Required

Using decision tree analysis:

(a)   calculate the expected value of the new project without a market research survey;

(b)   calculate the expected present value of continuing with the old range;

(c)   calculate the expected present value of the new project if the market research survey is carried out;

(d)   recommend a course of action to the firm.

5.10   Lecture example – Relevant costs (Marchbank Ltd)

Marchbank Ltd has been asked to produce a one-off batch of marbled paper. The sales team spent 20 man hours getting the contract at a cost of £20 per man hour, but have not yet fixed a final price.

The contract will need the following:

600 kg of material X	(Note 1)
200 kg of material Y	(Note 2)
300 kg of material Z	(Note 3)
200 hours of skilled labour	(Note 4)
100 hours of unskilled labour	(Note 5)

Notes

(1)   There are 300 kg of X in stock, which cost £3 per kg. The current purchase price is £4 per kg. Marchbank Ltd normally uses X to make cardboard, but sometimes sells it for £5.50 per kg.

(2)   There are 250 kg of material Y in stock, which cost £2.50 per kg. Its current purchase price is £3 per kg. If Marchbank Ltd does not accept the contract, it will either dispose of Y at a cost of 50p per kg disposed of, or sell it for £2 per kg, after incurring additional processing costs of £2.75 per kg.

(3)   There are 300 kg of material Z in stock, which cost £7.50 per kg. Z is no longer available, but until now has been used by Marchbank Ltd in a product giving a contribution of £3 per unit, after deducting the cost of Z. Each unit of the product includes 1 kg of Z.

(4)   Skilled labour is salaried, with an average salary of £20,800 per annum. Assume that there are 52 weeks in the year and the working week is 35 hours.

(5)   Unskilled labour is paid on an hourly basis at £6 per hour. The contract will have to be done in overtime, which is paid at time and a half.

(6)   Variable overheads are recovered at £4 per labour hour worked.

(7)   Fixed overheads are recovered at £10 per labour hour worked.

(8)   The contract will need a machine which has a net book value of £5,200. Depreciation is charged on the reducing balance basis at 20% per annum. The depreciation charge appropriate to the duration of the project is £60. The management accountant estimates that the machine's true loss of value is £10 per week. If the machine were not used in the contract it would be sold for £4,800.

Required

(a)   What is the minimum price which Marchbank Ltd should accept for the contract?
(b)   How would this price alter if the machine in Note 8 were not going to be sold?

5.11 Wymark Electronics plc (M87)

Wymark Electronics plc has been offered a fixed price contract to manufacture 12 specialised robotic work stations at £102,732 each. Four work stations would be made and sold each year and the contract would run for three years from 1 July 19X7. The following estimates have been made for the contract.

Equipment: Special equipment will have to be bought and paid for on 1 July 19X7. The minimum amount required for the contract costs £150,000 and this could be resold on 30 June 19X0 for £50,000. Ideally, Wymark wishes to keep initial investment as low as possible but work studies show that additional equipment would reduce semi-skilled labour costs by 1% for each additional £1,000 of equipment. Equipment, over and above the minimum, can only be purchased in increments of £1,000, has no resale value and must be paid for on 1 July 19X7.

Labour: Each of the work stations will require 2,000 hours of skilled labour and 4,000 hours of semi-skilled labour with current rates of £6 and £4 per hour respectively. During the first year it is expected that skilled labour will be in short supply and that skilled labour for the contract will have to be redeployed from existing work where there is a contribution of £8 per hour, net of labour costs. If the contract is accepted an existing technical manager, who was to have been made redundant, will continue to be employed on a permanent basis. His current salary is £18,000 pa and his redundancy terms were to have been a £30,000 lump sum payable on 1 July 19X7 and a pension of £4,000 pa (not inflation-proofed).

Overheads: Overheads are absorbed at the rate of £20 per skilled labour hour as follows:

	£
Fixed overhead	13
Variable overhead	7
	20

Wages, salaries and overheads are expected to increase at 10% pa compound.

Materials

Material	Quantity per work station	Current stock	Original cost per unit	Current purchase price per unit	Current realisable value per unit
	units	units	£	£	£
X	20	170	600	850	650
Y	15	60	500	550	200

Material X is used regularly by Wymark for its existing production but Y is used rarely and if not used for the new contract would have to be disposed of immediately. In addition to the two materials mentioned, the work stations each require 10 microchip circuits which would have to be bought in. No price is yet available but Wymark is confident that it will be able to obtain a price that will be fixed for the duration of the contract. Replacement prices and current realisable values of X and Y are expected to increase at the rate of 15% pa compound.

Wymark has a cost of capital of 16% in money terms and it can be assumed that all payments and revenues arise on the last day of the year to which they relate unless otherwise stated.

Price changes are deemed to take place annually at midnight on 30 June and because of its wish to enter this market, Wymark is prepared to accept this contract on a breakeven basis.

Required

(a)   Calculate the maximum price per circuit that Wymark should pay assuming that the circuits are purchased in three batches, payment is made at the end of each year and the minimum amount of equipment is purchased.   (14 marks)

(b)   Calculate the minimum amount of additional equipment which should be purchased assuming that it is discovered that the microchip circuits cannot be bought at less than £1,200 each.   (6 marks)

Note: Ignore taxation.   **(Total 20 marks)**

5.12   Information for decision-making (M93)

The overriding feature of information for decision-making is that it should be relevant for the decision being taken. However, decision-making varies considerably, at different levels within an organisation thus posing particular difficulties for the management accountant.

Required

(a)   Describe the characteristics of decision-making at different levels within an organisation.   (6 marks)

(b)   Explain how the management accountant must tailor the information provided for the various levels.   (5 marks)

(c)   Give an example of a typical management decision, state at what level this would normally be taken and what specific information should be supplied to the decision-maker.   (6 marks)
                    (Total 17 marks)

6   LINEAR PROGRAMMING

6.1   Lecture example – Tartan mill

A mill manufactures two kinds of tartan cloth: Royal Stuart (A) and Hunting Stuart (B). 1 yard of tartan A requires 8 oz of red wool, $2^{1}/_{2}$ oz of yellow wool and 2 oz of green wool, whilst 1 yard of tartan B is made up of 10 oz of red wool, 1 oz of yellow wool and 4 oz of green wool. The amounts of wool available in a given period are 5,000 lb of red, 1,250 lb of yellow and 1,875 lb of green. Both types of tartan can be produced on the same machines and both can be woven at a rate of 12 yards per hour. A total of 750 machine hours is available in the given period. The profit per yard is 40p for tartan A and 80p for tartan B.

Required

(a)   Given that the company must produce at least 3,000 yards of tartan A to fulfil firm orders, how much of each type of tartan should be manufactured in order to maximise profit?   (8 marks)

(b) If the profit per yard for tartan A remains constant at 40p, by how much can the profit per yard for tartan B change before the optimal product mix changes?

(3 marks)

(c) By how much would the maximum profit from part (a) be increased if there were no need to produce the minimum of 3,000 yards of A? (3 marks)

(d) Calculate and interpret the shadow (dual) price of 1lb green wool. (4 marks)

(e) Resolve the basic problem using the simplex method. (4 marks)

(Total 22 marks)

6.2   Standard and de-luxe (M91)

A small firm produces two qualities of a product – standard and de-luxe. The contribution per unit is £100 for the standard and £300 for the de-luxe.

Each model requires 1 hour per unit in the machine shop and 40 machining hours are available per week. The standard model can be assembled and finished in 2.5 hours per unit but the de-luxe takes 10 hours per unit. There are 200 hours per week available for assembly and finishing.

Market research suggests that the maximum weekly sales of the de-luxe model will be 18 units.

The products use a special component, of which only 1,200 are currently available per week. Each standard unit uses 25 components and each de-luxe unit needs 50.

Required

(a) Analyse the current position and recommend a weekly production plan, showing its contribution. (10 marks)

Whilst keeping to the de-luxe sales limit, the firm would like to maximise contribution and realises that this may mean paying more to increase the supply of some of the resources required. It is not possible to increase the machining hours but assembly hours and the number of components can be increased as follows.

Resource	*Additional amount above existing prices to increase supply*
Assembly hours	£12 extra per hour for hours above 200
Component	£1 extra per component for components above 1,200

(b) Assess whether it is worthwhile increasing the supply of assembly hours and components. (6 marks)

(c) Recommend a revised weekly production plan, showing its contribution. (6 marks)

(Total 22 marks)

6.3   Caterpillar China Co

The Caterpillar China Co Ltd produces a range of five similar products, A, B, C, D and E. The following table shows the quantity of each of the required inputs necessary to produce one unit of each product, together with the weekly inputs available and the selling price per unit of each product.

	Product					Weekly inputs available
Inputs	A	B	C	D	E	
Raw materials (kg)	6.00	6.50	6.10	6.10	6.40	35,000
Forming (hours)	1.00	0.75	1.25	1.00	1.00	6,000
Firing (hours)	3.00	4.50	6.00	6.00	4.50	30,000
Packing (hours)	0.50	0.50	0.50	0.75	1.00	4,000
Selling price (£)	40	42	44	48	52	

The costs of each input are as follows:

Materials	£2.10 per kg
Forming	£3.00 per hour
Firing	£1.30 per hour
Packing	£8.00 per hour

Required

(a)   In order to maximise the weekly contribution to profit a linear programming package on a computer is to be used.

Formulate this problem so that the data can be input, giving both the objective function and the constraints. State briefly the assumptions necessary for your model to be suitable.   (9 marks)

(b)   The output from the computer package produces the following final tableau of a simplex solution to this problem.

Basis	A	B	C	D	E	X	S	T	U	Value
A	1	1.18	1.04	0.46	0	0.36	0	0	−2.29	3,357
S	0	−0.34	0.23	0.02	0	−0.18	1	0	0.14	321
T	0	1.37	2.97	2.28	0	−0.27	0	1	−2.79	9,482
E	0	−0.09	−0.02	0.52	1	−0.18	0	0	2.14	2,321
	0	1.26	1.06	0.51	0	2.02	0	0	8.81	105,791

Where A, B, C, D and E are the weekly production levels for the five products; X is the amount of raw materials that falls short of the maximum available; S, T, U are the respective number of hours short of the maximum weekly input of forming time, firing time, and packing time.

Use this tableau to find the optimum weekly production plan for the Caterpillar China Co. Describe the implications of using this plan in terms of the unused resources and overall contribution to profit.   (4 marks)

(c)   In the context of this problem explain the meaning of 'the dual or shadow price of a resource'.

(5 marks)

(d)   There is a proposition that the company manufactures an additional product which would sell at £50 per unit. Each unit made would need 6 kg of raw materials, 1 hour of forming time, 5 hours of firing time and 1 hour to pack.

Is this a worthwhile proposition?

(2 marks)

(Total 20 marks)

7   NETWORK ANALYSIS

7.1   Assert

Estimated information about the activities involved in a forthcoming project is as follows:

Activity	Preceding activity	Normal duration in days	Normal activity cost (£)	Additional cost of activity for each day saved (£)	Minimum possible duration in days
A	–	5	700	200	4
B	A	4	750	275	2
C	A	10	1,250	225	6
D	B	3	500	125	2
E	B	8	1,000	100	5
F	C	12	1,050	150	6
G	D	5	600	50	3
H	D	6	900	150	3
J	E	2	400	-	2
K	G	7	850	75	4

Overhead costs are £250 per day.

(a)   Assuming no activities are crashed:

(i)   sketch the project network and calculate the normal time of completion and total cost (including overheads);

(ii)   calculate the float of each activity and explain what these figures indicate.

(8 marks)

(b)   Calculate the minimum possible time in which the project could be completed and the minimum total cost (including overheads) for which this minimum time could be achieved.

(6 marks)

(c)   Calculate the minimum total cost (including overheads) for which the project could be completed and state the corresponding project duration.

(6 marks)

(Total 20 marks)

7.2 Floating labour

(a) Draw the network for the following series of activities.

Activity	Duration	Men required
1 – 2	16	2
1 – 3	20	6
1 – 6	30	4
2 – 5	15	3
3 – 4	15	2
3 – 5	10	5
4 – 5	3	2
4 – 6	16	4
5 – 6	12	4

(b) Calculate total float, free float and independent float for each activity and isolate the critical path.

(c) Represent the activities on a Gantt chart, assuming that each activity starts at its earliest time, and indicate the total float for each activity by dotted lines.

(d) Use the number of men required for each activity to attach a work load histogram to your chart and differentiate between the load for critical activities and other activities by shading.

(e) If the available capacity is 10 men in any 1 week and all the men are interchangeable, move the activities with float, to minimise the amount of time that the labour force is overloaded.

Comment on your result. **(15 marks)**

7.3 Project crash (M93)

An engineering team has to install a new computer-controlled work cell and management wants the job to be completed in as short a time as possible without incurring unnecessary expense.

The tasks contained in the job have been analysed and are as follows:

Task	Preceding task	Normal duration (working days)	Normal cost £	Reduced duration (working days)
A	–	8	3,200	5
B	A	14	8,400	11
C	A	10	5,000	7
D	A	12	7,200	8
E	B	4	2,000	3
F	C	6	4,200	4
G	E	10	6,000	7
H	B,F	22	11,000	15
I	G,H	14	5,600	11
J	C	8	4,800	7
K	D	6	3,000	4
L	I,J,K	8	4,000	5

When the reduced duration is used, the cost increase is directly proportional to the ratio of normal to reduced duration. As an example, task A would cost £5,120 at five days' duration. Tasks can only be undertaken at either normal or reduced duration.

Specialist equipment has to be hired for the entire project on a weekly basis, ie. if equipment is required for nine working days then it must be hired for two weeks and paid for on this basis. Each week's hire costs £10,000.

The installation team can work a five- or six-day working week. Six-day working increases total installation costs (excluding equipment hire) by 20%.

Required

(a) Draw a project planning diagram showing clearly the critical path, project duration and which activities are at normal duration and which are at reduced duration;

(10 marks)

(b) Prepare a cost statement based on the plan developed in (a) showing what the position would be with five-day and six-day working. (8 marks)

(c) Make a recommendation as to how the project should be organised, together with any concerns you have about the plan or the analysis. (4 marks)

(Total 22 marks)

7.4 Network analysis (M92)

A large contracting organisation uses network analysis for project planning and control.

A major project is being considered for which the target time is a maximum of 42 months and the target cost a maximum of £55 million. The project consists of four main elements - A, B, C and D - which are subject to considerable uncertainty. These elements are shown on Diagram 1, together with their possible durations, costs and probabilities. The diagram also shows all the possible paths through the network.

Diagram 1

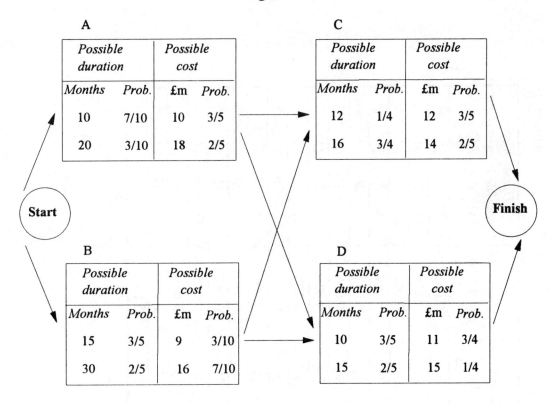

The 16 possible paths through the network have been tabulated and are shown in Table 1 which gives the individual element durations, their probabilities, the joint probability of each path and the duration of the possible critical paths.

Path	Element A Duration	Prob.	Element B Duration	Prob.	Element C Duration	Prob.	Element D Duration	Prob.	Joint probability	Duration of possible critical paths AC	AD	BC	BD
1	10	7/10	15	3/5	12	1/4	10	3/5	0.063	22	20	27	25
2	10	7/10	15	3/5	16	3/4	15	2/5	0.126	26	25	31	30
3	10	7/10	15	3/5	12	1/4	15	2/5	0.042	22	25	27	30
4	10	7/10	15	3/5	16	3/4	10	3/5	0.189	26	20	31	25
5	10	7/10	30	2/5	12	1/4	10	3/5	0.042	22	20	42	40
6	10	7/10	30	2/5	16	3/4	15	2/5	0.084	26	25	46	45
7	10	7/10	30	2/5	12	1/4	15	2/5	0.028	22	25	42	45
8	10	7/10	30	2/5	16	3/4	10	3/5	0.126	26	20	46	40
9	20	3/10	15	3/5	12	1/4	10	3/5	0.027	32	30	27	25
10	20	3/10	15	3/5	16	3/4	15	2/5	0.054	36	35	31	30
11	20	3/10	15	3/5	12	1/4	15	2/5	0.018	32	35	27	30
12	20	3/10	15	3/5	16	3/4	10	3/5	0.081	36	30	31	25
13	20	3/10	30	2/5	12	1/4	10	3/5	0.018	32	30	42	40
14	20	3/10	30	2/5	16	3/4	15	2/5	0.036	36	35	46	45
15	20	3/10	30	2/5	12	1/4	15	2/5	0.012	32	35	42	45
16	20	3/10	30	2/5	16	3/4	10	3/5	0.054	36	36	46	40

Required

(a) Calculate the probability of achieving the target duration. (6 marks)

(b) Prepare a table (similar to Table 1) showing the 16 possible costs of the project and their joint probabilities. (8 marks)

(c) Calculate the probability of achieving the target cost. (4 marks)

(d) Explain what guidance this type of time and cost analysis may provide for management. (4 marks)

(Total 22 marks)

8 SIGNIFICANCE TESTING

8.1 Textile finishing

In a textile finishing process, the average time taken is 6.4 hours. A series of eight trials is made with a modified process in an attempt to reduce this time. The following are obtained:

6.1, 5.9, 6.3, 6.5, 6.2, 6.0, 6.4, 6.2.

Has the modification succeeded in reducing the average processing time? **(10 marks)**

8.2 Mail order arrears (M93)

A mail-order company has 100,000 customers who choose goods from a catalogue and pay for them in weekly instalments. The company is concerned about the number of accounts in arrears. It wonders if there is any relationship between the amount of the initial purchase and whether an account is in arrears.

A random sample of 200 current accounts is taken and it is found that 40 are in arrears.

Some analysis has been carried out on this sample and the results are as follows:

For the 40 accounts in arrears

$$\Sigma x = £6,480$$
$$\Sigma x^2 = £1,102,250$$

where x = the amount of the original purchase.

For the 160 accounts not in arrears

Mean initial purchase = £152
Standard deviation of purchases = £39

Required

(a) Calculate 95% confidence limits for the percentage of all accounts which are in arrears. (6 marks)

(b) Calculate estimates of the mean and standard deviation of the 40 accounts in arrears. (4 marks)

Financial Training

(c)   Determine whether there is any statistical evidence of a difference between the mean initial purchases of the 40 accounts in arrears and of the 160 not in arrears.

(4 marks)

(d)   Interpret the results you have calculated and give any assumptions you have made

(3 marks)

(Total 17 marks)

8.3   Debtors (M87)

A company which has a range of profitable products is experiencing serious cashflow problems. The management accountant has decided to analyse the data relating to debtors, for she suspects that those debtors who owe more to the company are the ones who are taking longer to settle. A sample of 400 debts is produced and is analysed under the following headings:

(1)   Period outstanding *beyond* the normal credit period

        1 – 2 weeks: slow
        3 – 4 weeks: very slow
        5 – 6 weeks: warning letter
        7 – 8 weeks: legal action

(2)   Amount of debt

        £1,000 – 1,999: slow
        £2,000 – 2,999: medium
        £3,000 – 3,999: large
        £4,000 – 4,999: substantial

The clerks in the department have undertaken an examination of the 400 debts and have produced the table below:

	Slow	Very slow	Warning letter	Legal action
Small	12	15	16	17
Medium	15	17	21	27
Large	17	26	26	41
Substantial	26	32	37	55

Required

(a)   Use the chi-squared test to substantiate, or refute the suspicion of the management accountant.

(15 marks)

(b)   Explain carefully what is meant by the term 'significance' in the present context, and how a 'hypothesis test' differs from a 'test of significance'.

(5 marks)

(Total 20 marks)

8.4   Quattro plc (M91)

Quattro plc has four divisions – A, B, C and D. Each division manufactures the same goods and the group management wishes to compare the efficiency level of each division as measured by the number of faulty items manufactured.

A random sample is taken in each division as follows.

Division	Sample size	Number of faulty items
A	400	25
B	500	29
C	450	29
D	500	40

Required

(a)   Assess whether the evidence suggests there is any significant difference between the level of efficiency in the four divisions.   (12 marks)

(b)   State the assumptions on which the test used in (a) is based.   (5 marks)
                                                                        (Total 17 marks)

9   QUEUING THEORY

9.1   Heath Robinson Engineering

At a tool service centre in the factory of the Heath Robinson Engineering Co Ltd, the arrival rate is two per hour and the service potential is three per hour. The hourly wage paid to the attendant at the service centre is £1.50 per hour and the hourly cost of a machinist away from his work is £4.00.

(a)   State the assumptions on which simple queuing theory is based.   (5 marks)

(b)   Calculate the average number of machinists being served or waiting to be served at any given time.   (2 marks)

(c)   Calculate the average time a machinist spends on waiting for service.   (3 marks)

(d)   Calculate the total cost of operating the system for an eight-hour day.   (4 marks)

(e)   Calculate the cost of the system if there were two attendants working together *as a team*, each paid £1.50 per hour and each able to service on average two customers per hour.   (6 marks)
                                                                        (Total 20 marks)

9.2   Homebase (M89)

Each Saturday a large home improvement store experiences congestion at its credit card verification point which is at present staffed by one employee. Observation has revealed that customers arrive at an average rate of 38 per hour and that it takes an average of 1½ minutes for the telephone verification of a credit card.

It is felt that customers are being lost and the management accountant has proposed that a second employee be stationed at the verification point. The employee would be paid £2.50 per hour for the 12 hours that the store is open on Saturday and it would be necessary to install a second telephone at a one-off cost of £100.

Evidence from another store suggests that over 20 weeks following the introduction of a second verification employee the number of credit card transactions rose by about 10%. Typically, the mean value of a credit card transaction is £25 and currently there are about 456 transactions on a Saturday.

The average gross profit percentage for the store is 15%.

Required

(a)   Calculate the average queue lengths and average times a credit card customer would have to wait in the queue with both one and two assistants, assuming a single queue;

(For $C = 2$, $P_0 = 0.319$)

Multi-channel queuing formulae:

Average time a customer is in the queue (including times there is no queue)

$$= \frac{(\rho c)^c}{c!(1-\rho)^2 c\mu} P_o$$

Average number of customers in the queue $= \dfrac{\rho(\rho c)^c}{c!(1-\rho)^2} P_o$ (6 marks)

(b)   Advise management whether a second verification employee should be provided and give two other factors which should be considered in making the decision.   (4 marks)

(c)   Explain the assumptions upon which queuing theory is based and state whether you think these are realistic or unrealistic.   (10 marks)

(Total 20 marks)

10   CAPITAL INVESTMENT APPRAISAL

10.1   Alphabet Group plc (M88)

You have recently been appointed as management accountant attached to the headquarters of the Alphabet Group plc, with special responsibility for monitoring the performance of the companies within the group. Each company is treated as an investment centre and every month produces an operating statement for the group headquarters. Summaries of the statements for companies X and Y, which make similar products selling at similar prices, for the last month showed a typical situation:

Extract from company monthly operating statements

		X £'000	Y £'000
	Sales	600	370
less	Variable costs	229	208
=	Contribution	371	162
less	Controllable fixed overheads (including depreciation on company assets)	65	28
=	Controllable profit	306	134
less	Apportioned group costs	226	119
=	Net profit	80	15
	Company assets	£6.4m	£0.9m
	Estimated return on capital employed (on annual basis)	15%	20%

Although both companies are earning more than the target return on capital of 12%, there is pressure on interest rates which means that this rate must be increased soon and the board is concerned at the relatively low return achieved by X.

Required

(a) Compare and discuss the relative performance of the two companies as shown in the summarised operating statements. (10 marks)

(b) Redraft the operating statements using an alternative performance measurement to return on capital employed and interpret them against a background of rising interest rates. (5 marks)

(c) Critically compare the use of return on capital employed and the alternative performance measure used in (b) to assess the performance of investment centres.

(5 marks)

(Total 20 marks)

10.2 Exewye (M89)

A2Z plc supports the concept of terotechnology or life-cycle costing for new investment decisions covering its engineering activities. The financial side of this philosophy is now well established and its principles extended to all other areas of decision-making.

The company is to replace a number of its machines and the production manager is torn between the Exe machine, a more expensive machine with a life of 12 years, and the Wye machine with an estimated life of six years. If the Wye machine is chosen it is likely that it would be replaced at the end of six years by another Wye machine. The pattern of maintenance and running costs differs between the two types of machine and relevant data are shown below.

		Exe £		Wye £
Purchase price		19,000		13,000
Trade-in value		3,000		3,000
Annual repair costs		2,000		2,600
Overhaul costs	(at year 8)	4,000	(at year 4)	2,000
Estimated financing costs averaged over machine life		10% pa		10%pa

Required

(a) Recommend, with supporting figures, which machine to purchase, stating any assumptions made. (10 marks)

(b) Describe an appropriate method of comparing replacement proposals with unequal lives.

(4 marks)

(c) Describe life cycle costing and give the benefits that are likely to accrue from its use. Support your answer with examples of changes in practice that could occur from adopting this philosophy. (6 marks)

(Total 20 marks)

10.3 RS plc (M90)

RS plc manufactures domestic food mixers. It is investigating whether or not to accept a three-year contract to make a new model for sale through a supermarket chain. The contract uses skilled labour which cannot be increased above that currently available and RS plc will receive a fixed price of £42 per mixer for all the mixers it can produce in the three-year period. The following estimates have been made:

Capital investment	£50,000 payable now, with nil scrap value
Additional overhead	£25,000 per annum
Materials	£30 per mixer
Labour	£6 per hour

The factory manager knows from experience of similar machines that there will be a learning effect for labour. He estimates that this will take the form:

Cash flow

$$y = ax^{-0.3}$$

where	y	=	average labour hours per unit
	a	=	labour hours for first unit
	x	=	cumulative production

He estimates that the first mixer will take 10 hours to produce and that the fixed amount of labour available will enable 5,000 mixers to be produced in the first year.

Apart from the capital investment, all cashflows can be assumed to arise at year-ends.

The company has a cost of capital of 15%.

Required

(a) Calculate the NPV of the proposed contract.   (16 marks)

(b) State which other factors need to be considered before a final decision is made

(6 marks)

(Total 22 marks)

10.4 AB Ltd (M91)

(a) AB Ltd is reviewing its credit control activities. At present, debtors pay at the end of the second month after the sale (for example, January sales are paid for at the end of March).

It is estimated that by recruiting additional staff and pursuing more active credit control policies, debts could be collected one month earlier than at present. The extra costs for the first month would be £2,000. Due to the effect of automation, these costs are expected to decrease at 0.25% per month indefinitely.

Credit sales in the first month are expected to be £250,000 with a monthly growth of 0.5% which is expected to continue indefinitely. The cost of capital is 1.25% per month.

Required

Appraise the proposed in-house credit control system and advise whether it would be worthwhile.   (10 marks)

(b)   If AB Ltd decides to change its credit control system, an option being considered is to have the whole operation dealt with externally by a computer bureau. The bureau has quoted a fixed rate of £5,000 per month plus an initial systems and programming charge. This would reduce AB Ltd's existing administrative costs by £4,000 per month indefinitely and avoid the £2,000 extra costs mentioned above.

Required

(i)   State the maximum amount that should be paid for the initial systems charge.

(6 marks)

(ii)   Indicate what other factors should be considered before a final decision is taken about the change in credit policy.

(6 marks)

Note: Ignore general inflation and taxation.   **(Total 22 marks)**

11   INFORMATION TECHNOLOGY AND SIMULATION

11.1   Data collection (N90)

'Considerable effort goes into the design of sophisticated information systems, many of which rely for their success on the quality of the data collection process that precedes the system . . . yet sometimes these collection processes are far from satisfactory. Why, as trained accountants, do we often close our eyes to the inadequacy of the data collection processes and still believe in the figures we report to management?'

Extract from article by Bentley (in *Management Accounting,* January 1989).

(a)   Describe typical problems and inadequacies encountered in data collection processes.

(5 marks)

(b)   Explain the key objectives of effective data collection with regard to the quantity of information, accuracy and timing.

(5 marks)

(c)   Describe how a decision-maker's information needs could be reflected in the data collection process.

(7 marks)

(Total 17 marks)

11.2   Simulation (M92)

(a)   A company has been having problems with stockouts for one of its components and is contemplating making alterations either to the reorder quantity or to the reorder level, or to both.

Before making a decision, the company wishes to explore whether any guidance can be obtained by simulating the operation of the system.

The pattern of weekly demand over the past few years has been as follows.

Weekly demand (Units)	Frequency
500	10
525	15
550	30
575	50
600	55
625	60
650	40
675	20
700	10
725	5

Ordering costs are £20 per order and the carrying cost is £5 per annum per unit. The estimated loss when an order cannot be met is £12 per unit. When stock reaches the preset order point a replenishment order is issued.

Required

Describe, using a flowchart or other means, how a simulation model for this problem might work. (12 marks)

(b)   Using a reorder point of 2,500 and an order quantity of 2,000, a simulation of 20 weeks' operations has been run on a computer and the following summary produced.

Simulation summary

Number of periods	20 weeks	Carrying cost	£1,984.13
Average inventory	1,031.8 units	Ordering cost	£120.00
Orders	6	Stockout cost	£20,580.00
Stockouts	1,715.0 units	Total cost	£22,684.13
Average demand	606.3 units		
Lead time	4 weeks		

Required

Interpret the above summary and suggest what could be done next to make the simulation more realistic. (5 marks)

(Total 17 marks)

11.3   DB plc (M90)

DB plc operates a conventional stock-control system based on reorder levels and economic ordering quantities (EOQ). The various control levels were set originally based on estimates which did not allow for any uncertainty and this has caused difficulties because, in practice, lead times, demands and other factors do vary.

As part of a review of the system, a typical stock item, Part No X206, has been studied in detail as follows.

Data for Part No X206

Lead times	Probability
15 working days	0.2
20 working days	0.5
25 working days	0.3

Demand per working day	Probability
5,000 units	0.5
7,000 units	0.5

Note: It can be assumed that the demands would apply for the whole of the appropriate lead time.

DB plc works for 240 days per year and it costs £0.15 pa to carry a unit of X206 in stock. The reorder level for this part is currently 150,000 units and the reorder cost is £1,000.

Required

(a)   Calculate the level of buffer stock implicit in a reorder level of 150,000 units.

(4 marks)

(b)   Calculate the probability of a stockout.   (2 marks)

(c)   Calculate the expected annual stockouts in units.   (3 marks)

(d)   Calculate the stock-out cost per unit at which it would be worthwhile raising the reorder level to 175,000 units.   (3 marks)

(e)   Discuss the possible alternatives to a reorder level EOQ inventory system and their advantages and disadvantages.   (5 marks)

(Total 17 marks)

Answers

1 COST ASCERTAINMENT AND COST BEHAVIOUR

1.1 Maneller Ltd

(a)

			Number of aircraft	
			240	360
			£m	£m
Direct material	240 @ £3m		720	720
	120 @ £2.7m		–	324
Direct labour	(W1/W2)		1,228.8	1,617.6
			1,948.8	2,661.6
Development and testing			220	220
Production facility			20	20
Other fixed indirect costs			100	150
			2,288.8	3,051.6

(i) Breakeven price for 240 aircraft $= \dfrac{2{,}288.8}{240} = $ £9.5 million

(ii) Breakeven price for 360 aircraft $= \dfrac{3{,}051.6}{360} = $ £8.5 million

(b) The additional revenue will be:

	£m
50 aircraft @ £8.6m	430
Less price reduction 280 aircraft @ £0.4m	(112)
	318

The additional costs will be:

	£m
Direct materials 50 aircraft @ £2.7m	135
Direct labour (W3)	161
	296

Net increase in revenue	£22

The above analysis indicates that the company should accept the order, but, as the decision is marginal, other factors should be taken into account.

Notes

(1)   It has been assumed that Tolly obtains 10% discount for parts on all orders over 240. (An alternative assumption might be that discount is only granted on order size of 120 aircraft.)

(2)   It has been assumed that the other fixed indirect costs are incurred whilst the project is continuing, in this case three years, irrespective of the number of aircraft sold in year 3.

Workings

(1)   Tabulation

Batch no	Cumulative quantity	Cumulative cost £m	(80%) Average cost £m	Cost per unit £m
1	30	300	300	10
2	60	480	240	8
3	120	768	192	6.4
4	240	1,228.8	153.6	5.12

Therefore labour cost for 240 aircraft would be £1,228.8 million.

(2)   Formula

Y = cumulative average time per batch of 30 = ax^{-b}

Where a = £300m

$x = \dfrac{360}{30}$

$-b = \dfrac{\log 0.8}{\log 2}$

$Y = 300 \times 12^{-0.321928} = 134.80394$

Therefore labour cost for 360 aircraft $= \dfrac{134.80394}{30} \times 360 = £1,617.6$ million

(3)   For 330 units (280 ordered + 50 extra order)

$Y = 300 \times \dfrac{330^{-0.321928}}{30} = 138.63337$

Therefore labour cost for 330 aircraft $= \dfrac{138.63337}{30} \times 330 = £1,525$ million

For 280 units

$$Y = 300 \times \frac{280^{-0.321928}}{30} = 146.16361$$

Therefore labour cost for 280 aircraft $= \dfrac{146.16361}{30} \times 280 = £1,364$ million

Therefore labour cost for extra 50 aircraft $= £161$ million

1.2 Cost behaviour

(a) The traditional approach to cost behaviour analysis is to assume that costs vary linearly with the activity level. This can be represented graphically as below.

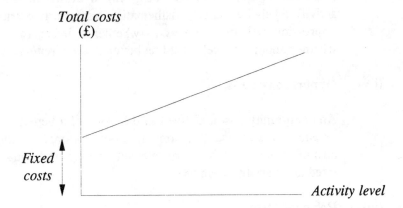

The intercept on the y-axis represents the fixed costs for the period. The gradient of the line represents the variable cost per unit. The total cost is the sum of the fixed costs and variable costs, which can be expressed algebraically as follows.

Total costs = Fixed costs + (Activity level × Variable cost per unit)

In practice it is observed that the set of points collected for a particular activity do not exactly fall on a straight line as above. If they are close to a line, then simple linear regression analysis can be carried out to identify the line of best fit through the observed points, and the differences between the points and the line can be put down to random fluctuations. In other situations the points may be nowhere near a straight line. This could have arisen due to any of the following factors.

(i) The relationship between cost and activity level could be curvilinear rather than straight-line linear. For example a quadratic expression may hold between activity level x and total costs C of the form $C = ax^2 + bx + c$. Such an expression would describe a parabola rather than a straight line.

(ii) A straight line may be a fair approximation to cost behaviour within a finite range of activity level, but beyond this range either below or above, the linear relationship breaks down.

(iii) The traditional model assumes that activity level is the only determinant of cost, ie. that simple regression applies. In practice multiple regression is more likely, with total cost depending on a number of factors (eg. activity level and the number of machine breakdowns).

(iv) No notice has yet been taken of inflation. It is likely that both fixed costs and variable cost per unit will increase over time in line with general inflation.

(v) Other external factors may also impact upon costs, such as the state of the weather, or the day of the week.

(vi) Certain costs are indivisible and will behave in a step function as activity level increases. An example is full-time employees, which must be hired and released one by one rather than in fractions of people.

(b) Other possible approaches to analysing cost behaviour include the following.

(i) **Drawing a scattergraph**

If a scattergraph (or scatter diagram) is drawn of the observed costs and activity levels before any mathematical analysis is carried out, an immediate impression will be given as to whether a linear model is appropriate, or whether another model would be better in the circumstances.

(ii) **Opportunity costs**

An opportunity cost is defined as the value of a benefit sacrificed in favour of an alternative course of action. In a decision-making context the opportunity cost of an item will be more relevant than its traditional breakdown between fixed and variable elements.

(iii) **Relevant costs**

Decisions should be taken on the basis of examining the costs and revenues which are relevant to that particular decision, ignoring completely the costs and revenues which are unaffected by that decision. Whether a cost is relevant is more important than knowing its breakdown between fixed and variable elements.

1.3   New environment

(a) Traditional management accounting performance measures such as budgetary control and standard costing are best suited to stable production processes since budgets and standards are usually based on past performance. Clearly past performance is only a useful predictor of the future if conditions are stable.

The modern manufacturing environment is characterised by rapid technological changes, work produced to specific customer needs and high quality produce. In such an environment the traditional measures referred to above find it hard to keep up. Similarly the reduction in direct labour as a proportion of total cost and the move towards automated processes such as CAD/CAM make the traditional classification and analysis of labour costs redundant.

Traditional accounting systems lay very little emphasis on non-financial matters such as quality and response time. It is, therefore, largely true that traditional techniques are irrelevant or misleading in the modern world and new methods are needed to evaluate such aspects of production.

(b) Management accountants can adopt new methods to suit the modern environment such as activity-based costing (ABC). ABC identifies the activities which cause costs, known as 'cost drivers', calculates the costs per unit of activity and charges the activity costs to the products which use those activities. This helps in the move away from traditional overhead absorption based on direct labour hours.

In addition, traditional techniques such as standard costing may be adapted and made more flexible so that labour costs are subsumed within variable overheads and automated processes are monitored to arrive at standard times per batch which together with standard cost rates will provide the target for actual costs to be compared against.

Further non-financial performance measures must be devised to assess quality, innovation and customer satisfaction.

2 REGRESSION AND CORRELATION

2.1 Coefficient of determination

(a) The coefficient of determination, r^2, is given by the formula:

$$r^2 = \frac{\left(n\Sigma xy - (\Sigma x)(\Sigma y)\right)^2}{\left(n\Sigma x^2 - (\Sigma x)^2\right)\left(n\Sigma y^2 - (\Sigma y)^2\right)}$$

(Note the question actually gives the formula wrongly in that the square is missing in the numerator.)

This is calculated first using $x = x_1$ and again using x_2.

y against x_1

Substituting the summations given, we get:

$$r^2 = \frac{\left((10 \times 58,040) - (113 \times 4,550)\right)^2}{\left((10 \times 1,533) - 113^2\right)\left((10 \times 2,451,300) - 4,550^2\right)}$$

$$= \frac{66,250^2}{2,561 \times 3,810,500}$$

$$= \mathbf{0.4498}$$

y against x_2

$$r^2 = \frac{\left((10 \times 121,000) - \left(212 \times 4,550^2\right)\right)}{\left((10 \times 6,120) - 212^2\right)\left((10 \times 2,451,300) - 4,550^2\right)}$$

$$= \frac{246,400^2}{16,256 \times 3,810,500}$$

$$= \mathbf{0.9801}$$

Comment

The value of r^2 represents the proportion of the total variation in y that can be attributed to the variation in x, so that the higher its value, the more closely the variables are related.

For y (sales) and x_1 (local advertising), r^2 is about 0.45, whereas for y (sales) and x_2 (regional advertising), r^2 is about 0.98.

Thus monthly sales are much more closely related to regional advertising expenditure than they are to local advertising expenditure, contradicting the stated assertion.

(b)   Here the dependence of sales (y) on local advertising (x_1) and regional advertising (x_2) jointly, ie. in combination, is being measured. The coefficient of multiple correlation of 0.99 measures the proportion of the variation in y that can be attributed to the variation in x_1 and x_2 jointly and is the bi-variate equivalent of r^2. Since r^2 for y on x_2 alone is 0.98, we can say that there is no real evidence that prediction of monthly sales from both local and regional advertising is any better than prediction from regional advertising alone, ie. local advertising expenditure effectively adds nothing to the potential accuracy of the prediction.

Despite this the multiple regression equation of y on x_1 and x_2 has been calculated. This takes the form $y = a + bx_1 + cx_2$, where a, b and c are determined from the summary data.

The sales forecast for the stated outlet has been obtained by substituting $x_1 = 12$ (ie. local advertising £12,000) and $x_2 = 30$ (ie. regional advertising for outlet 8, £30,000), in the multiple regression equation to give a predicted value of monthly sales y of 597.333 or £597,333.

(**Note:** The actual computation of a, b and c by the candidate is complicated and would not be required.)

Value and limitations of regression analysis in sales forecasting

If it is known or suspected that sales may depend on a number of other variables, eg. advertising expenditure then regression analysis is a concise mathematical method of using sample data to (i) determine which variables are most useful for prediction purposes and (ii) predict sales using the calculated regression equation.

It is also possible to attach limits of *error* to a prediction. Provided a number of assumptions are valid, this is generally a better, though more complex, method of sales forecasting than one based on 'hunch' or 'rule-of-thumb'.

A number of assumptions are made in regression analysis, which if contravened may make sales predictions suspect. For example, a regression equation calculated at a particular point in time will not necessarily be valid at a future point in time, so that the equation would need to be continuously updated.

Other factors in sales forecasting

It is assumed that this relates to the specific company in the question. Thus, as well as local and regional advertising expenditure, factors that could influence sales are:

(i)   degree of competition;
(ii)   size of outlet in terms of floor area and number of staff employed;
(iii) general socio-economic level in the area.

There is, of course, no exhaustive list and candidates may think of several other factors.

2.2   Cecil Beaton plc

(a)

	(Units in '000) x	(Contribution in £'000) y	x^2	xy
	150	162	22,500	24,300
	180	184	32,400	33,120
	200	184	40,000	36,800
	230	248	52,900	57,040
	760	778	147,800	151,260

$$b = \frac{n\Sigma xy - \Sigma x \Sigma y}{n\Sigma x^2 - (\Sigma x)^2} = \frac{(4 \times 151,260) - (760 \times 778)}{(4 \times 147,800) - (760 \times 760)}$$

$$= \frac{605,040 - 591,280}{591,200 - 577,600}$$

$$= \frac{13,760}{13,600} = 1.012$$

$$a = \frac{\Sigma y - b\Sigma x}{n} = \frac{778 - (1.012 \times 760)}{4}$$

At planned output 260,000 the contribution is 2.22 + 1.012 (260)

= 265.34 = £265,340

(b)   95% confidence limit is

265.34 ± 4.303 × 14.5

= 265.34 ± 62.39

Upper limit   £327,730   say £328,000
Lower limit   £202,950   say £203,000

These are the limits within which we can be 95% certain the actual value of the contribution will fall.

(c)   Linear regression is a simple statistical technique for finding the line of best fit for a given set of data. Once found it may then be used for forecasting values of the dependent variable.

However, there are limitations which must be borne in mind when interpreting results:

–   forecasting by extrapolation is liable to give inaccurate results due to circumstances not foreseen in the original analysis;

–   not all relationships between variables are linear and a more complex analysis may be needed.

3   BUDGETARY CONTROL AND PROFIT IMPROVEMENT

3.1   Processors Ltd

(a)   **Calculation of initial selling price at 1 January**

(i)   Budgeted output and sales, 20,000 kg

(ii)   Variable costs

	£'000	£ per kg
Materials		
23,000 kg at £10 per kg		
(£11.50 usage per kg)	230	11.50
Labour		
360,000 hours at £0.80 per hour		
(18 hours per kg)	288	14.40
Overhead		
Power: 2,400,000 units at £0.01 per unit	24	1.20
Distribution: 20,000 kg at £2.40 per kg	48	2.40
	590	29.50

(iii)   Fixed costs per month

	£'000		
Works overhead	20		
Administration	14		
Distribution	1		
Selling	7.5		
	42.5 (× 12)	510	25.50

(iv)   Total costs — 1,100 — 55.00

(v)   Profit margin (20%) — 220 — 11.00

(vi)   Sales and selling price — 1,320 — 66.00

(b)   **Statements showing revised budgeted profit for the year**

		Half year ended	
	£	30 June £	31 December £
Contribution per kg shown by original budget			
Selling price	66		
Variable costs	29.5	36.5	36.5
Adjustments arising from decisions taken and events occurring			
(i) Increase in selling price		–	2.4
			38.9
(ii) Increase in variable costs 5% × £29.5		–	1.475
		36.5	37.425

Output and sales	kg	kg
Total per original budget	10,000	10,000
Estimated increase 2.5%	250	250
	10,250	10,250
Anticipated decrease due to higher selling price ($\frac{2.40}{0.20} \times 20.5$)		246
	10,250	10,004

Budgeted profit	£	£
Contribution		
10,250 × £36.5	374,125	
10,004 × £37.425		374,400
Less fixed cost per original budget £510,000		
Half year	255,000	
half year + 1%		257,550
Revised budgeted profit	119,125	116,850

3.2   Sizer

(a)   **Budgetary control**

(i)   **Aims and advantages**

The aims of a budgetary control system are to plan, control and coordinate the activities of the business in the short term, and specifically:

(1)   to establish human responsibilities in concrete terms;

(2)   to maximise the results of operations and the return on capital investment;

(3)   to establish cost centres, and co-ordinate activities between these centres and departments;

(4)   to plan the capital needs of the business and the working capital required;

(5)   to establish an effective system for the supply of control information;

(6)   to provide a basis for comparison between actual performance and plan.

Advantages of a budgetary control system

(1)   It clearly establishes the overall aims of the business and individual targets for departments and cost centres.

(2)   It provides for information as a guide to control, and action to effect control of current operations.

(3)   It caters for constant review of decision-making to take account of current developments in the business.

(4)   It establishes responsibilities in departments and personnel and encourages maximum performance by personal motivation.

(5)   It provides for co-ordination of the short-term and long-term plans of the business.

(6)   It provides the basis for the development of standard costs and greater cost control.

(7)   It assists management to assess alternative uses of scarce resources.

(ii)   **Five main budgets used in a system of budgetary control**

(1)   **Sales budget** – showing number of units sold, unit selling price and total sales revenue analysed perhaps by product, area, time or some other appropriate basis.

(2)   **Production budget** – using the figures from the sales budget (if demand was the principal budget factor) this would show sales, opening and closing finished stock levels and production. This could be analysed as the sales budget and might well have supporting schedules showing materials, labour and manufacturer overhead costs.

(3)   **Expense budget** – based on the figures for production and sales details of selling, administration, financial and research expenses

could be estimated; these expenses where possible should be analysed into their fixed and variable elements.

(4) **Cash budget** – knowing the estimate for sales and costs, with details of creditors and debtors periods or when certain expense items fall due it would be possible to find the cash receipts and payments on, say, a monthly basis. This would be used to indicate interest costs in the financial expenses budget.

(5) **Capital expenditure budget** – looking primarily at the production budget, but also reviewing other areas of a company's activities, an indication can be gained of capital expenditure requirements. In addition to just 'slotting these into' the cash budget, some investment appraisal calculations would appear in such a budget showing both costs and benefits; these benefits may well be in qualitative rather than necessarily financial forms.

(b) **Zero-base budgeting levels**

(i) **Nature or ZBB**

ZBB is a formalised system of budgeting for the activities of an enterprise as if each activity were being performed for the first time (hence zero base).

(ii) **Steps in ZBB**

ZBB involves:

– developing *decision packages* for each company activity;
– evaluating and ranking these packages; and
– allocating resources to the various activities accordingly.

Decision packages contain information about: *function* of an activity; *goal* of that department; measure of performance; *costs and benefits* from different ways of organising an activity (at different levels of funding); *consequences* of not performing an activity.

These packages should be reviewed and an organisation's commitment to each activity decided.

(iii) **Areas where most effective**

The ZBB approach is best applied to *service* and support areas rather than manufacturing operations.

(iv) **Advantages and disadvantages**

Disadvantages are that it takes up a great deal of management *time*. It generates lots of *paper*. It requires education and *training*. Results may be initially disappointing.

Advantages are that it establishes *minimum requirements* from service departments. It produces a plan to work to when more resources are available. It makes managers think about what they're doing. It establishes *priorities*. It can be carried out annually, a few activities per year or when crises are envisaged.

3.3   LMN Co

(a)

LMN Co
Budgeted profit and loss account for the quarter ended 31 March 19X1

	£	£
Sales (W1)		360,000
Cost of goods sold		
Opening stock	66,500	
Production costs (W2)	274,760	
Less: Closing stock (W3)	(119,654)	
		(221,606)
Gross profit		138,394
Administration overhead (W4)	69,000	
Bad debts (W5)	10,800	
		(79,800)
Net profit		58,594

Workings

(1)   Unit sales = 1,000 + 1,400 + 1,600 = 4,000
Value of sales = 4,000 × £90 = £360,000

(2)   Budgeted stock at 1 January 1991 = 1,200 units
Budgeted sales in January 1991 = 1,000 units
∴ Constant ratio each month = 1.2

	Jan (units)	Feb (units)	Mar (units)	Apr (units)	Total (units)
Opening stock	1,200	1,680	1,920	2,160	
Closing stock	1,680	1,920	2,160		
∴ Stock increase	480	240	240		
Sales	1,000	1,400	1,600		
∴ Production required	1,480	1,640	1,840		4,960
∴ Overtime required		140	340		480

	£
So total variable production costs = 4,960 × (12 + £24 + £8)	218,240
Cost of overtime = 480 × £24	11,520
Fixed production overhead = 3 × £15,000	45,000
	274,760

(3) Closing stock $= \dfrac{2,160}{4,960} \times £274,760 = £119,654$

(4) Administration overhead $= 3 \times £23,000 = £69,000$

(5) 97% of sales are collected, so 3% must be bad debts.
Total bad debts $= 3\% \times £360,000 = £10,800$

(b)
LMN Co
Cash budgets for the first three months of 19X1

	January £	February £	March £
Receipts			
Current month's sales (30%)	27,000	37,800	43,200
Previous month's sales (67%)	78,390	60,300	84,420
	105,390	98,100	127,620
Payments			
Materials (1,480 × £12, etc.)	17,760	19,680	22,080
Labour (normal, 1,480 × £24, etc.)	35,520	39,360	44,160
Labour (overtime, 140 × £24, etc.)	–	3,360	8,160
Variable overhead (1,480 × £8, etc.)	11,840	13,120	14,720
Fixed overhead (less depreciation)	11,500	11,500	11,500
Administration overhead	23,000	23,000	23,000
	99,620	110,020	123,620
Net cashflow	5,770	(11,920)	4,000

(c) Net cash movement for the quarter $= £5,770 - £11,920 + £4,000 = -£2,150$.

The budgeted profit in part (a) can be reconciled to this figure as follows:

LMN Co
Reconciliation of budgeted profit with net cash movement

	£	£
Budgeted profit for the quarter		58,594
Less: Increase in debtors		
Sales less bad debts (£360,000 – £10,800)	349,200	
Receipts (£105,390 + £98,100 + £127,620)	331,110	
		(18,090)
Add: Depreciation charged (3 × £3,500)		10,500
Less: Increase in finished stocks (£119,654 – £66,500)		(53,154)
Net cash movement for the quarter		(2,150)

3.4 Japanese companies

(a) 'Physical measures' are used where items are measured in their physical units rather than in monetary amounts. For example, the amount of good material output from a process could be measured in kilograms, rather than stating these kilograms at a standard value to give a pound sterling amount.

'Non-financial indices' are index numbers obtained from comparing two amounts measured in physical terms rather than in monetary amounts. Often such indices are calculated at a series of points in time to determine the trend of the values. For example, the good material output in kilograms in 1981 could be the base period value, with output for each successive year calculated as an index number based on 1981.

(b) Three useful non-financial indices could be as follows.

(i) **Sales returns : sales**

Such an index number could be used as a measurement of customer satisfaction with the company's products. High returns suggest that customers do not like what they are being provided with. If goods are returned because of faulty workmanship, the index can also be used as a quality control tool assessing the quality of the production department as well as the inspection department.

(ii) **Idle time : total labour time**

Efficient management of a company's labour resources should mean a low proportion of idle time for the workforce. The index number produced can be used to assess how effectively labour is being used.

(iii) **Deliveries made late : deliveries made on time**

Customers will be content only if our company delivers goods at the times when promised. This index number therefore gauges the potential dissatisfaction of customers from our delivery scheduling. It can also be examined to assess whether such scheduling was realistic in the first instance.

(c) There are several traditional cost and management accounting practices that are inappropriate in modern conditions. Examples are given below.

(i) Overhead has traditionally been absorbed on the basis of direct labour hours. In today's manufacturing environment the proportions of total cost represented by direct materials and direct labour may be very small, leading to absurdly large overhead recovery rates. Other methods of absorbing overheads are likely to be more appropriate.

(ii) Cost and management accountants spend a large proportion of their time generating monthly reports, whose production is seen as an end in themselves. A typical split of time might be 90% producing the schedules, and only 10% analysing them to give information for the basis of decision-making. There is no point producing any management report if it is simply going to be filed away without being looked at. Such reports must be properly analysed, and acted upon.

(iii) A similar problem arises in the budget process. Hours of time are spent arguing on what figures should go into future periods' budgets, but much less time is often spent in investigating the causes of budget variances.

(iv) Standard costing systems usually set one standard for each cost and revenue item, and try to use this standard as the benchmark for all purposes arising. This is an impossible ambition to achieve: 'different standards for different purposes' is the only realistic approach.

(v) There is often an over-emphasis on financial accounting and total absorption costing within management accounting systems. Only a marginal costing system can identify opportunity costs for the purpose of efficient decision-making.

(vi) There is often an over-emphasis on short-term profitability at the expense of long-term development. All costs are variable in the long run, and long term maximisation of contribution has to be seen as the ideal objective of business in that context.

3.5 B Ltd

(a) **Budgeted production**

	Period 1	Period 2	Period 3	Period 4
Opening stock	4,000	2,500	3,300	2,500
Less: Sales	(15,000)	(20,000)	(16,500)	(21,000)
Less: Closing stock	(2,500)	(3,300)	(2,500)	(3,000)
Budgeted production	13,500	20,800	15,700	21,500

(b)   **Cost budget for period 4**

	£'000	£'000
Direct labour		
Normal rate 21,500 × £20 (W1)	430	
Bonus rate 3,500 × £10 (W1)	35	
		465
Direct material		
21,500 × £8 (W2)		172
Production overhead		
Variable 21,500 × £5 (W3)	107.5	
Fixed	50.0	
		157.5
Depreciation		40
Administration overhead		
Variable 21,500 × £2 (W4)	43	
Fixed	65	
		108
Selling overhead		
Variable 21,000 × £1 (W5)	21	
Fixed	45	
		66
		1,008.5

Workings

(1)   Direct labour rate (period 1) = $\dfrac{£270,000}{13,500}$ = £20/unit

To find the bonus paid for production above 18,000 units:

	£'000
Period 2 – normal rate (20,800 × £20)	416,000
Budgeted cost	444,000
Bonus paid	28,000

Bonus rate = $\dfrac{£28,000}{20,800 - 18,000}$ = £10/unit

(2)   **Direct materials**

Direct materials rate = $\dfrac{£108,000}{13,500}$ = £8/unit

---

(3)   **Production overhead**

	Period 1	*Period 2*	*Period 2 – Period 1*
Cost £	117,500	154,000	36,500
Production	13,500	20,800	7,300
Variable cost per unit			£5

Fixed cost = £117,500 – 13,500 × £5 = £50,000

(4)   **Administration overheads**

	Period 1	*Period 2*	*Period 2 – Period 1*
Cost £	92,000	106,600	14,600
Production	13,500	20,800	7,300
Variable cost per unit			£2

Fixed cost = £92,000 – 13,500 × £2 = £65,000

(5)   **Selling overheads**

	Period 1	*Period 2*	*Period 2 – Period 1*
Cost £	60,000	65,000	5,000
Production	15,000	20,000	5,000
Variable cost per unit			£1

Fixed cost = £60,000 – 15,000 × £1 = £45,000

(c)   **Budget variances**

	Budget £'000	*Actual* £'000	*Variances* £'000
Direct labour	465	458	7.0F
Direct materials	172	176	4.0A
Production overhead	157.5	181	23.5A
Depreciation	40	40	–
Administration overhead	108	128	20.0A
Selling overhead	66	62	4.0F
	1,008.5	1,045	36.5A

(d)   **Criticism of assumptions for cost budgets**

(i)   Variable costs vary linearly with either production or sales.

(ii)   Fixed costs remain fixed within the relevant range. There could be a step change at 21,000 units which has not been taken into account.

(iii)   Depreciation is constant at increasing levels of production.

(iv)   Stockholding costs are fixed and do not vary with stock levels.

3.6   Flexible budgets

(a)   It is rare that all variable costs vary with the same variable, and the relationships are unlikely to be linear. Direct costs may come closest - particularly materials, although wastage and bulk discounts can distort the pattern; labour is only going to be reasonably close if it is paid on a strict hourly/production basis - but most workers will have some form of minimum wage.

Overheads are generally classified into variable and fixed parts; this classification is sometimes quite difficult to get clear cut. The fixed element can vary on a 'stepped' basis over wider ranges of activity levels, and the variable overhead element is often the most difficult to fit to a simple linear relationship with volume. The use of activity-based costing goes some way towards assessing this variability more 'accurately'.

(b)   The purpose of setting up flexible budgets is to have as good an estimate as possible of expected costs and revenues at different levels of activity. These are then compared with actual costs for the particular level achieved, and significant variances highlighted on a regular report.

Clearly, if the original standards and relationships used in preparation of the budget are inaccurate, the report may be quite misleading. Seemingly significant variances, subsequently investigated at a monetary and time cost, may in fact be quite innocuous; whereas smaller ones that are ignored could in fact indicate an out of control operation.

(c)   Rather than trying to use one 'blanket' flexing factor (production, labour hours, etc.) for all costs, more detailed analysis need to be carried out for each individual cost.

This can get quite complex, perhaps involving the use of multi-variable regression techniques; but can be simplified, particularly for overheads by identifying possible 'cost drivers' for each cost and using historic data to assess which can be used as the most accurate predictor.

If it becomes apparent after the event that the costs were affected by other factors than those included in the original budget (eg. changes in price and/or availability of resources, market trends) a revised budget could be drawn up incorporating these factors.

Comparison against the revised budgets (operational variances) will then give more meaningful information to management about the internal operations of the business. The remaining variances (between revised and original budgets) would be classified as 'planning' variances.

4 STANDARD COSTING AND VARIANCE ANALYSIS

4.1 AC/DC Co

			£
(a)	Total overhead	600 units	4,989
		500 units	4,489
		100	500

The variable overhead rate is $\dfrac{£500}{100}$ = £5 per unit

Variable overhead hourly rate = $\dfrac{£2,925}{2,340 \text{ hours}}$ = £1.25

Standard time = $\dfrac{£5}{£1.25}$ = 4 hours

(b)

		£
Materials 4 sheets × £1.12	4.48	
2 spools × £2.39	4.78	
		9.26
Labour (4 hours × £2.50)		10.00
Variable overhead (4 hours × £1.25)		5.00
Fixed overhead (4 hours × (£2.10 − 1.25))		3.40
Standard unit cost		27.66

(c)

	£
Sheets 3,000 × £0.02 (F)	60 (F)
Spools 1,500 × £0.01 (U)	15 (U)
Materials price variance	45 (F)

(d)

			£
Sheets	(550 × 4) − 2,215 =	−15 × £1.12	16.80 (U)
Spools	(550 × 2) − 1,106 =	−6 × £2.39	14.34 (U)
Materials usage variance			31.14 (U)

(e)   Direct labour rate variance

(2,113 hours × £2.50) − £5,409.28   =   £126.78 (U)

(f)   Direct labour efficiency variance

(550 units × 4 hours) − 2,113 hours   =   87 hours (F) × 2.50
                                      =   £217.50 (F)

(g)   Variable overhead expenditure variance

(2,113 hours × £1.25) − £2,769   =   £127.75 (U)

(h)   Variable overhead efficiency variance

87 hours (F) × £1.25   =   £108.75 (F)

(i)   Fixed overhead budget variance

£2,110 − (2,340 hours × £0.85)   =   £121 (U)

(j)   Fixed overhead volume variance

2,340 hours − (550 × 4 hours)   =   140 hours (U) × £0.85
                                =   £119 (U)

4.2   Ruggerball Ltd

(a)   (i)   Budgeted and actual contributions for period 7.

Schedule reference	£	£	£
Budgeted contribution			24,000
Sales margin variances			
(i) Price		4,000 (F)	
(ii) Contribution			
Lost through three-day week	9,600		
Gained through labour efficiency	1,600		
		8,000 (A)	
			4,000
			20,000

Cost variances	*Favourable*	*Adverse*	
Materials			
(iii) Price − Bladders		800	
(iv) − Leather		5,733	
(v) Usage of Leather	2,533		
Labour			
(vi) Rate of pay		500	
(vii) Idle time due to three-day week		1,800	
(viii) Efficiency	300		
	2,833	8,833	6,000
Actual contribution			14,000

Schedules

Sales margin variances

(Expected production based on three-day week = 60% × 6,000 = 3,600 balls)

(i)	Price variance 4,000 @ £1	£4,000 (F)	
(ii)	Contribution variance (6,000 – 4,000) = 2,000 @ £4	£8,000 (A)	

	£	
Lost through three-day week (40% × 6,000) @ £4	9,600	(A)
Gained through efficiency (4,000 – 3,600) @ £4	9,600	(F)
	8,000	(A)

Material variances

		£	
(iii)	Price		
	Actual cost of bladders used	2,800	
	Standard cost	2,000	
		800	(A)
(iv)	Actual cost of leather used	13,333	
	Standard cost	7,600	
		5,733	(A)

		£
Note:	Actual cost of packing materials	867
	Standard cost $\dfrac{4,000}{6,000 \times £1,300}$	867
		–

		Bales	
(v)	Usage		
	Actual usage of leather for 4,000 balls	100	
	Standard usage of leather (4,000 – 6,000) × 200	133 1/3	
		33 1/3	
	@ £76 per bale	£2,533	(F)

Answers

Labour variances

(vi) Rate of pay: 5,000 hours @ 10p   £500 (A)

(vii) Idle time due to three-day week
40% × 5,000 hours = 2,000 hours @ 90p   £1,800 (A)

(viii) Efficiency

	Hours
Actual hours (based on three-day week)	3,000
Standard hours for 4,000 units (4,000 − 6,000) × 5,000 hours)	3,333
	333

@ 90p per hour   £300 (F)

(ii) The adverse leather price variance combined with the favourable leather usage variance suggest that the firm may possibly be using a higher grade of leather than that envisaged when the budget was constructed. If this is the case and the higher selling price can be attributed to the better quality leather then the change in policy has resulted in a small gain to the firm (£4,000 + £2,533) − £5,733 = £800.

If additionally, the increased labour efficiency was attributable to the higher grade of leather used, then the £1,900 gain shown due to labour efficiency would be a direct consequence of the material quality change. This illustrates the importance of management flexibility under changing economic circumstances and indicates the problems (and importance) of attributing variances to causes on a total effects basis, rather than the conventional fragmented approach.

(b) The expected cost of investigation is given by:

Cost of investigation + cost of correction when required

= £(160 + 0.4 × 350)

= £300

The expected saving to be made would not be greater than 0.4 × £600

= £240

Therefore if expected values are the criterion to be used, this variance is not worthy of investigation.

4.3 Learning effects

(a) Learning coefficient (materials) $= \dfrac{\text{Log}(1-0.05)}{\text{Log } 2}$

$= \dfrac{-0.02228}{0.30103} = -0.074$

(b)   Batch 28 of month 6 (= 160th batch overall)

    (i)   Standard labour hours
           = standard labour hours for 1st 160 batches   (160y)
           less standard labour hours for 1st 159 batches   (159y)

$$= 160\,(500)(160)^{-0.322} - 159\,(500)(159)^{-0.322}$$
$$= 15{,}609 - 15{,}542 = 67 \text{ hours}$$

    (ii)   Standard materials
$$= 160\,(55)\,(160)^{-0.074} - 159\,(55)\,(159)^{-0.074}$$
$$= 6{,}045 - 6{,}010 = 35 \text{ hours}$$

The above calculations show the expected hours/units specifically for the last batch.

Note: An alternative approach would be to take the cumulative average hours/materials per batch at 160 batches as the standard.

    ie. labour: $500\,(160)^{-0.322} = 97.55$ hours $\cong 98$ hours
            materials: $55(160)^{-0.074} = 37.78$ hours $\cong 38$ hours

Answers to (b) and (c) have been given for both these approaches.

Standard cost of last batch

	£	*Alternative* £
67(98) labour hours at £8/hour	536	784
35(38) units materials @ £100/unit	3,500	3,800
Variable overheads 67(98) hours @ £15/hour	1,005	1,470
	5,041	6,054

(c)

	£	Variance	*Alternative* £	Variance
Labour				
Actual hours at actual rate	978		978	
Labour rate		58A		58A
Actual hours at standard rate				
(115 × £8)	920		920	
Labour efficiency		384A		136A
Standard hours at standard rate	536		784	
Direct materials				
Actual wage at actual price	3,977		3,977	
Materials price		123F		123F
Actual wage at standard price	4,100		4,100	
(41 × £100)				
Material usage		600A		300A
Standard wage at standard price	3,500		3,800	

	£	Variance	*Alternative* £	Variance
Variable overheads				
Actual hours at actual rate	1,685		1,685	
Variable overhead rate		40F		40F
Actual hours at standard rate (115 × £15)	1,725		1,725	
Variable overhead efficiency		720A		255A
Standard hours at standard rate	1,005		1,470	

Summary

	£	£	£	£
Standard cost		5,041		6,054
Direct labour variances				
– rate	58A		58A	
– efficiency	384A	442	136A	194
Direct materials variance				
– price	123F		123F	
– usage	600A	477	300A	177
Variable overhead variances				
– rate	40F		40F	
– efficiency	720A	680	225A	215
Actual cost		6,640		6,640

(d) All the efficiency/usage variances are adverse indicating that more hours/units of material were necessary than the learning effect calculations showed. This may be due to one or both of:

(i) an inaccurate learning factor being used [planning]
(ii) the workforce not performing as well as they could [operational]

The labour rate variance was also adverse indicating that the hours worked cost more than £8/hour. This may be because of unexpected wage rises or possibly the presence of idle time – ie. non-productive hours paid. Absorption of this cost into productive hours will increase the rate.

Materials and overhead price/rate variances are favourable; a cost saving has been made on acquiring these resources.

4.4   Mix variances

Sales variances

1   Actual sales in actual mix at actual profit margins (computed with cost of sales at standard)

		£	£	£
X	100 × (10 – 8)	200		
Y	120 × (16 – 12)	480		
Z	180 × (19 – 15)	720		
	400		1,400	

2   Actual sales in actual mix at standard profit margins

		£	£	
X	100 × 2	200		Sales price variance
Y	120 × 3	360		£60 (A)
Z	180 × 5	900		
	400		1,460	

3   Actual total sales in standard mix at standard profit margins

		£	£	
X (1)	80 × 2	160		Mix
Y (2)	160 × 3	480		£20 (F)
Z (2)	160 × 5	800		
	400		1,440	

4   Budgeted sales in standard mix at standard profit margins

		£	£	
X	100 × 2	200		Quantity
Y	200 × 3	600		£360 (A)
Z	200 × 5	1,000		
	500		1,800	

Assumption

Whenever mix variances are computed, we are assuming that the products are substitutes one for another. It is therefore valid and meaningful to compute the impact of such substitutions on the reported profit.

If this assumption is invalid, three separate sets of price and volume variances would be more useful.

Materials mix variances

Actual expenditure (actual quantity × actual cost)

		£
L		11,000
M		14,000
N		37,400
		62,400

Actual quantities at standard costs

Price
5,600 F

L	5,000 × £2	10,000	
M	14,000 × £1	14,000	
N	11,000 × £4	44,000	68,000

30,000

Mix
(3,000) A

Total quantity input in standard mix at standard price

$$30,000 \text{ lb} \times \frac{325}{150} \qquad \qquad 65,000$$

Yield
(3,250) A

Standard cost of actual production

$$19,000 \text{ lb} \times \frac{325}{100} \qquad \qquad 61,750$$

4.5 Conan

(a) (i)

Distribution centre A	*Copiers* £'000	*Personal computers* £'000	*Word processors* £'000	*Total* £'000
Revenue	2,400	1,920	1,440	5,760
Transfer costs	(2,000)	(1,600)	(1,200)	(4,800)
Commission	(80)	(96)	(60)	(236)
Advertising costs				(350)
Distribution costs				(155)
				219

Therefore profit for region A = £219,000

(ii) *Distribution centre B*

	Copiers £'000	Personal computers £'000	Word processors £'000	Total £'000
Revenue	2,760	580	1,650	4,990
Transfer costs	(2,400)	(500)	(1,500)	(4,400)
Commission	(72)	(29)	(75)	(176)
Distribution costs				(180)
				234

Therefore profit for region B = £234,000

(b) *Reconciliation of profit figures*

	£'000 F	£'000 A	£'000
Profit for region B			234
Sales variances (W1)			
Price	284		
Mix	145		
Quantity		59	370
			604
Cost variances			
Commission (W2)			
Price		23.2	
Mix		54.4	
Quantity	17.6		
Advertising expenditure		350	
Distribution (W3)			
Volume	18		
Expenditure	7		
	42.6	427.6	(385)
Profit in region A			219

Workings

(1) **Sales variances**   £'000

Actual quantity in actual mix @ actual profit
    (£5,760,000 – 4,800,000)   960
Actual quantity in actual mix @ standard profit
    (1,000 @ £300 + 320 @ £800 + 1,200 @ 100)   676
Actual quantity in standard mix @ standard profit
    $2,520 @ \dfrac{590,000}{2,800}$ 531
Budgeted quantity in standard mix @ standard profit   590

Therefore
    Sales price variance   = £(960,000 – 676,000) =   £284,000 (F)
    Sales mix variance   = £(676,000 – 531,000) =   £145,000 (F)
    Sales quantity variance = £(531,000 – 590,000) =   £59,000 (A)

(2)	**Commission variances**		£'000

Actual quantity in actual mix @ actual commission   236

Actual quantity in actual mix @ standard commission
$$(1,000 @ £60 + 320 @ £290 + 1,200 @ £50) \qquad 212.8$$

Actual quantity in standard mix @ standard commission
$$2,520 \ @ \ \frac{176,000}{2,800} \qquad 158.4$$

Standard quantity in standard mix @ standard commission   176

Therefore

Commission price variance	=	£(236,000 – 212,800)	=	£23,200 (A)
Commission mix variance	=	£(212,800 – 158,400)	=	£54,400 (A)
Commission quantity variance	=	£(158,400 – 176,000)	=	£17,600 (F)

(3)	**Distribution expenses**	£

Actual total quantity @ actual expenditure   155,000

Actual total quantity @ standard expenditure
$$2,520 \ @ \ \frac{180,000}{2,800} \qquad 162,000$$

Budgeted total quantity @ standard expenditure   180,000

Distribution expenditure variance	=	£(155,000 – 162,000)	=	7,000	(F)
Distribution volume variance	=	£(162,000 – 180,000)	=	18,000	(F)

4.6   Thorpe Ltd

(a)   Traditional variance analysis

Alpha   £

Material price variance
£51,840 – (10,800 × £3)   19,440 (A)

Material usage variance
(10,000 – 10,800) × £3   2,400 (A)

Total variance   21,840 (A)

Beta

Material price variance
700 × (£30 – £25)   3,500 (F)

Material usage variance
(750 – 700) × £30   1,500 (F)

Total variance   5,000 (F)

(b) **Planning and operational variances**

Alpha

	£
Total planning variance $10,000 \times (£4.50 - £3.00)$	15,000 (A)

which could be analysed as follows:

	£
Uncontrollable $10,000 \times (£4 - £3)$	10,000 (A)
Possibly avoidable $10,000 \times (£4.50 - £4)$	5,000 (A)
Operational variances	
Material usage $(10,000 - 10,800) \times £4.50$	3,600 (A)
Material price $10,800 \times (£4.5 - £4.8)$	3,240 (A)
	6,840 (A)
Total variance	21,840 (A)

Beta

	£
Planning variance	
Uncontrollable 750 tonnes $\times (£30 - £23)$	5,250 (F)
Operational variances	
Material price $700 \times (£23 - £25)$	1,400 (A)
Material usage $(750 - 700) \times £23$	1,150 (F)
	250 (A)
Total variance	£5,000 (F)

Workings

	Quantity	Unit price	Total cost
Alpha	kg	£	£
Original flexed budget (gamma)	10,000	3	30,000
Revised flexed budget (delta)	10,000	4	40,000
Revised flexed budget (gamma)	10,000	4.5	45,000
Actual (gamma)	10,800	4.8	51,840
Beta	tons	£	£
Original flexed budget	750	30	22,500
Revised flexed budget	750	23	17,250
Actual	700	25	17,500

4.7 POV Ltd

(a) **Reconciliation using conventional variances**

			£
Budgeted contribution (2,500 × £78)			195,000
Sales volume variance (350 units × £78)			27,300 F
Flexed budgeted contribution			222,300

Variances	F £	A £	
Materials price (12,450 × (£18 − £20))	24,900		
Materials usage (2,850 × 4 − 12,450) £20		21,000	
Labour rate (18,800 × £(8 − 7))		18,800	
Labour idle time (400 × £7)		2,800	
Labour efficiency (2,850 × 6 − 18,400) £7		9,100	
	24,900	51,700	
			26,800 A
Actual contribution			195,500

(b)   **Reconciliation using planning and operational variances**

	£	£
Original budgeted contribution (2,500 × £78)		195,000
Planning variances (W)		
Materials 2,500 units × £(74.25 − 80)	14,375 F	
Labour 2,500 units × £(48 − 42)	15,000 A	
		625 A
Revised budgeted contribution (2,500 × £77.75)		194,375
Operational variances		
Sales volume (350 units × £77.75)		2,721.25 F
Flexed revised budgeted contribution		221,587.50

Cost variances	F £	A £	
Materials price (12,450 × (£18 − £16.50))		18,675	
Materials usage			
(2,850 × 4.5 − 12,450) £16.50	6,187.5		
Labour rate	–	–	
Labour idle time (400 × £8)		3,200	
Labour efficiency (2,850 × 6 − 18,400) £8		10,400	
	6,187.5	32,275	
			26,087.50 A
Actual contribution			195,500.00

Workings

Revised standard cost card

	£
Materials 4.5 kg @ £16.50	74.25
Labour 6 hours @ £8 (note)	48.00
	122.25
Selling price	200.00
Contribution	77.75

Note: This assumes that the increase from £6.50 per hour (without bad weather bonus) to £8 per hour is entirely due to the planning decision to use the alternative raw material.

(c)   Planning and operational variances highlight the effects of bad budgeting separately from aspects of operational performance. They enable actual results to be compared against an up-to-date and realistic target. In this case, the revised analysis reveals:

(i) better than expected material usage, perhaps the new material was not as difficult to work with as expected;

(ii) an adverse price variance, perhaps because the company paid more for improved quality;

(iii) poor labour efficiency despite the incentive of a higher rate of pay per hour.

4.8 County Preserves

(a) **Ingredients planning variances deemed uncontrollable** (W1)

Fruit extract	(£0.16 – £0.19) × 400 kg	£12 (A)
Glucose syrup	(£0.10 – £0.12) × 700 kg	£14 (A)
		£26 (A)

(b) **Ingredients operating variances deemed controllable** (W2)

Fruit extract	– price (£0.19 – £0.18) × 428 kg	£4.280 (F)
	– usage (400 kg – 428 kg) × £0.19	£5.320 (A)
Glucose syrup	– price (£0.12 – £0.12) × 742 kg	–
	– usage (700 kg – 742 kg) × £0.12	£5.040 (A)
Pectin	– price (£0.332 – £0.328) × 125 kg	£0.500 (F)
	– usage (99 kg – 125 kg) × £0.332	£8.632 (A)
Citric acid	– price (£2 – £0.95) × 1 kg	£1.050 (F)
	– usage (1 kg – 1 kg) × £2	–
		£13.162 (A)

Note that labour variances are not required.

(c) **Comments**

The advantages of using the operational and planning approach include the following:

(i) Changing business conditions will often mean that standards would otherwise become outdated.

(ii) The calculation of operational variances for managers helps to identify those variances under their control.

(iii) Realistic standards and variances should help to improve the motivation of managers.

(iv) The approach helps to evaluate the accuracy of the original standard and is useful for planning purposes.

The disadvantages of using the operational and planning approach include the following:

(i) It is difficult to determine a revised standard which is seen to be objective and accepted by all concerned.

(ii)   More work is involved for the accounting and management staff.

(iii)   As there will be an element of subjectivity in determining the revised standard, there may be pressure from operational managers to have their own variances classified as planning or uncontrollable variances.

(d) Mix and yield variances (using revised standard prices) (W3)

	Fruit extract kg	£	Glucose syrup kg	£	Pectin kg	£	Citric acid kg	£	Total kgs	£
Standard price × actual mix	428	81.32	742	89.04	125.00	41.5	1.00	2.00	1,296.00	213.86
Mix variance (W4)	4 (F)	0.76	14 (F)	1.68	18.08 (A)	(6.0)	0.08 (F)	0.16	– (A)	(3.40)
Standard price × standard mix	432	82.08	756	90.72	106.92	35.5	1.08	2.16	1,296.00	210.46
Normal loss 3%									38.88	–
Expected output (at standard cost)									1,257.12	210.46
Actual output (at standard cost)									1,164.00	194.87
Yield variance (W5, W6)									93.12 (A)	15.59

	£	
Total mix variance	3.40	(A)
Yield variance	15.59	(A)
	18.99	(A)

(e)   **Total variance for the batch** (W7)

	£
Actual cost of 1.164 kg of jam	268.030
Standard cost of 1.164 kg of jam	227.368
Total variance	40.662 (A)

Workings

(1)   The uncontrollable planning variances are the price rises attributable to causes outside the control of the firm. These price variances are evaluated with the *standard* usage, as the *actual* usage will contain some operational variances.

(2)   The operational variances are the normal price and usage variances, after taking account of the revised standard prices for fruit extract and glucose syrup (£0.19 per kg for fruit extract and £0.12 per kg for glucose syrup).

(3)   The mix and yield variances can be calculated by a number of different methods. Note that they are based on the revised standard prices for fruit extract and glucose syrup.

(4)   The mix variance is calculated by comparing the *actual* mix for 1,296 kg with the *standard* mix for 1,296 kg of input. The normal proportions for 1,200 kg of input are given in the standard cost data. These normal proportions must be applied to the actual input to determine the standard mix as follows:

$$\text{Fruit extract} \qquad \frac{400}{1,200} \times 1,296 \ = \ 432 \text{ kg}$$

$$\text{Glucose syrup} \qquad \frac{700}{1,200} \times 1,296 \ = \ 756 \text{ kg}$$

$$\text{Pectin} \qquad \frac{125}{1,200} \times 1,296 \ = \ 135 \text{ kg}$$

$$\text{Citric} \qquad \frac{1}{1,200} \times 1,296 \ = \ 1.08 \text{ kg}$$

The resulting variances (in kg) are evaluated at the standard price per kg (revised standard for fruit extract and glucose syrup).

(5)   The yield variance is calculated by comparing the expected output from 1,296 kg of input, after accounting for the normal loss, with the actual output from 1,296 kg of input. Note that the normal loss does not have a cost or value, in accordance with the conventions of process costing. The normal loss expected from 1,296 kg of input is 38.88 kg, resulting in 1,257.12 kg of expected output. The actual output was 1,164 kg. The yield variance is evaluated at the standard cost per unit of output (see W6).

(6)   The standard cost per kg of output (in this case using the revised standard prices for fruit extract and glucose syrup) is calculated as follows:

Standard cost data per batch

	£
Fruit extract 400 kg × £0.19 per kg	76.000
Glucose syrup 700 kg × £0.12 per kg	84.000
Pectin 99 kg × £0.332 per kg	32.868
Citric acid 1 kg × £2 per kg	2.000
Standard cost for 1,200 − (3% of 1,200) = 1,164 kg	194.868

Standard cost per kg $\dfrac{£194.868}{1,164 \text{ kg}}$ = £0.1674123

The yield variance is valued as 93.12 kg × £0.1674, ie. £15.59

(7)   The total variance for the batch (using the original standards and including labour costs) has been calculated by comparing the actual cost of 1,164 kg of output, with the standard cost of 1,164 kg of output.

The actual cost is:

	£
Fruit extract 428 kg × £0.18 per kg	77.04
Glucose syrup 742 kg × £0.12 per kg	89.04
Pectin 125 kg × £0.328 per kg	41.00
Citric acid 1 kg × £0.95 per kg	0.95
Labour 20 hours at £3 per hour	60.00
	268.03

The standard cost is:

	£
Fruit extract 400 kg × £0.16 per kg	64.000
Glucose syrup 700 kg × £0.10 per kg	70.000
Pectin 99 kg × £0.332 per kg	32.868
Citric acid 1 kg × £2 per kg	2.000
Labour 18 hours at £3.25 per hour	58.500
	227.368

5   MARGINAL COSTING AND DECISION-MAKING

5.1   Types of cost

(a)   *Opportunity cost* – The greatest benefit foregone as a result of choosing a course of action (eg. use of a fixed asset which could otherwise be sold).

Marginal costs – The additional cost of producing one more unit of output (eg. production costs for 10 units is £20 and for 11 units is £23; the marginal cost of the 11th unit is £3).

Imputed costs – A cost, not necessarily incremental, which is charged to a unit of output or a project (eg. the cost of existing fixed assets charged to a project).

Differential costs – The difference in costs between two alternatives (eg. internal production costs £10 per unit, whereas purchase costs £12 per unit; the differential costs of purchase are £2 per unit).

(b)   The contradiction in the quoted statement arises because marginal costs, differential costs and opportunity costs are usually one and the same thing.

The imputed costs may be notional and so are different from the rest.

(c)   Fixed costs will only be relevant costs if they are affected by the decision being taken. This might arise if they are stepped or avoidable. Fixed costs which are static in the short term may become variable in the longer term and so become relevant costs.

5.2   Letters

(a)   **Calculate fixed costs per unit**

	Alpha	Beta	AB plc
Production (units)	20,000	40,000	–
Machinery time (hours)	2	1	–
Total machining time	40,000	40,000	80,000
Fixed costs	–	–	£480,000
Absorbed: rate per hour	–	–	£6

Calculate contributions

	Alpha £		Beta £
Selling price	25		50
Variable costs	(20 – 12) 8	(40 – 6)	34 (total costs – fixed costs)
Contribution	17		16
Hours	2		1
Contribution per hour	8.50		16

Therefore the company should make Beta to meet maximum demand and use the balance for Alpha.

Units	Alpha	Beta	£
50,000 Beta uses 50,000 hours	–	50,000	
15,000 Alpha uses $\dfrac{30,000 \text{ hours}}{80,000 \text{ hours}}$	15,000	–	
Unit contribution	17	16	
Total contribution	£255,000	£800,000	1,055,000
Fixed costs			(480,000)
Profit			575,000

The existing plan is stated as £500,000 profit and is thus not optimal.

(b)   The pricing system used in the existing plan is a 'cost plus' system which may be criticised as

–   demand is ignored, which here exceeds supply
–   it does not lead to the best allocation of scarce resources.

However, the system is widely used in practice as

–   it is a simple system which allows delegation of pricing decisions
–   it is the only feasible system in a jobbing industry.

It needs to be used in a framework which recognises the relevance of demand and market conditions.

(c)   **Table 2**

Price-demand relationships for Alpha and Beta

Alpha (let A = 10 of units sold)

P	A
£20	45
£30	15

$$\therefore P = 35 - 10/30\ A$$

$30 + (10 \times \frac{1}{2})$

£35	0

Beta (let B = 10 of units sold)

P	B
£45	70
£55	30

$$\therefore P = 62.5 - 10/40\ B$$

$55 + (10 \times \frac{3}{4})$

£62.5	0

Marginal revenue functions

$$R_A = 35A - \frac{2}{3}A^2 \qquad \therefore MR_A = 35 - \frac{2}{3}A$$

$$R_B = 62.5B - \frac{1}{4}B^2 \qquad \therefore MR_B = 62.5 - \frac{1}{2}B$$

Maximum profits when MR = MC

Alpha

$MR = 35 - 1/3\,A = MC = 8$

$$\therefore A = \frac{27 \times 3}{2} = 40.5, \text{ ie. } 40{,}500 \text{ units}$$

$$\therefore P = 35 - (10/3 \times 40.5) = £21.50$$

5.3 EX Ltd

(a) Usage of resources at maximum call-off levels:

		Part A		*Part B*
		(7,000)		(9,000)
Alloy	@ 1.6 kg	11,200 kg	@ 1.6 kg	14,400 kg
Line S	@ 0.6 hrs	4,200 hrs	@ 0.25 hrs	2,250 hrs
Line T	@0.5 hrs	3,500 hrs	@ 0.55 hrs	4,950 hrs

Thus, if Part A is made, the restricting resource would be Line S capacity; whereas the production of Part B is restricted by both alloy availability and Line T capacity.

$$\text{Maximum Part A } \frac{4{,}000}{0.6} = 6{,}666 \text{ units}$$

Maximum Part B

$$= \text{lower of } \frac{13{,}000}{1.6} = 8{,}125$$

$$\text{and } \frac{4{,}500}{0.55} = 8{,}182 \qquad \text{ie. } 8{,}125 \text{ units}$$

Contribution earned

(i) per unit

		Part A	*Part B*
		£	£
Price		145	115
Alloy	(1.6 × £12.50)	(20)	(20)
Variable overhead			
– Line S	(0.6/0.25 × £80)	(48)	(20)
– Line T	(0.5/0.55 × £100)	(50)	(55)
		27	20

(ii) maximum possible

Part A	6,666 × £27	=	£179,982
Part B	8,125 × £20	=	£162,500

Thus Part A should be made

(b) From (a) EX Ltd will earn £179,982 : the maximum call-off (7,000 units Part A) will not be met due to restriction in Line S capacity.

(c)

	Part A		Part B	
	hrs	£	hrs	£
Loss of sales revenue				
(6,666 × £14.50/8,125 × £11.50)		(96,657)		(93,437.50)
Unused machine hours				
Line S	–	–		
(4,000 – 8,125 × 0.25)			1,968	118,080
Line T (4,500 – 6,666 × 0.5)	1,167	70,020		
(4,500 – 8,125 × 0.55)			31	1,860
Increase/(decrease) in contribution		26,637		26,502.50
Original contribution		179,982		162,500
Revised contribution		153,345		189,002.50

Thus the company should now manufacture Part B, yielding a new contribution of £189,002.50

(**Note:** It has been assumed that £60 is paid only for each *whole* unused machine hour : if fractions of hours are also allowed, Part B's credits would be
Line S : 1,968.75 × £60 = £118,125
Line T : 31.25 × £60 = £1,875
giving a revised contribution of £189,062.50

5.4 Lecture solution – Decision theory

(a) **Table of profits**

		Order quantity			
		200	300	400	500
Demand	Probability				
150	(0.3)	1,000	(1,500)	(4,000)	(6,500)
250	(0.2)	3,000	2,500	–	(2,500)
350	(0.3)	3,000	4,500	4,000	1,500
450	(0.2)	3,000	4,500	6,000	5,500
Expected profit		2,400	2,300	1,200	(900)
Minimum profit		1,000	(1,500)	(4,000)	(6,500)
Maximum profit		3,000	4,500	6,000	5,500

(i) Highest expected profit will be £2,400 with an order quantity of 200 units.
(ii) Maximin: order quantity 200 units
(iii) Maximax: order quantity 400 units

Table of regrets

	Order quantity			
	200	300	400	500
Demand				
150	0	2,500	5,000	7,500
250	0	500	3,000	5,500
350	1,500	0	500	3,000
450	3,000	1,500	0	500
Maximum regret for each order quantity	3,000	2,500	5,000	7,500

∴ Minimax regret: order quantity 300 units.

(b)   With perfect knowledge of the demand level the most suitable order quantity can be selected.

Demand = 150 (Prob 0.3)

	£
Order 200 : profit 1,000 × 0.3	300

Demand = 250 (Prob 0.2)

Order 200 : profit 3,000 × 0.2	600

Demand = 350 (Prob 0.3)

Order 300 : profit 4,500 × 0.3	1,350

Demand = 450 (Prob 0.2)

Order 400 : profit 6,000 × 0.2	1,200
Expected profit with perfect information	3,450
Expected profit without perfect information (a) (i)	(2,400)
Maximum to be paid for information	1,050

(i)

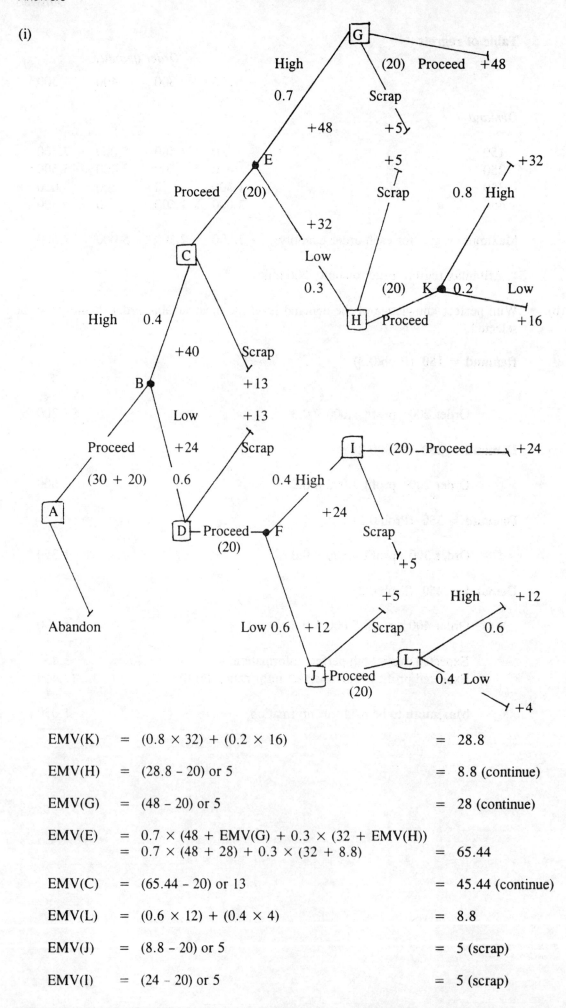

$$EMV(K) = (0.8 \times 32) + (0.2 \times 16) = 28.8$$

$$EMV(H) = (28.8 - 20) \text{ or } 5 = 8.8 \text{ (continue)}$$

$$EMV(G) = (48 - 20) \text{ or } 5 = 28 \text{ (continue)}$$

$$EMV(E) = 0.7 \times (48 + EMV(G)) + 0.3 \times (32 + EMV(H))$$
$$= 0.7 \times (48 + 28) + 0.3 \times (32 + 8.8) = 65.44$$

$$EMV(C) = (65.44 - 20) \text{ or } 13 = 45.44 \text{ (continue)}$$

$$EMV(L) = (0.6 \times 12) + (0.4 \times 4) = 8.8$$

$$EMV(J) = (8.8 - 20) \text{ or } 5 = 5 \text{ (scrap)}$$

$$EMV(I) = (24 - 20) \text{ or } 5 = 5 \text{ (scrap)}$$

$$\text{EMV(F)} \quad = \quad 0.4 \times (24 + 5) + 0.6 \times (12 + 5) \qquad\qquad = \quad 21.8$$

$$\text{EMV(D)} \quad = \quad (21.8 - 20) \text{ or } 13 \qquad\qquad = \quad 13 \text{ (scrap)}$$

$$
\begin{aligned}
\text{EMV(B)} \quad &= \quad 0.4 \times (40 + \text{EMV(C)}) + 0.6 \times (24 + \text{EMV(D)}) \\
&= \quad 0.4 \times (40 + 45.44) + 0.6 \times (24 + 13) \\
&= \quad (0.4 \times 85.44) + (0.6 \times 37) \qquad\qquad = \quad 56.376
\end{aligned}
$$

$$\text{EMV(A)} \quad = \quad 56.376 - 50 \qquad\qquad = \quad 6.376$$

Therefore the company should proceed immediately but scrap after one year if sales are low.

(ii) Let probability of high sales in Year 2 given high sales in Year 1 be p.

The first calculation this affects is:

$$
\begin{aligned}
\text{EMV(E)} \quad &= \quad p(48 + 28) + (1 - p)(32 + 8.8) \\
&= \quad 76p + 40.8(1 - p) \\
&= \quad 35.2p + 40.8
\end{aligned}
$$

$$
\begin{aligned}
\text{EMV(C)} \quad &= \quad (35.2p + 40.8 - 20) \text{ or } 13 \\
&= \quad 35.2p + 20.8 \text{ (since this is greater than 13 even if p is zero)}
\end{aligned}
$$

$$
\begin{aligned}
\text{EMV(B)} \quad &= \quad 0.4 \times (40 + \text{EMV(C)}) + 0.6 \times (24 + \text{EMV(D)}) \\
&= \quad 0.4 \times (40 + 35.2p + 20.8) + (0.6 \times 37) \\
&= \quad 24.32 + 14.08p + 22.2 \\
&= \quad 14.08p + 46.52
\end{aligned}
$$

$$\text{EMV(A)} \quad = \quad 14.08p + 46.52 - 50 = 14.08p - 3.48$$

Thus the decision will not change provided $14.08p > 3.48$

ie. $p > \dfrac{3.48}{14.08} \sim 0.25$

The probability can fall to 0.25 before the decision changes, a fall of

$$\dfrac{0.7 - 0.25}{0.7} \times 100\% \sim 64\%$$

So the decision is very insensitive to this probability.

5.5 Standard and deluxe

(a)

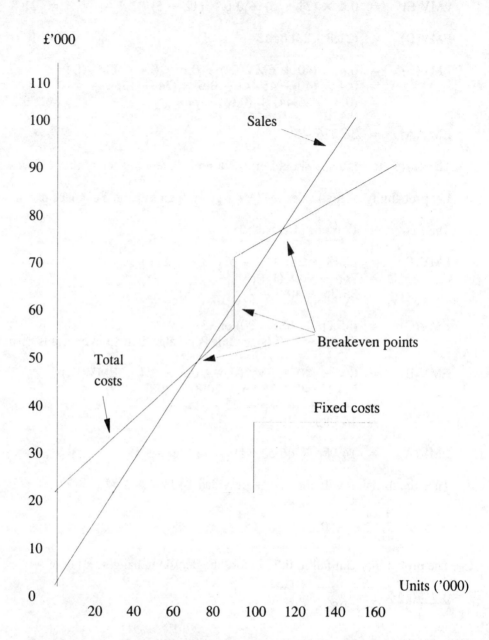

£'000

Graph 1: Breakeven chart for standard quality

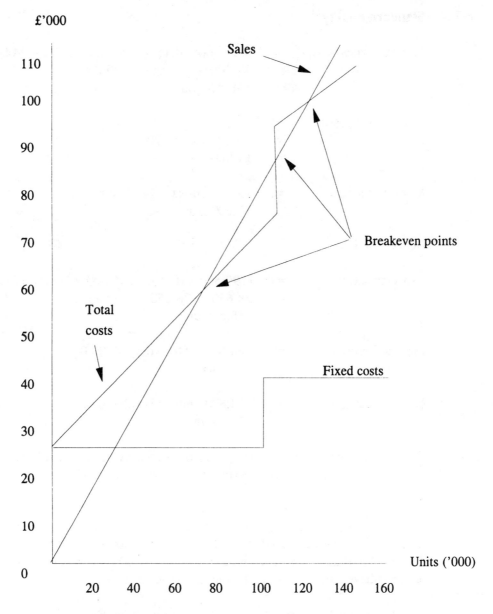

£'000

Graph 2: Breakeven chart for deluxe quality

(b)   Graph 1 shows the breakeven chart for standard quality products. Between 0 and 79,000 units, a loss is reported. At 80,000 units the company breaks even. Between 80,001 and 99,999 units, a profit is reported. At 100,000 units (the discontinuity point for fixed costs) the company makes a loss. Between 100,001 units and 139,999 units, a loss is reported. At 140,000 units the company breaks even. Above 140,000 units, a profit is reported.

Graph 2 shows the breakeven chart for deluxe quality products. Between 0 and 71,428 units, a loss is reported. Between 71,429 units and 99,999 units, a profit is reported. Between 100,000 units and 114,285 units, a loss is reported. Above 114,285 units, a profit is reported.

Each chart provides management with information concerning the sales levels at which they should aim. However no quantitative measure is given of the relative risk of the two products.

(c) **Standard quality**

Expected sales	=	$(172,000 \times 0.1) + (160,000 \times 0.7) + (148,000 \times 0.2)$
	=	$17,200 + 112,000 + 29,600$
	=	$158,800$ units

So expected profits	=	$158,800 \times (7 - 4.5) - 350,000$
	=	$397,000 - 350,000$
	=	£47,000

| Margin of safety | = | $158,800$ units $- 140,000$ units |
| | = | $18,800$ units |

Deluxe quality

Expected sales	=	$(195,500 \times 0.3) + (156,500 \times 0.5) + (109,500 \times 0.2)$
	=	$58,650 + 78,250 + 21,900$
	=	$158,800$ units

| Expected profits | = | $158,800 \times (10 - 6.5) - 400,000$ |
| | = | £155,800 |

| Margin of safety | = | $158,800$ units $- 114,286$ units |
| | = | $44,514$ units |

(d) We can see that deluxe quality products have a larger expected profit, but do not want to advise management to launch these until the product's risk has been taken into account.

One quick measure of a product's risk is the range of possible outcomes. The range of demand for standard products is $172,000 - 148,000 = 24,000$ units. The range of demand for deluxe products is $195,500 - 109,500 = 86,000$ units. So deluxe products have a higher risk and a higher expected return.

One way to relate the risk to the return is to examine the coefficients of variation of the two products, that is the standard deviation divided by expected values. These are calculated as follows.

Standard quality

x	p	px	$(x - \bar{x})$	$p(x - \bar{x})^2$
172,000	0.1	17,200	13,200	17,424,000
160,000	0.7	112,000	1,200	1,008,000
148,000	0.2	29,600	(10,800)	23,328,000
		158,800		41,760,000

$$\bar{x} = \Sigma px = 158,800 \text{ units}$$

$$\sigma = \sqrt{\Sigma p(x - \bar{x})^2} = \sqrt{41,760,000} = 6,462 \text{ units}$$

$$\text{The coefficient of variation} = \frac{6,462}{158,800} = 0.041$$

Deluxe quality

x	p	px	$(x - \bar{x})$	$p(x - \bar{x})^2$
195,500	0.3	58,650	36,700	404,067,000
156,000	0.5	78,250	(2,300)	2,645,000
109,500	0.2	21,900	(49,300)	486,098,000
		158,800		892,810,000

$\bar{x} = \Sigma px = 158{,}800$ units

$\sigma = \sqrt{\Sigma p(x - \bar{x})2} = \sqrt{892{,}810{,}000} = 29{,}880$ units

The coefficient of variation $= \dfrac{29{,}880}{158{,}800} = 0.188$

So in relative terms, we see that the risk of the deluxe quality product is more than four times as great as the risk of the standard product. Whether the company should expose itself to this risk in pursuit of the greater expected profits is a decision that can only be taken by management themselves in the light of the risk characteristics that they wish to adopt.

5.6 XYZ plc

(a) We must choose between a price of £13.50 or £14.50 a unit, on the basis of the highest expected outcome with at least an 80% chance of breaking even.

Price set at £13.50 per unit

Demand (units)	Probability	Contribution per unit £	Probability	Total contribution £	Combined probability
45,000	0.3	6.50	0.15	292,500	0.045
		7.00	0.65	315,000	0.195
		7.30	0.20	328,500	0.060
60,000	0.5	6.50	0.15	390,000	0.075
		7.00	0.65	420,000	0.325
		7.30	0.20	438,000	0.100
70,000	0.2	6.50	0.15	455,000	0.030
		7.00	0.65	490,000	0.130
		7.30	0.20	511,000	0.040
					1.000

Last year fixed costs were 75,000 × £3 = £225,000

This year fixed costs are expected to be:

	£
0.3 × 225,000 × 1.50	101,250
0.5 × 225,000 × 1.25	140,625
0.2 × 225,000 × 1.10	49,500
	291,375

We see that even the lowest anticipated total contribution is larger than the expected fixed costs, so we expect a 100% chance of making a profit next year.

Price set at £14.50 per unit

Demand (units)	Prob- ability	Contribution per unit £	Prob- ability	Total contribution £	Combined probability	Cumulative probability
35,000	0.3	7.50	0.15	262,500	0.045	] Loss =
		8.00	0.65	280,000	0.195	] 0.3
		8.30	0.20	290,500	0.060	]
55,000	0.5	7.50	0.15	412,500	0.075	)
		8.00	0.65	440,000	0.325	) Profit =
		8.30	0.20	456,500	0.100	) 0.7
68,000	0.2	7.50	0.15	510,000	0.030	)
		8.00	0.65	544,000	0.130	)
		8.30	0.20	564,400	0.040	)
					1.000	

We see that we expect a 70% chance only of at least breaking even. There is an expected 30% chance of making a loss. The decision was therefore *not* made in accordance with group guidelines of requiring at least an 80% chance of breaking even.

(b)   **Comment on the estimates**

(i)   Where have the estimates come from? Are they just management's best guess based on past experience, or has external advice been sought, for example from expert consultants?

(ii)   Is it valid to assume that the unit variable costs, fixed costs and demand estimates are statistically independent? It would seem more likely that some dependence actually existed between the parameters, so that, for example, a high sales level would accompany a lower production cost per unit.

Other factors to have been considered

(i)   The model currently uses a small selection of discrete possibilities as the probability distribution for each parameter. A distribution with a wider range of possibilities could be tried, or a continuous probability distribution such as a normal distribution could be tried.

(ii)   Simulation runs could be carried out on a computer to test possible scenarios against the group guidelines.

(iii)   Other possible sales prices could be tried, for example £13, £14 and £15.

(iv)   Prices charged by competitors for similar products would be valuable information.

(c)   The group guidelines maximise the expected profits subject to at least an 80% chance of breaking even. This strategy appears to be fairly risk-averse in that only a maximum 20% probability of making a loss will be tolerated. Where a possible option exceeds this 20% threshold, even if it offers very large expected profits, it will not be accepted.

The group would be still more risk-averse if the 80% figure were increased to, say, 90%. At present the group attitude to risk appears to be moderately risk-averse.

5.7   Z Ltd

(a)   **Pricing and purchasing decisions**

	£	£
Selling price	15	20
Variable manufacturing costs (excluding materials)	3	3
Contribution (excluding materials)	12	17

	£	£
Advertising and selling costs	£25,000	£96,000
General fixed costs	£40,000	£40,000

Sales ('000 units)	36	28	18	28	23	13
	£'000	£'000	£'000	£'000	£'000	£'000
Option (i) for materials						
Contribution (as above)	432	336	216	476	391	221
Materials (£3 × 3 kg)	324	252	162	252	207	117
	108	84	54	224	184	104
Total fixed costs	65	65	65	136	136	136
Profit/(loss)	43	19	(11)	88	48	(32)
Probability	0.3	0.5	0.2	0.3	0.5	0.2
Expected profit/(loss)	12.9	9.5	(2.2)	26.4	24.0	(6.4)
Expected value		20.2			44.0	

Option (ii) for materials

Material requirement (kg)	108	84	54	84	69	39
Material purchases (kg)	108	84	54	84	69	50
Surplus (for sale) (kg)	–	–	–	–	–	11

	£'000	£'000	£'000	£'000	£'000	£'000
Contribution (as above)	432	336	216	476	391	221
Materials (£2.75 per kg)	297	231	148.5	231	189.75	137.5
Surplus sold at £1 per kg	–	–	–	–	–	(11)
	135	105	67.5	245	201.25	94.5
Total fixed costs	65	65	65	136	136	136
Profit/(loss)	70	40	2.5	109	65.25	(41.5)
Probability	0.3	0.5	0.2	0.3	0.5	0.2
Expected profit/(loss)	21.0	20.0	0.5	32.7	32.625	(8.3)
Expected value		41.5			57.025	

Note that the minimum requirement of 50,000 kg only results in surplus material with the lowest level of expected sales, ie. 13,000 units.

Option (iii) for materials

Material requirement (kg)	108	84	54	84	69	39
Material purchases (kg)	108	84	70	84	70	70
Surplus (for sale) (kg)	–	–	16	–	1	31

	£'000	£'000	£'000	£'000	£'000	£'000
Contribution (as above)	432	336	216	476	391	221
Materials (£2.50 per kg)	270	210	175	210	175	175
Surplus sold at £1 per kg	–	–	(16)	–	(1)	(31)
	162	126	57	266	217	77
Total fixed costs	65	65	65	136	136	136
Profit/(loss)	97	61	(8)	130	81	(59)
Probability	0.3	0.5	0.2	0.3	0.5	0.2
Expected profit/(loss)	29.1	30.5	(1.6)	39.0	40.5	(11.8)
Expected value		58.0			67.7	

The highest expected profit of £67,700 results from a selling price of £20 and buying a minimum of 70,000 kg of material at a cost of £2.50 per kg.

(b)   **Expected profit (£'000)**

Expected sales *Purchasing option*	*Optimistic*		*Most likely*		*Pessimistic*	
(i)	43	88	19	48.00	(11.0)	(32.0)
(ii)	70	109	40	65.25	2.5	(41.5)
(iii)	97	130	61	81.00	(8.0)	(59.0)

For the best result:

Profit	130.0	81.0	2.5
Probability	0.3	0.5	0.2
Expected profit	39.0	40.5	0.5

	£'000
Total expected profit with perfect information	
39.0 + 40.5 + 0.5	80.0
Expected profit from (a) above	67.7
	———
Maximum price for perfect information	12.3
	———

Note: This question is an excellent test of your ability to organise your thoughts and your workings in a clear, concise and logical manner.

5.8   Homeworker

(a)   **Maximum increased production availability**

(i)   **Current production capacity**

Per batch of 10 Homelathes

Machine hours required:	A	10
	B	14
	C	12
		——
		36 machine hours
		——

Maximum available capacity 4,752 machine hours.
Current production capacity 4,752 ÷ 36, ie. 132 batches.

(ii)   **Potential production capacity**

Buy	A	0
Make	B	14
Make	C	12
		——
		26 machine hours per batch
		——

Capacity 4,752, ie. 4,752 ÷ 26 = 182.8 batches
An increase of 182.8 − 132 = 50.8 or 38.5%

Buy	B	0
Make	A	10
Make	C	12

22 machine hours per batch

Capacity 4,752, ie. 4,752 ÷ 22 = 216 batches
An increase of 216 – 132 = 84 or 63.6%

Buy	C	0
Make	A	10
Make	B	14

24 machine hours per batch

Capacity 4,752, ie. 4,752 ÷ 24 = 198 batches
An increase of 198 – 132 = 66 or 50%

(b) **Financial implications – which component to buy out** (production availability limited to 50% increase)

Note that even if there was no limitation on the increase in production capacity, it would not necessarily be the best decision to buy component B. Although this course of action makes the best use of the available machine hours, it does not yet take into account the relative costs of buying the components. The optimum decision is the one that takes account of both of these factors.

(i) **Expected value of the component prices**

		A		B		C	
		Price	*EV*	*Price*	*EV*	*Price*	*EV*
		£	£	£	£	£	£
Pessimistic	0.25	96	24	176	44	149	37.25
Most likely	0.50	85	42.5	158	79	127	63.50
Optimistic	0.25	54	13.5	148	37	97	24.25
			80.0		160		125.00

(ii) **Present contribution per batch**

	£	£
Selling price		600
Variable cost of components	160	
Assembly costs (variable)	40	
Total variable costs		200
Contribution per batch		400

(iii) **Potential contribution from buying a component**

	A	B	C
	£	£	£
Variable cost of component	32	54	58
Expected purchase cost	80	160	125
Additional cost of purchase	48	106	67

Present contribution per batch	£400	£400	£400
Contribution if component purchased	£352	£296	£333
Potential number of batches	182.8	198 (note 1)	198
Total contribution	£64,346	£58,608	£65,934

Buying in component C offers the highest total contribution of £65,934, compared with the previous contribution of 132 batches × £400 = £52,800.

(c) **Profit statement for the period**

	£	£
Sales (198 batches)		118,800
Variable costs:		
Component A	6,336	
Component B	10,692	
Component C (purchased)	24,750	
Component D	2,376	
Component E	792	
Assembly costs (£40 × 198)	7,920	
		52,866
Contribution		65,934
Fixed cost (£316 × 132 batches)		41,712
Profit		24,222

Note that the fixed cost was originally absorbed at the rate of £316 per batch, when 132 batches were produced. Even though 198 batches will now be produced, there is no reason for the total fixed cost to change from its original level.

(d) **Other factors if management had decided to avoid risk**

(i) The price on which the decision to buy component C is based, is an expected value of a range of three prices, varying from £97 to £149. The most likely price is £127. Homeworker Ltd might wish to take account of the range of prices of the components, which contributes to the uncertainty.

(ii) The price charged by General Machines Ltd is to be based on audited figures, ie. actual costs. There is therefore no incentive for General Machines to exercise adequate cost control, as inefficiencies can be passed on by means of higher prices.

(iii) If Homeworker Ltd is to buy the entire production requirements of component C from General Machines Ltd, the firm will be wholly dependent on one supplier for delivery dates, suitable quality and price. Any disruption in the supply of component C will cause severe problems for Homeworker Ltd.

(iv) Although it was stated in part (c) that there was no reason why the total fixed cost should change from its original level, it is quite possible that an increase in production, and especially assembly, of 50% of the original output, will result in an increase in fixed cost.

(v) The marketing department has estimated a 50% increase in demand next period, and production is being geared up to produce an extra 50%. However, if this estimate is optimistic, Homeworker Ltd will be left with high levels of stock which has been produced at an increased cost. The firm should be sure that both sales and production levels can be achieved before making the decision to buy in one of the components.

5.9 Ices

(a) **No market research**

High demand

	£'000	*Factors*	*PV* £'000
T_{1-3}	40	2.11	84.4
T_{4-6}	30	3.33 − 2.11	36.6
			121.0

Low demand

	£'000	*Factors*	*PV* £'000
T_{1-3}	15	2.11	31.65
T_{4-6}	10	3.33 − 2.11	12.20
			43.85

Expected NPV = $(0.75 \times 121) + (0.25 \times 43.85) = 101.713$

(b)   **Continuing present range**

	£'000	*Factors*	*PV* £'000
T_1	28.500	0.83	23.655
T_2	27.075	0.69	18.682
T_3	25.721	0.58	14.918
T_4	24.435	0.48	11.729
T_5	23.213	0.40	9.285
T_6	22.053	0.33	7.277
			85.546

(c) and (d)

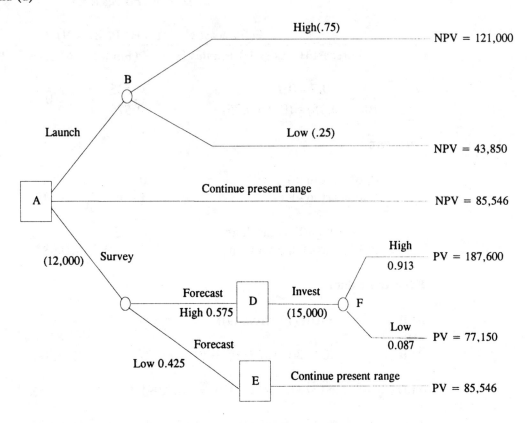

With survey

High demand

	£'000	*Factors*	*PV* £'000
T_{1-3}	60	2.11	126.6
T_{4-6}	50	3.33 – 2.11	61.0
			187.6

Low demand

	£'000	*Factors*	*PV* £'000
T_{1-3}	25	2.11	52.75
T_{4-6}	20	3.33 – 2.11	24.40
			77.15

Probabilities (using Bayes' theorem):

$$P(\text{Sales H/Forecast H}) = \frac{P(\text{Forecast H / Sales H}) \; P(\text{Sales H})}{\text{Total P (Forecast H)}}$$

$$= \frac{P(\text{Forecast H / Sales H}) \; P(\text{Sales H})}{P(\text{Forecast H / Sales H}) \; P(\text{Sales H}) + P(\text{Forecast H / Sales L}) \; P(\text{Sales L})}$$

$$= \frac{0.7 \times 0.75}{(0.7 \times 0.75) + (0.2 \times 0.25)} = \frac{0.525}{0.575} = 0.913$$

Therefore:

P(forecast high)	=	0.575
P(forecast low)	=	1 – 0.575 = 0.425
P(Sales high/Forecast high)	=	0.913
P(Sales low/Forecast high)	=	1 – 0.913 = 0.087

Expected values

At B : £101,713 (from (a))

At F : $(0.913 \times 187,600) + (0.087 \times 77,150) = £177,991$

At D : £177,991 – £15,000 = £162,991

At C : $(0.575 \times 162,991) + (0.425 \times 85,546) = £130,007$

At A :
Launch	£101,713
Continue present range	£85,546
Survey	£118,007

Answer to (c) £118,077

Answer to (d) Undertake survey with extra investment if the forecast is high.
EV = £118,077

5.10 Lecture solution - Relevant costs (Marchbank Ltd)

(a)

	£
Sales team time - sunk	–
Material X – replacement cost as used regularly in business 600 × 4	2,400
Material Y – 200 kg in stock: disposal cost saved 200 × 0.5	
(sale is not relevant as costs 75p per kg; 500 kg disposed of anyway)	(100)
Material Z – lost sale proceeds 300 × (3 + 7.50)	3,150
Skilled labour – salaried, so no incremental cost	-
Unskilled labour – 100 × 6 × 1.5	900
Variable overheads (200 + 100) × 4	1,200
Fixed overheads – no incremental cost	-
Machine – loss of value (see working)	30
Minimum price	7,580

(b) The price would fall by £30, as the loss of value of the machine would be irrelevant.

Working

This year's depreciation charge $5,200 \times 20\% = £1,040$

∴ Project's duration $\dfrac{60}{1,040} \times 52$ (see note 4) = 3 weeks

∴ True loss of value is $10 \times 3 = £30$

5.11 Wymark Electronics plc

(a) **Maximum price per circuit to be paid**

As the maximum price is not immediately evident from the data, it is best to work through the following stages:

Step 1 – Determine the cashflows for each of the three years, taking account of the inflation level applicable to each item of cost.

Step 2 – Discount the cashflows using the required cost of capital of 16% in money terms.

Step 3 – Determine the maximum amount payable for the circuits.

Step 1 – Cashflows, taking account of inflation

	19X7/X8	19X8/X9	19X9/X0
Inflows			
Revenue 4 × £102,732	410,928	410,928	410,928
Disposal of machine	–	–	50,000
Outflows			
Equipment (1/7/X7)	(150,000)	–	–
Labour			
Skilled 4 × 2,000 × £6	(48,000)	(+10%) (52,800)	(+10%)(58,080)
Semi-skilled 4 × 4,000 × £4	(64,000)	(+10%) (70,400)	(+10%)(77,440)
Opportunity cost of			
skilled labour 4 × 2,000 × £8	(64,000)	–	–
Technical manager –			
redundancy 1/7/X7	30,000		
– salary	(18,000)	(+10%) (19,800)	(+10%)(21,780)
– pension – not paid	4,000	4,000	4,000
Overhead			
Variable 4 × 2,000 × £7	(56,000)	(+10%) (61,600)	(+10%)(67,760)
Materials			
X – 4 × 20 × £850			
purchase price	(68,000)	(+15%) (78,200)	(+15%)(89,930)
Y – 4 × 15 × £200			
realisable value (1/7/X7)	12,000	–	–
– 4 × 15 × £550			
purchase price		(+15%) (37,950)	(+15%)(43,642)
	———	———	———
Net cashflow 1/7/X7	(132,000)	94,178	106,296
30/6/X8	96,928		
	———	———	———

Step 2 – Discount the cashflows at 16%

1/7/X7	£132,000	outflow	× 1.000	(132,000)
30/6/X8	£96,928	inflow	× 0.86	83,358
30/6/X9	£94,178	inflow	× 0.74	69,692
30/6/X0	£106,296	inflow	× 0.64	68,029
				———
Net cash inflow				89,079
				———

Step 3 – Determine maximum payable for the circuits

Cost for 40 microchip circuits – fixed at start of contract (1/7/X7) £89,079 ÷ 2.25 = £39,591 pa.

Cost per circuit £39,591 ÷ 40 = £990

(b)   **Minimum amount of additional equipment**

Expected purchase price of circuits	£1,200
Breakeven purchase price of circuits	£990
Difference in cost per circuit	£210
Annual requirement 40 circuits	£8,400
Cumulative present value factor	× 2.25
Additional discounted cost	£18,900

This amount must be saved from the cost of semi-skilled labour. This is currently:

	£
Year 1 £64,000 × 0.86	55,040
Year 2 £70,400 × 0.74	52,096
Year 3 £77,440 × 0.64	49,562
	156,698

The present value effect of a 1% reduction in semi-skilled labour is as follows:

	£
Labour cost reduction £156,698 × 1%	1,567
Capital cost increase	1,000
Net present value saving	567

Total saving required	£18,900
Net saving per £1000 equipment	£567

The equipment required to generate the total saving would be:

$$\frac{£18,900}{£567} \times £1,000 \quad = \quad £33,333$$

Rounded up   =   £34,000

5.12   Information for decision-making

(a)   The different levels of management will be involved in decision-making of varying time scales:

Strategic decision-making - the longer-term decisions, for the next five – ten years of the business. These will be taken by the top level of management. The decisions will more in the nature of targets - ie. what is to be achieved rather than how it is to be done.

Tactical decision-making - taken by the 'middle tier' of management, concerning the operations over the next one or two years. This will start to formulate plans to achieve the longer-term objectives, including choice of products and markets, allocation of resources, etc.

Operational decision-making - these are the day-to-day decisions made by 'local' management, that will have very clear quantifiable objectives, often cost/revenue based; eg. choosing between types and suppliers of resources, deciding on credit terms and generally reacting to changing local circumstances.

(b) **Information requirements**

Strategic decisions

Most of the information needed at this level will be related to the external environment - the economy and its potential effects on the particular industry sector(s); the markets for the current and proposed products/services; technological changes expected; potential future legislation and taxation changes and their possible effects, etc. Much of this will be qualitative and by necessity in general terms. This information will need to be updated at least annually.

Tactical decisions

More detailed qualitative and quantitative information will be needed here, both external and internal - expected market sizes and shares, set-up costs for new ventures, breakeven activity levels, expected resource availability over the next year, training and internal expertise required for new areas of work, expected salary rises, etc. This information would be updated monthly.

Operational decisions

These will be made largely on the basis of detailed internal quantitative information. This will include detailed monthly budgets, cashflows and comparisons with actual; suppliers' prices; sales records and patterns; stock reports; machine down times; staff costs etc. Daily or weekly updating will be needed at this level.

(c) A tactical decision would be whether to close an internal service department and contract out the work instead, eg. data processing, canteen, machine maintenance, etc.

The information required on which to base this decision will include:

(i) detailed historic costs analyses for the department over the last few years;

(ii) forecast activity levels of relevant user departments to assess future usage;

(iii) closure costs (redundancy, committed leases);

(iv) tenders from prospective contractors including costs, timing, back-up, additional services;

(v) potential effects on staff morale, especially where significant redundancies are involved; possible redeployment of staff.

6 LINEAR PROGRAMMING

6.1 Lecture solution – Tartan mill

(a)   Let   x = number of sq ft of red board produced per day
            y = number of sq ft of blue board produced per day

Since total output cannot exceed 3,000 sq ft

$$x + y \leq 3,000 \qquad\qquad (1)$$

Red board requires 0.5 litres/sq ft of chemical A.
Blue board requires 0.3 litres/sq ft of chemical A.
The maximum daily supply of chemical A is 1,200 litres.

$$\therefore \quad 0.5x + 0.3y \leq 1,200 \qquad\qquad (2)$$

Red board requires 0.525 litres/sq ft of chemical B.
Blue board requires 0.75 litres/sq ft of chemical B.
The maximum daily supply of chemical B is 2,100 litres.

$$\therefore \quad 0.525x + 0.75y \leq 2,100 \qquad\qquad (3)$$

Also, since the amounts of board produced each day cannot be negative

$$x \geq 0 \qquad\qquad (4)$$
$$y \geq 0 \qquad\qquad (5)$$

Equations (1) - (5) define the constraints and all feasible solutions lie in the unshaded area on the graph below (ONQRS).

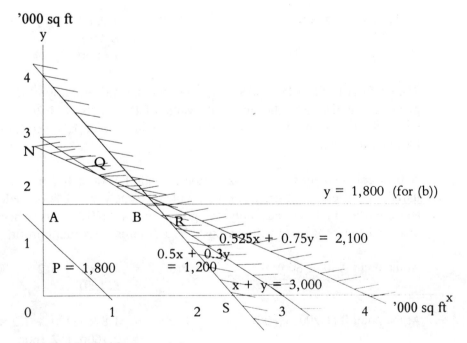

Daily profit P = 1.8x + 1.2y

The line for P = 1,800 is shown by a dotted line on the graph.

The line of maximum profit is the one parallel to the line for P = 1,800 which is the furthest away from the origin but which still touches the polygon ONQRS. By inspection this is the line passing through R. Now R lies at the intersection of the two lines:

$$0.5x + 0.3y = 1,200 \text{ and } x + y = 3,000$$

Solving these for x and y, R is (1,500, 1,500)

$$\therefore P = (1.8 \times 1,500) + (1.2 \times 1,500)$$
$$= 4,500p$$
$$\textbf{Profit} = \textbf{£45}$$

Alternative method

If it is not obvious after drawing the graph which point line is required, the profit can be calculated at each of the extreme points of the feasibility polygon and the maximum value produced gives the answer.

At the origin 0   Profit $= (1.8 \times 0) + (1.2 \times 0) = £0$

At the point N (0, 2,800)   Profit $= 1.8 \times 0 + 1.2 \times 2,800$
$$= 3,360p$$
$$= £33.60$$

At the point Q $\left(\dfrac{2,000}{3}, \dfrac{700}{3} \right)$ Profit $= 1.8 \times \dfrac{2,000}{3} + 1.2 \times \dfrac{7,000}{3}$
$$= 0.6 \times 2,000 + 0.4 \times 7,000$$
$$= 1,200p + 2,800p$$
$$= £40$$

At the point S (2,400, 0)   Profit $= 1.8 \times 2,400 + 1.2 \times 0$
$$= 4,320p$$
$$= £43.20$$

The profit at R was £45, which is greater than the value at any of the other extreme points and is therefore the maximum value of P = 1.8x + 1.2y over the polygon ONQRS. To obtain this the manufacturer should produce 1,500 sq ft each of red and blue board per day.

(b)   A firm commitment to supply a customer with 1,800 sq ft per day of blue board introduces an extra constraint to the problem, namely y ≥ 1,800. When this line is added to the graph the feasibility polygon becomes ANQB. Since this area does not include the point R there will obviously be a different maximum profit.

At the point A (0, 1,800)   Profit $= 1.8 \times 0 + 1.2 \times 1,800$
$$= £21.60$$

At the point B (1,200, 1,800)   Profit $= 1.8 \times 1,200 + 1.2 \times 1,800$
$$= 2,160p + 2,160p$$
$$= £43.20$$

Comparing the values for A, B, N and Q we see that maximum profit occurs at B, when x = 1,200 and y = 1,800.

(c)   The critical constraints are:

Supply of chemical A $0.5x + 0.3y \le 1{,}200$
Machine capacity $x + y \le 3{,}000$

The dual price for chemical A can be found by assuming one more litre to be available.

The optimal solution then lies at the intersection of:

	$0.5x + 0.3y$	$= 1{,}201$	(6)
and	$x + y$	$= 3{,}000$	(7)
Multiply (6) by 2	$x + 0.6y$	$= 2{,}402$	(8)
Subtract (8) from (7)	$0.4y$	$= 598$	
	y	$= 1{,}495$	
Substitute in (7)	x	$= 3{,}000 - 1{,}495$	
		$= 1{,}505$	

Profit $= 1.8x + 1.2y = (1.8 \times 1{,}505 + 1.2 \times 1{,}495)$ pence
$= £45.03$

Thus one extra litre of chemical A increases the profit by 3p.

$\therefore$ Dual price for chemical A $= 3\text{p/litre}$

Interpretation 1

The dual price gives the maximum premium it is worth paying to obtain more of a scarce resource. In this case, if extra supplies of chemical A can be purchased for no more than 3p on top of the original price, then it will be worth buying some extra.

The dual price for machine capacity can be found by assuming an extra square foot can be produced.

The optimal solution now lies at the intersection of:

	$0.5x + 0.3y$	$= 1{,}200$	(9)
and	$x + y$	$= 3{,}001$	(10)
Multiply (9) by 2	$x + 0.6y$	$= 2{,}400$	(11)
Subtract (11) from (10)	$0.4y$	$= 601$	
	y	$= 1{,}502.5$	
Substitute in (10)	x	$= 3{,}001 - 1{,}502.5$	
		$= 1{,}498.5$	

Profit $= 1.8x + 1.2y = (1.8 \times 1{,}498.5 + 1.2 \times 1{,}502.5)$ pence
$= £45.003$

Thus the extra machine capacity to produce one more square foot gives an increase in profit of 0.3 pence.

$\therefore$ Dual price for machine capacity $= 0.3\text{p/sq ft}$

Interpretation 2

It will be worth increasing the machine capacity if it will cost less than 0.3p/sq ft over and above the original cost.

Alternative approach, via the dual problem.

Primal problem is: maximise $1.8x + 1.2y$

subject to:

machine capacity constraint $x + y \leq 3{,}000$	(M)
chemical A constraint $0.5x + 0.3y \leq 1{,}200$	(A)
chemical B constraint $0.525x + 0.75y \leq 2{,}100$	(B)
and $x, y \geq 0$	

then dual problem is: minimise $3{,}000M + 1{,}200A + 2{,}100B$

subject to:

'x constraint' $M + 0.5A + 0.525B \geq 1.8$
'y constraint' $M + 0.3A + 0.75B \geq 1.2$
and $M, A, B \geq 0$

where M = dual price of machine capacity for one square foot
        A = dual price of one litre of chemical A
        B = dual price of one litre of chemical B

However, from the solution to the primal problem we know that the chemical B constraint is non-critical $\therefore B = 0$

In other words, the dual problem simplifies to:

minimise $3{,}000M + 1{,}200A$

subject to:

x constraint $M + 0.5A \geq 1.8$

y constraint $M + 0.3A \geq 1.2$ $(M, A \geq 0)$

In fact, since the other constraints in the primal are critical we can say that M and A are both non-zero, ie. $M, A > 0$. The graph is, roughly, going to look like this:

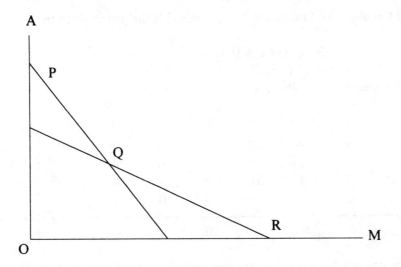

We know that the solution point is going to be P, Q or R, but Q is the only one of these points at which both A and M are non-zero. Thus we need to solve simultaneously the two constraint lines:

$$M + 0.5A = 1.8 \qquad (1)$$
$$M + 0.3A = 1.2 \qquad (2)$$

$$(1) - (2) \qquad 0.2A = 0.6$$

$$A = 3$$

$$\text{substitute in (1)} \qquad M + 1.5 = 1.8$$

$$M = 0.3$$

giving the same dual values as with the previous method.

(d)   The shadow price of 1oz green wool is the increase in contribution (profit) available from an increase of 1lb in the availability of green wool; ie. the constraint will change to

$$2x + 4y \le 30.016$$

The optimal solution will again be on any point between the intersections of this new constraint with the vertical axis and the red wool constraint. Taking the former: when $x = 0$, $y = 7,504$, and $p = 0.8 \times 7,504 = £6,003.20$

Thus the maximum profit has risen by £3.20, which is thus the shadow or dual price of 1lb of green wool. The mill should be prepared to pay up to £3.20 *premium* to obtain each extra pound of green wool (until it is no longer the limiting factor).

(e)   The inequalities for the constraints are

$$8x + 10y \le 80,000$$
$$2.5x + y \le 20,000$$
$$2x + 4y \le 30,000$$
$$x + y \le 9,000 \qquad\qquad x \ge 0, \ y \ge 0$$

and the objective function to be maximised is the profit given by

$$P = 0.4x + 0.8y$$

The initial simplex tableau is

x	y	a	b	c	d	
8	10	12	0	0	0	80,000
$5/2$	1	0	1	0	0	20,000
2	4	0	0	1	0	30,000
1	1	0	0	0	1	9,000
−0.4	−0.8	0	0	0	0	0

since column 2 has the largest negative indicator, this is chosen as the pivot column.

Dividing all the positive entries in this column into the entries of the last column, the results are:

$$\frac{80,000}{10} = 8,000; \quad \frac{20,000}{1} = 20,000; \quad \frac{30,000}{4} = 7,500; \quad \frac{9,000}{1} = 9,000$$

The smallest value is 7,500; hence 4 is the pivot element.

Perform the following row operations on the tableau

$$R_3' = \tfrac{1}{4}R_3, \ R_1' = R_1 - 10R_3', \ R_2' = R_2 - R_3', \ R_4' = R_4 - R_3', \ R_5' = R_5 + \tfrac{4}{5}R_3'$$

This has the effect of reducing the pivot element to 1 all other entries in the pivot column to zero.

The resulting tableau is

x	y	a	b	c	d	
3	0	1	0	−2.5	0	5,000
2	0	0	1	−0.25	0	12,500
0.5	1	0	0	0.25	0	7,500
0.5	0	0	0	−0.25	1	1,500
0	0	0	0	0.2	0	6,000

This is a final tableau since there are no negative indicators.

Interpretation

For any column with one entry of 1 and all other entries zero, the value of the variable is the value in the last column in the same row as the 1. All variables with columns not in this format are zero.

For the above tableau

$$x = 0 \quad y = 7,500 \quad a = 5,000 \quad b = 12,500 \quad c = 0 \quad d = 1,500$$

where a, b, c and d are the slack variables.

Thus maximum profit is £6,000 when 7,500 yards of tartan B are produced with none of tartan A (as found in (c) above).

The slack variables give the following information:

$$a = \text{surplus red wool}$$
$$b = \text{surplus yellow wool}$$
$$c = \text{surplus green wool}$$
$$d = \text{spare production capacity in yardage}$$

The values for these variables can be easily checked.

When 7,500 yards of tartan B are woven the amounts of red, yellow and green wool used will be 75,000oz, 7,500oz and 30,000oz, respectively. The maximum available amounts of each colour are 80,000oz, 20,000oz and 30,000oz.

Thus

$$a = 80,000 - 75,000 = 5,000$$
$$b = 20,000 - 7,500 = 12,500$$
$$c = 30,000 - 30,000 = 0$$

The maximum possible production in the given time is 9,000 yards, but in the solution for maximum profit only 7,500 yards were produced leaving 1,500 yards of spare production capacity (ie. $d = 1,500$).

Note also that the dual prices are given in the bottom row for each of the resources - thus the dual prices for red wool, yellow wool and production capacity (the 'a', 'b' and 'd' columns) are zero, whilst that for green wool is £0.20/oz or £3.20/lb as found in (d).

6.2 Standard and de-luxe

(a) This is a standard two-variable linear programming problem.

Let x be the number of standard units produced per week.
Let y be the number of de-luxe units produced per week.

The objective function is to maximise weekly contribution, represented by:

$$C = 100x + 300y$$

The constraints are as follows.

$x + y$ - 40		(machining hours)
$2.5x + 10y$ - 200		(assembly and finishing hours)
y - 18		(maximum sales)
$25x + 50y$ - 1,200		(special components)
x, y - 0		(non-negativity)

Such a problem can be solved graphically.

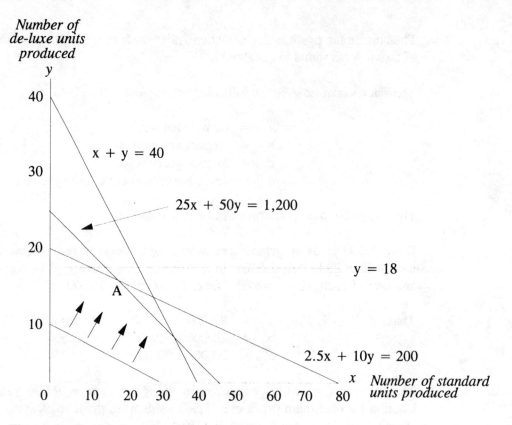

Figure 1: Production plan for a small firm

The optimal point is at point A on the graph. This is at the intersection of:

$$25x + 50y = 1,200$$
$$2.5x + 10y = 200$$

$$25x + 100y = 2,000$$
$$50y = 800$$
$$y = 16$$
$$x = 16$$

I recommend a weekly production plan of 16 standard models and 16 de-luxe models. The contribution earned each week is $100x + 300y = (100 \times 16) + (300 \times 16) = £6,400$.

Special components and assembly and finishing hours are fully used up to their available maximum levels. There are 8 hours unused for machining time still available each week under this plan.

(b) The simplest approach is to calculate the dual prices of both assembly hours and number of components. We currently are constrained by this problem:

Maximise $100x + 300y$
Subject to $2.5x + 10y \leq 200$
$25x + 50y \leq 1,200$
$x, y \geq 0$

The dual prices emerge as the solutions to the dual problem.

Let A = the dual price of assembly time (£/hour)

Let B = the dual price of components (£/component).

The dual problem is as follows:

Minimise   200A + 1,200B
Subject to   2.5A + 25B   ≥   100
                10A + 50B   ≥   300
                     A, B   ≥   0

This problem can also be solved graphically.

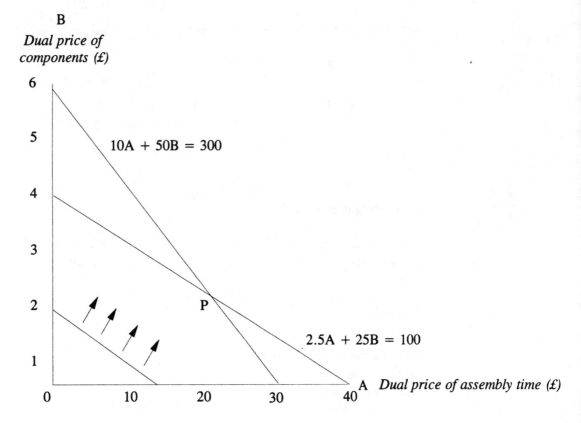

B
Dual price of components (£)

10A + 50B = 300

P

2.5A + 25B = 100

A *Dual price of assembly time (£)*

Figure 2: Dual problem

The solution can be read off the graph to be A = £20/hour, B = £2/component

As we are being offered additional assembly hours and components at prices less than the dual prices, it will be worthwhile increasing the supply of both assembly hours and components beyond the position in part (a) since the benefits will exceed the costs.

(c)   The limiting factors will now be the maximum de-luxe sales limit of 18 per week and the 40 machining hours available per week.

We start from a position of producing 16 standard units and 16 de-luxe units per week. We have spare machining capacity to produce 8 additional units (40 hours maximum less the 32 hours currently being used).

Each additional standard unit will involve:

Contribution = £100

		£
Costs	– Assembly 2.5 hrs @ £12	30
	– Components 25 components @ £1	25
		55

Net contribution = £45

Each additional de-luxe unit will involve:

Contribution = £300

			£
Costs	–	Assembly 10 hrs @ £12	120
	–	Components 50 components @ £1	50
			170

Net contribution = £130

To maximise contribution, we therefore choose our 8 additional units to be 2 de-luxe (to reach the 18 maximum) and the remaining 6 to be standard.

The revised recommended weekly production plan is to make 18 de-luxe models and 22 standard models.

	£
Contribution = From part (a)	6,400
Additional standards 6 × 45	270
Additional de-luxes 2 × 130	260
	6,930

6.3 Caterpillar China Co

(a) In order to obtain the objective function we first need the costs per unit for each product. These are found by multiplying the amount of each resource needed for a unit of a product by the unit costs (eg. product A – cost of materials = 6 × 2.1 = £12.60).

A table of costs can then be constructed as follows.

Resource	Product				
	A	B	C	D	E
Raw materials	12.60	13.65	12.81	12.81	13.44
Forming	3.00	2.25	3.75	3.00	3.00
Firing	3.90	5.85	7.80	7.80	5.85
Packing	4.00	4.00	4.00	6.00	8.00
Total (£)	23.50	25.75	28.36	29.61	30.29

By subtracting the costs from the selling price we get the contributions:

	Product				
	A	B	C	D	E
Selling price (£)	40.00	42.00	44.00	48.00	52.00
Costs	23.50	25.75	28.36	29.61	30.29
Contribution (£)	16.50	16.25	15.64	18.39	21.71

So, the objective function to be maximised is P = **16.50A + 16.25B + 15.64C + 18.39D + 21.71E**

where A, B, C, D and E are the weekly production figures for the five products.

The *constraints* can be written down directly from the table, ie.

Materials: 6.00A + 6.50B + 6.10C + 6.10D + 6.40E - 35,000

Forming: 1.00A + 0.75B + 1.25C + 1.00D + 1.00E - 6,000

Firing: 3.00A + 4.50B + 6.00C + 6.00D + 4.50E - 30,000

Packing: 0.50A + 0.50B + 0.50C + 0.75D + 1.00E - 4,000

The main assumption is that all units manufactured are sold since if this is not the case the full maximum profit contribution will not be realised. Also both costs and revenue are assumed to rise linearly with the number of units produced and sold. It is also assumed that no time capacity, eg. forming hours, is lost if production is switched from one product to another.

(b)   Only variables appearing in the basis column have non-zero values. Thus the table shows that for maximum profit, the weekly production plan consists of:

> 3,357 units of product A
> 2,321 units of product E
> 0 units of B, C and D

Overall maximum profit contribution (£)

$$= (3,357 \times 16.50) + (2,321 \times 21.71) = £105,779 \text{ per week}$$

Unused (slack) resources

From the table, S = 321, T = 9,482; X and U are both 0

∴ There are (i)   no unused raw materials;

(ii)   321 unused forming hours;

(iii)   9,482 unused firing hours;

(iv)   no unused packing hours.

(c)   Dual or shadow price represents the amount of additional contribution that would result from acquiring one additional unit of a given resource, or the loss in contribution that would result from being deprived of one unit of the resource.

Thus for resources not fully used, in this case forming hours and firing hours, the shadow prices are zero, since losing or acquiring time in these areas has no effect on maximum profit. These are indicated in the table by zeroes in the last row under S and T.

The shadow prices for the fully used resources, ie., materials and packing hours are £2.02 per kg and £8.81 per hour respectively. Thus acquiring one additional kg of raw materials would produce an additional contribution of £2.02 and acquiring an extra hour of packing time would produce an additional contribution of £8.81.

(d)   For the proposed new product, the **cost** per unit will be:

$$(6 \times 2.10) + (1 \times 3.00) + (5 \times 1.30) + (1 \times 8.00) = £30.10$$

Selling price = £50 per unit

So contribution per unit = 50 − 30.10 = £19.90

From previously the fully used ('scarce') resources are materials (X) and packing (U) with shadow prices £2.02 and £8.81 respectively. Each unit of the new product will result in a deprivation of 6 kg of materials and one hour of a packing, ie. a reduction in existing contribution of $(6 \times 2.02) + (1 \times 8.81) = £20.93$. Since this exceeds the contribution of £19.90 per unit for the new product, it is not a worthwhile proposition to introduce the new product.

7   NETWORK ANALYSIS

7.1   Assert

(a)   (i) and (ii)

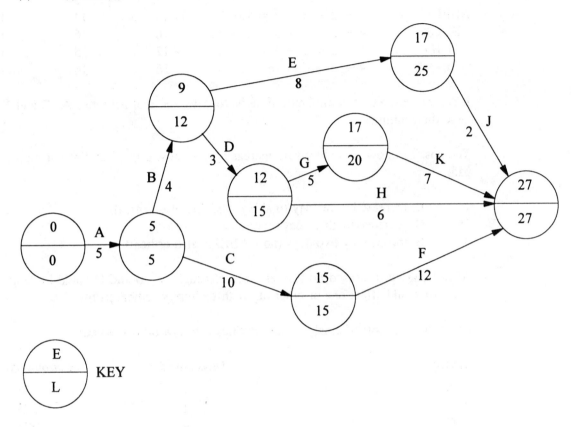

Activity	Latest time (L) for end event	–	Earliest time (E) for start event	–	Activity duration	=	Total float
A	5	–	0	–	5	=	0
B	12	–	5	–	4	=	3
C	15	–	5	–	10	=	0
D	15	–	9	–	3	=	0
E	25	–	9	–	8	=	8
F	27	–	15	–	12	=	0
G	20	–	12	–	5	=	3
H	27	–	12	–	6	=	9
J	27	–	17	–	2	=	8
K	27	–	17	–	7	=	3

The total float of an activity is the time by which it can be delayed without altering the total time taken for the project. Activities with a total float of zero are critical, ie. A, C and F.

Normal time 27 days.

Normal cost 27 × 250 + 8,000 = £14,750

(b) The minimum possible time is most easily found by crashing every activity to its minimum.

Path	Duration (days)	Amended duration (see later)		
		1	2	3
ABEJ	4 + 2 + 5 + 2 = 13	14	14	16
ABDGK	4 + 2 + 2 + 3 + 4 = 15	16	16	16
ABDH	4 + 2 + 2 + 3 = 11	12	15	15
ACF	4 + 6 + 6 = 16	16	16	16

It can be seen that the minimum time is 16 days and that activities A, C and F must be at their minima.

The cost can now be reduced by increasing the most costly activity not on a critical path:

1: B, increase by one day (making ABDGK also critical)
2: H, increase by three days
3: E, increase by two days (now ABEJ is also critical)

ABDH can be increased no further since although, A, B and D could be lengthened to do so would affect one or other of the three jointly critical paths.

The additional cost of crashing the activities can now be calculated:

Activity	Days saved	Additional cost (£)
A	1	200
B	1	275
C	4	900
D	1	125
E	1	100
F	6	900
G	2	100
H	Nil	Nil
J	Nil	Nil
K	3	225
		2,825

Therefore minimum total cost for duration of 16 days is £8,000 + £2,825 + (16 × £250) = £14,825.

(c) The minimum total cost is best found by systematically crashing the cheapest activities on the critical paths (provided always that the cost of crashing the critical path by one day shall now exceed the cost of overhead thus saved, £250)

Path	Duration (days)	Amended duration			
		1	2	3	4
ABEJ	19	19	18	18	18
ABDGK	24	24	23	21	20
ABDH	18	18	17	17	17
ACF	27	24	23	21	20

1   Activity F is the cheapest (to crash) on Path ACF, it should be crashed by three days, at which point ABDGK becomes jointly critical.

2   ACF *and* ABDGK can be reduced by crashing A (cost 200) or one of B, D, G or K plus either C or F. The cheapest of these latter options is F plus G (cost 200). We will crash A, because it lies on all four paths, but the maximum is only one day.

3   Now we will crash F plus G by two days (limited by G).

4   Still ACF and ABDGK must be crashed together. The cheapest remaining method is F plus K (cost 225) by one day (now limited by F).

The cheapest way of crashing ACF and ABDGK is now C plus K, but at 225 + 75 = 300 (250) it would not be worthwhile.

Activity	Days saved	Additional cost £
A	1	200
F	6	900
G	2	100
K	1	75
		1,275

The minimum cost is thus £8,000 + £1,275 + (20 × £250) = £14,275 with an associated minimum time of 20 days.

7.2   Floating labour

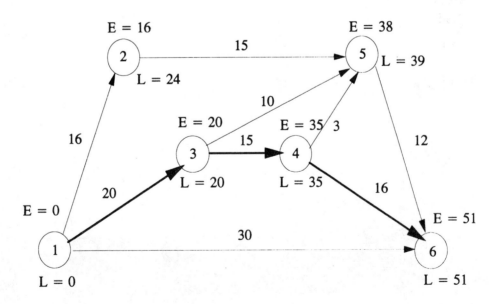

The formulae for various types of float are:

(i)   Total float = L(end) − E(start) − duration
(ii)   Free float = E(end) − E(start) − duration
(iii) Independent float = E(end) − L(start) − duration

The values can now be tabulated.

Activity	Duration	E(start)	E(end)	L(end)	L(start)	TF	FF	IF
1 – 2	16	0	16	24	0	8	0	0
1 – 3	20	0	20	20	0	0	0	0
1 – 6	30	0	51	51	0	21	21	21
2 – 5	15	16	38	39	24	8	7	0
3 – 4	15	20	35	35	20	0	0	0
3 – 5	10	20	38	39	20	9	8	8
4 – 5	3	35	38	39	35	1	0	0
4 – 6	16	35	51	51	35	0	0	0
5 – 6	12	38	51	51	39	1	1	0

Activities are critical if the total float is zero.

The critical path is therefore:

1 – 3, 3 – 4, 4 – 6

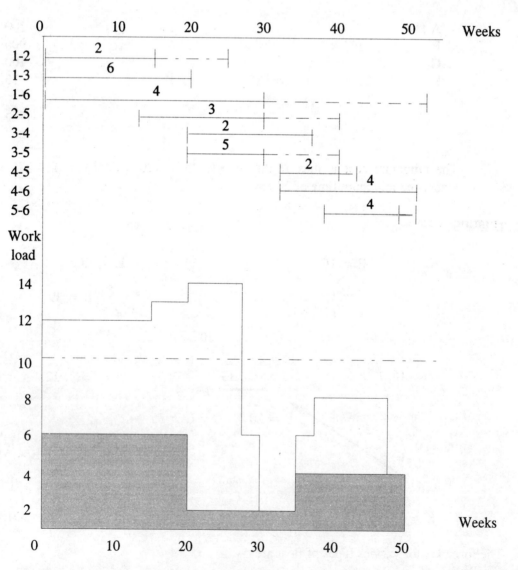

The shaded area shows the work load for the critical activities (ie. those with zero float). These critical activities cannot be moved without extending the total time for the project, which is unacceptable, and so the minimisation of overloading must be achieved by moving the remaining activities by an amount up to their total float.

which is unacceptable, and so the minimisation of overloading must be achieved by moving the remaining activities by an amount up to their total float.

In the above situation the labour force is overloaded for 30 weeks. In the revised chart following the overloading only occurs in 20 weeks.

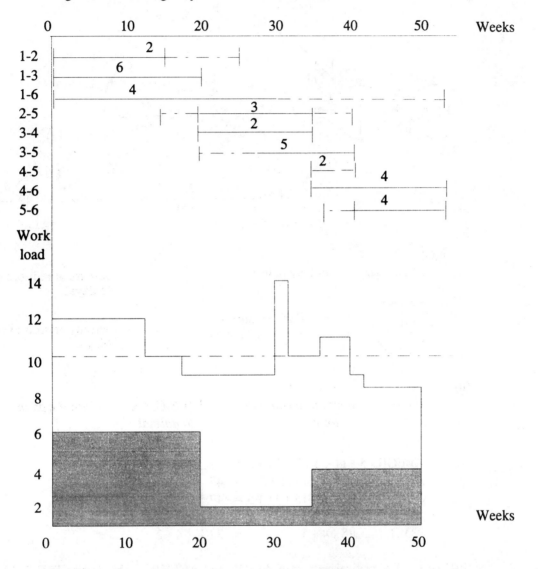

Although this arrangement gives the minimum length of time for overloading it may well not be the situation chosen in practice because of the 'spike' occurring in week 29. This feature could be removed by advancing activity 3 – 5 by 1 week, but this in turn would lengthen the project time since 3 – 5 is a critical activity. However, within the context of local circumstances, this arrangement may be judged acceptable.

7.3   Project crash

(a)   The easiest way to arrive at the absolute minimum time (at minimum call) for the project which tasks are at normal and reduced durations is to:

   (i)   draw network and determine the paths through it;

   (ii)   take all paths down to their reduced durations;

   (iii)   leave all activities on the resulting critical path at reduced durations;

(iv)   determine which of the remaining activities can be increased back up to normal duration without affecting overall project time to effect.

(i)

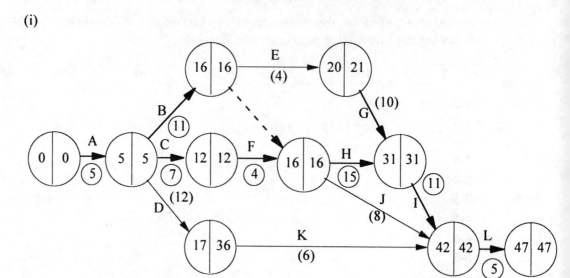

Key

- - - - ▶   = critical path

⑤   = activity at reduced duration (5 days)

(E | L)   E = Earliest start time
L = Latest start time

( )   = activity at normal duration (days)

(ii)

Paths	Reduced durations total	D,E,G,J,K to normal durations	Final duration
ABEGIL	5+11+3+7+11+5 = 42	+1+3	46
ABHIL	5+11+15+11+5 = 47		47
ACFHIL	5+7+4+15+11+5 = 47		47
ACJL	5+7+7+5 = 24	+1	25
ADKL	5+8+4+5 = 22	+4+2	28

(iii)&(iv)   The critical paths are ABHIL and ACFHIL. This leaves D,E,G,J,K that could potentially go back to normal duration. In fact, all can be adjusted back without affecting minimum project time of 47 days.

(b) **Five-day working week**

	Installation		£
	A	$3,200 \times 8/5$	5,120
	B	$8,400 \times 14/11$	10,691
	C	$5,000 \times 10/7$	7,143
	D		7,200
	E		2,000
	F	$4,200 \times 6/4$	6,300
	G		6,000
	H	$11,000 \times 22/15$	16,133
	I	$5,600 \times 14/11$	7,127
	J		4,800
	K		3,000
	L	$4,000 \times 8/5$	6,400
			————
			81,914

Equipment hire

$\dfrac{47}{5}$ = 10 weeks @ £10,000		100,000
		————
		181,914
		————

Six-day working week

Installation	$81,914 \times 1.2$	£98,297
Equipment hire		

$\dfrac{47}{6}$ = 8 weeks @ £10,000		£80,000
		————
		£178,297
		————

(c) Based upon the above analysis the project should be undertaken with the activities A, B, C, F, H, I, L, at the reduced duration, with a six-day working week.

With six-day working only one day's slippage is allowable before another week's hire of equipment is required, as opposed to three days for five-day working. It may be better to use five-day working at first and switch to six-day working if slippage occurs.

7.4 Network analysis

(a) **Probability of achieving target duration of 42 months**

(Since most paths in Table 1 are less than 42 months, it will be quickest to identify those greater than 42.)

Path	Duration of (maximum) critical path	Joint probability
6	46	0.084
7	45	0.028
8	46	0.126
14	46	0.036
15	45	0.012
16	46	0.054
		───────
		0.340
		───────

$\therefore$ Probability $(\leq 42 \text{ months}) = 1 - 0.34 = 0.66$

(b) **Table of possible costs and joint probabilities**

Path	Element A £m	Prob.	Element B £m	Prob.	Element C £m	Prob.	Element D £m	Prob.	Joint probability	Total cost £m
1	10	0.6	9	0.3	12	0.6	11	0.75	0.081	42
2	10	0.6	9	0.3	14	0.4	15	0.25	0.018	48
3	10	0.6	9	0.3	12	0.6	15	0.25	0.027	46
4	10	0.6	9	0.3	14	0.4	11	0.75	0.054	44
5	10	0.6	16	0.7	12	0.6	11	0.75	0.189	49
6	10	0.6	16	0.7	14	0.4	15	0.25	0.042	55
7	10	0.6	16	0.7	12	0.6	15	0.25	0.063	53
8	10	0.6	16	0.7	14	0.4	11	0.75	0.126	51
9	18	0.4	9	0.3	12	0.6	11	0.75	0.054	50
10	18	0.4	9	0.3	14	0.4	15	0.25	0.012	56
11	18	0.4	9	0.3	12	0.6	15	0.25	0.018	54
12	18	0.4	9	0.3	14	0.4	11	0.75	0.036	52
13	18	0.4	16	0.7	12	0.6	11	0.75	0.126	57
14	18	0.4	16	0.7	14	0.4	15	0.25	0.028	63
15	18	0.4	16	0.7	12	0.6	15	0.25	0.042	61
16	18	0.4	16	0.7	14	0.4	11	0.75	0.084	59

(c) **Probability of achieving target cost of £55 million**

As before, selecting those over £55 million:

Path	Cost £m	Joint probability
10	56	0.012
13	57	0.126
14	63	0.028
15	61	0.042
16	59	0.084
		0.292

$\therefore$ Probability ($\leq$ £55 million) = $1 - 0.292 = 0.708$

(d) The analysis gives guidance as to the likelihood of meeting targets and thus avoiding penalties or excessive costs. These will in turn reflect the level of risk attached to the project so that alternative projects may be evaluated in comparison.

8 SIGNIFICANCE TESTING

8.1 Textile finishing

Sample mean $= \dfrac{\Sigma x}{n} = \dfrac{49.6}{8} = 6.2$

Sample SD, S

$$= \sqrt{\left(\Sigma(x - \bar{x})^2 / (n - 1)\right)}$$

$$= \sqrt{\left(\frac{0.28}{7}\right)}$$

$$= 0.2$$

(a) Null hypothesis: the sample came from a population with a mean of 6.4 hours.

(b) Alternative hypothesis: the sample came from a population with a mean of less than 6.4 hours.

(c) Significance level 5%.

(d) One-tailed test, 5% level: critical value is $t_{.05}$ with $(8 - 1) = 7$ degrees of freedom. Critical value of $t_{.05}$ is 1.895.

(e) $t = \dfrac{\bar{x} - \mu}{s / \sqrt{n}} = \dfrac{6.2 - 6.4}{0.2 / \sqrt{8}} = -2.83$

(f)   The null hypothesis is rejected and the test shows that the average process time has been significantly reduced.

8.2   Mail order arrears

(a)   95% confidence limits for proportions

$$= p \pm 1.96 \sqrt{\frac{pq}{n}}$$

$$= 0.2\left(\frac{40}{200}\right) \pm 1.96 \sqrt{\frac{(0.2)(0.8)}{200}}$$

$$= 0.2 \pm 0.055 \qquad\qquad = 0.145 - 0.255 \qquad (14\tfrac{1}{2}\% - 25\tfrac{1}{2}\%)$$

(b)   For 40 accounts in arrears

$$\text{mean} = \bar{x} = \frac{\sum x}{n} = \frac{£6,480}{40} = £162$$

$$\text{standard deviation, SD} = \sqrt{\frac{\sum(x-\bar{x})^2}{n-1}} = \sqrt{\frac{\sum x^2 - n\bar{x}^2}{n-1}}$$

$$= \sqrt{\frac{£1,102,250 - 40(162)^2}{39}}$$

$$= £36.69$$

(c) H_0:   the two samples are taken from populations with the same mean ie. $\mu_1 = \mu_2$

H_1:   the samples come from populations with different means $\mu_1 = \mu_2$

Standard error for differences between means

$$= \sqrt{\frac{S_1^2}{n_1} + \frac{S_2^2}{n_2}} = \sqrt{\frac{26.69^2}{40} + \frac{39^2}{160}} = \sqrt{43.16} = 6.57$$

H_0 will be rejected if $|Z| > 1.96$ [5% significance level]

$$z = \frac{(\bar{x}_1 - \bar{x}_2) - 0}{\text{SE}} = \frac{162 - 152}{6.57} = 1.52$$

Thus H_0 is not rejected - there is no statistical evidence that the mean initial purchases are significantly for accounts in arrears from those not.

(d)   There does not appear to be any relationship between the amount of the initial purchase and the likelihood of the account going into arrears.

The assumptions made in the hypothesis test are:

(i)   the populations can be reasonably approximated by normal distributions;
(ii)   the samples were drawn at random;

(iii)   the samples are unbiased.

8.3   Debtors

(a)   A test of association (chi-squared test) is required to see if there is any relationship between amount of debt and settlement time.

The **hypotheses** are as follows:

Null hypothesis, H_0 – No relationship between size of debt and settlement time.

Alternative hypothesis, H_1 – There is a relationship between size of debt and settlement time.

The observed frequencies (O) should be first set out together with the row and column totals as follows.

	Slow	Very slow	Warning letter	Legal action	Total
Small	12	15	16	17	60
Medium	15	17	21	27	80
Large	17	26	26	41	110
Substantial	26	32	37	55	150
Total	70	90	100	140	400

The expected frequencies (E) are then computed using the basic rule:

$$E = \frac{\text{Row total} \times \text{column total}}{\text{Grand total}}$$

eg. Small/slow, $E = \dfrac{60 \times 70}{400} = 10.5$

Table of expected frequencies (E)

	Slow	*Very slow*	*Warning letter*	*Legal action*
Small	10.5	13.5	15	21
Medium	14	18	20	28
Large	19.25	24.75	27.5	38.5
Substantial	26.25	33.75	37.5	52.5

χ^2 is then $\sum (O-E)^2/E$

$$= \frac{(12-10.5)^2}{10.5} + \frac{(15-13.5)^2}{13.5} + \ldots \frac{(55-52.5)^2}{52.5}$$

$$= \textbf{2.22} \text{ (to two decimal places)}$$

Computational note

Individual values of $(O-E)^2/E$ do not need to be written down – the more quickly and accurately done using the calculator memory.

Using the chi-squared tables, the number of degrees of freedom is (Rows – 1)(Columns – 1) = (4 – 1)(4 – 1) = 9, so that a value of 16.919 is needed for chi-squared for 5% significance.

Since the calculated value is below this, **there is no evidence of a relationship between size of debt and time taken to settle**.

The suspicion of the MA is not substantiated.

(b) In the above context the *lack* of significance of chi-squared meant that the differences between observed and expected frequencies could be put down to 'chance' or 'sampling error' and could not be attributed to a possible relationship between size of debt and settlement time – the differences were not 'significant' in the statistical sense.

The question goes on to ask for the distinction between a 'hypothesis test' and a 'test of significance' but it has to be said that, as far as the *procedures* involved are concerned these two terms are generally regarded as synonymous.

A hypothesis is a belief that a particular statement is true, eg. that the mean length of steel rods is 10 cm and the 'hypothesis test' is then a procedure for deciding whether to accept the truth of this hypothesis or to accept an alternative which in the case cited would state that the mean has some other value. The procedure for deciding which hypothesis to accept is based on the computation of a 'test-statistic' (in the above example the sample mean) which has a known expected value under the original ('null') hypothesis. If the actual (observed) value of the test statistic differs from the expected value by more than could be accounted for by pure chance, then the original hypothesis is rejected in favour of the alternative.

A 'test of significance' follows the same basic procedure, but one could possibly differentiate between the two by a consideration of the way in which the final conclusion is made. In a test of hypothesis we compute the probability associated with the observed value of the test statistic and make the appropriate conclusion. Thus if the probability is below 1% there is 'strong evidence for rejecting the null hypothesis'; the conclusion therefore is expressed in terms of the degree of evidence against the null hypothesis. In a test of significance we fix a probability ('significance level') in advance and if the calculated probability is less than this we reject the null hypothesis and if it is more we accept it.

It should again be emphasised however that there is in effect little difference between these two approaches.

8.4 **Quattro plc**

(a) We will carry out χ^2 goodness of fit test.

Null hypothesis – There is no difference between the level of efficiency in the four divisions.

Alternative hypothesis – There is a significant difference between the level of efficiency in the four divisions.

	A		B		C		D		Total
	O	E	O	E	O	E	O	E	
Faulty	25	26.6	29	33.2	29	29.9	40	33.2	123
Non-faulty	375	373.4	471	466.8	421	420.1	460	466.8	1,727
Total	400		500		450		500		1,850

Tutorial note: The expected values in the contingency table above are calculated under the null hypothesis that the 123 faults should be spread evenly amongst the four divisions, in proportion to the number of items in the sample for each division.

For example, Division A expected $= \dfrac{123}{1,850} \times 400 = 26.6$

O	E	$\dfrac{(O-E)^2}{E}$
25	26.6	0.096
29	33.2	0.531
29	29.9	0.027
40	33.2	1.393
375	373.4	0.007
471	466.8	0.038
421	420.1	0.002
460	466.8	0.099
		2.193

Our observed X^2 statistic is $\sum \dfrac{(O-E)^2}{E} = 2.193$

There are $(m-1)(n-1) = (2-1)(4-1) = 3$ degrees of freedom. At the 95% confidence level, tables show a critical χ^2-statistic of 7.81. Our observed χ^2 is less than this, so we cannot reject the null hypothesis.

Our test has not provided evidence that there is a significant difference between the level of efficiency in the four divisions.

(b)   The χ^2 test in part (a) is based on the following assumptions.

(i)   That faults occur according to a normal distribution. This assumption that the population of faults complies with a normal distribution means that the χ^2 test is an example of a parametric test.

(ii)   That the observed data is not biased, so that each sample is a genuinely random sample drawn from that division.

(iii)   That efficiency level can properly be measured by the number of faulty items manufactured in each division. If one division had suffered a one-off breakdown during the period, or if another division carried on completely different operations from the other three, then such an assumpt... be valid.

(iv) That a 95% confidence level is appropriate for the test. If very in... decisions would be taken on the basis of the conclusion of the test, perhaps ... 99% level would be more appropriate.

9 QUEUING THEORY

9.1 Heath Robinson Engineering

(a) A simple queuing system comprises:

(i) a single service channel
(ii) a single waiting line
(iii) FIFO queue discipline
(iv) variable arrivals and service times following a Poisson distribution
(v) an infinite population of potential customers
(vi) no simultaneous arrivals
(vii) no bulk servicing

(b) Traffic intensity ρ = $\dfrac{\text{average service time}}{\text{average inter-arrival time}}$ = $2/3$

Average number in system = $\rho/(1-\rho) = \dfrac{2}{3} \div \dfrac{1}{3}$ = 2

(c) Average time spent in queue = $\dfrac{\rho^2}{(1-\rho)} \times \dfrac{1}{\lambda} = \dfrac{(2/3)^2}{1/3} \times \dfrac{1}{2}$ = $2/3$ hour

(d) Labour cost = $8 \times £1.50$ = £12

Average number of machinists away from work = 2

Cost of lost time = $2 \times £4 \times 8$ = £64

Total cost = £12 + £64 = £76

(e) $\rho = 1/2$

Average number in system = $\rho/(1-\rho) = 1$

Labour cost = $2 \times 8 \times £1.50$ = £24

Cost of lost time = $1 \times £4 \times 8$ = £32

Total cost = £24 + £32 = £56

Note: Since the question gave that the two attendants would be working as a team, the system in part (e) was treated as a simple queuing system with a service rate of 4 per hour.

9.2   Homebase

(a) (i) One server

$$p = \frac{\lambda}{\mu} \quad \frac{38}{40} = 0.95$$

(ii) Two server $p = \frac{\lambda}{c\mu}$

Number in queue

$$\frac{p\lambda}{\mu - \lambda} \equiv \frac{0.95 \times 38}{40 - 38} = 18.05 \text{ say } 18$$

Time in queue

$$\frac{\lambda}{\mu(\mu - \lambda)} \equiv \frac{38}{40(40 - 38)} = 28.5 \text{ min}$$

(b) Two servers $D = \dfrac{g}{Cm} \quad \dfrac{38 \times 1.1}{2 \times 40} = 0.5225$

Number in queue

$$\frac{p(pC)^c P_0}{C!(1-p)^2} \quad P_0 = \frac{0.5225(0.5225 \times 2)^2 \times 0.319}{2(1 - 0.5225)^2} = 0.4$$

Time in queue

$$\frac{(pC)^c P_0}{C!(1-p)^2 C} \quad P_0 = \frac{(0.5225 \times 2)^2 \times 0.319}{2(1 - 0.5225)^2 \times 2 \times 40} = 0.573 \text{ min}$$

in effect virtually no queue or waiting time.

(c) **Estimated benefit from second employee**

Benefit 10% additional transactions, ie.

$456 \times 10\% = 45.6$
× £25 average value sales   £1,140
× 15% margin contribution   171
Costs 12 × 2.50   (30)

Weekly gain   £141

This weekly gain will ease the initial installation cost of £100.

Other factors which may be considered (only two required):

(i)   goodwill of customers;
(ii)   availability of additional staff;
(iii) seasonality of business;
(iv)   additional sales revenue from customers with no time to shop.

(d) The major assumptions upon which queuing theory is based are:

(i)   arrivals follow the poisson distribution;
(ii)   the service rate follows a negative exponential distribution;
(iii) there is queue discipline and service discipline;
(iv)   no balking or reneging,
(v)   the rate of service at each point is identical, and
(vi)   there is time for the system to settle down to stability.

These assumptions are rigid and unlikely to be met in practice.

10 CAPITAL INVESTMENT APPRAISAL

10.1 Alphabet Group plc

(a)

	X £'000	X %	Y £'000	Y %
Sales	600	100	370	100
Less: Variable costs	229	38	208	56
Contribution	371	62	162	44
Less: Controllable fixed overheads	65	11	28	8
Controllable profit	306	51	134	36
Less: Apportioned group costs	226	38	119	32
Net profit	80	13	15	4

(1) X has a higher c/s ratio with 62%, compared with 44% for Y.

(2) X has a higher controllable profit percentage of 51%, compared with 36% for Y. However, Y's controllable fixed costs are only 8% of sales, compared with 11% for X.

(3) The apportioned group costs and the resulting net profit are not very helpful in judging the relative performance of the two companies.

(4) ROCE can be calculated on an *annual* basis, by adjusting the monthly profit figures to annual figures.

For company X £80 × 12 = £960.
For company Y £15 × 12 = £180.

The ROCE can be verified as:

$$\text{X} \qquad \frac{£960}{£6,400} \times 100 = 15\% \qquad\qquad \text{Y} \qquad \frac{£180}{£900} \times 100 = 20\%$$

On a ROCE basis, the performance of Y seems to be better, at 20%, than that of X.

(5) Both companies are earning more than the target ROCE of 12%.

(6) It is possible that the investment in X is more recent, more modern, at higher prices and with higher depreciation than Y.

(7) Sales to capital employed.

	X	Y
Sales (annual basis) / Capital employed	$\dfrac{£7,200}{£6,400} \times 100$	$\dfrac{£4,400}{£900} \times 100$
	= 112.5%	= 493.3%

Y has an extremely high level of sales compared with the capital employed, but those sales generate a relatively poor profit.

(b) The two major methods of performance evaluation are:

(i) based on absolute values (eg. ROCE);
(ii) based on relative values (eg. residual profit).

Operating statements – based on residual profit

	X £'000	Y £'000
Sales	600	370
Less: Variable costs	229	208
Contribution	371	162
Less: Controllable fixed overheads	65	28
Controllable profit	306	134
Less: Imputed interest (see note)	64	9
Controllable residual profit	242	125
Less: Apportioned group costs	226	119
Net residual profit	16	6

Note

The imputed interest is calculated as:

$$X - 12\% \times £6.4m \div 12 = £64,000 \text{ per month}$$
$$Y - 12\% \times £0.9m \div 12 = £9,000 \text{ per month}$$

With a background of rising interest rates, the imputed interest charge is likely to increase. This will affect X proportionately more than Y, as X has a much larger amount of capital employed, as measured by book values, on which the interest charge is based. If the assets were revalued to current cost, a more meaningful comparison would be possible.

(c) Essentially, ROCE uses absolute values, whereas residual profit uses relative values.

ROCE may not encourage managers to make investments which could be beneficial to the group as a whole. A high existing ROCE would make it difficult for managers to find suitable investments which at least match their current ROCE. This would not be in the group's interest if there were investments yielding more than the target rate of return. However, the residual profit method overcomes this problem, by clearly showing the minimum required rate of return.

Although the use of residual profit may lead to better investment decisions by managers, ROCE is much more widely used in practice.

10.2 Exewye

(a)

Exe: 12-year life

	Year	Cost	Discount factor	Discounted cost
		£		£
Purchases	0	19,000	1	19,000
Overhaul	8	4,000	0.47	1,880
Trade in	12	(3,000)	0.32	(960)
Annual repair	1–12	2,000	6.81	13,620
				33,540

Equivalent annual cost = £33,540 ÷ 6.81 = £4,925

Wye: Six-year life

	Year	Cost	Discount factor	Discounted cost
		£		£
Purchases	0	13,000	1	13,000
Overhaul	4	2,000	0.68	1,360
Trade in	6	3,000	0.56	(1,680)
Annual repair	1–6	2,600	4.36	11,336
				24,016

Equivalent annual cost = £24,016 ÷ 4.36 = £5,508

Recommendation: Purchase Exe

Assumptions

- Same performance, capacity, reliability and speed for each model.
- No inflation.
- 12-year estimates are as accurate as six-year estimates.
- Cashflows arise at year-ends.

(b)   Proposals with unequal lines can be compared using the concept of equivalent annual cost (EAC). This converts a net present value of cashflows for a period of several years into an annual cost to which it is equivalent. In this way sets of cashflows relating to varying periods are all expressed in common terms (ie. an annual amount).

(c) Life cycle costing is defined as 'a combination of management, financial, engineering and other practices, applied to physical assets in pursuit of economic life cycle costs (ie. its aim is to obtain the best use of physical assets at the lowest total cost to the entity)'.

These costs will include the capital cost and eventual residual value and increasing maintenance and running costs.

Examples of life cycle costing in practice would include

(i)   the operation of a fleet of cars;
(ii)   a switch to leasing from outright purchase of fixed assets;
(iii) expenditure on insulation and the reduction in heating bills in subsequent years.

10.3 RS plc

(a) To calculate the NPV of the proposed contract, we must discount the cashflows arising to the present time.

	Year 1 £	Year 2 £	Year 3 £
Cash receipts			
From sales (W1)	210,000	355,278	443,562
Cash payments			
Overhead	25,000	25,000	25,000
Materials (5,000 × £30, etc.)	150,000	253,770	316,830
Labour (3,884 × £6 each year)	23,304	23,304	23,304
	198,304	302,074	365,134
Net cashflow	11,696	53,204	78,428

The table of cash profiles can be drawn up as follows.

Time	Flow £	Discount factor at 15%	Present value £
0	(50,000)	1	(50,000)
1	11,696	0.87	10,176
2	53,204	0.76	40,435
3	78,428	0.66	51,762
			52,373

The NPV of the proposed contract is £52,373. Since the contract has a positive NPV, *prima facie*, it should be accepted.

Working

(1)   We are told that year 1 sales are 5,000 mixers. More units will be produced in the second and third years as the learning effect is experienced.

$$y = ax^{-0.3}$$

where y   =   average labour hours per unit
        a   =   labour hours for first unit
        x   =   cumulative production

In year 1,   y   = $10 \times 5,000^{-0.3}$
                   = 10×0.07768
                   =   0.7768 hours per unit

So the total hours used in year 1 = $5,000 \times 0.7768 = 3,884$ hours

Now let x = cumulative production after two years.

Average labour hours per unit after two years is given by:

$$y = \frac{2 \times 3,884}{x} = \frac{7,768}{x}$$

So $\dfrac{7,768}{x}$ = $10 \times {}^{-0.3}$

or $7,768$ = $10 \times {}^{0.7}$

    $x^{0.7}$ = 776.8

    x   = $^{0.7}\sqrt{776.8} = 13,459$ units after 2 years

So year 2 production = $13,459 - 5,000 = 8,459$ units

Similarly, let x = cumulative production after three years. Average labour hours per unit after three years is given by:

$$y = \frac{3 \times 3,884}{x} = \frac{11,652}{x}$$

So $\dfrac{11,652}{x}$ = $10 \times {}^{-0.3}$

or $11,652$ = $10 \times {}^{0.7}$

    $x^{0.7}$ = $1,165.2$

    x   = $^{0.7}\sqrt{1,165.2} = 24,020$ units after 3 years

So year 3 production = $24,020 - 13,459 = 10,561$ units

Sales each year are therefore:

Year 1	5,000 × £42	= £210,000
Year 2	8,459 × £42	= £355,278
Year 3	10,561 × £42	= £443,562

(b) Other factors needing to be considered before a final decision is made include the following.

(i) How accurate are the estimates given in the question likely to be?

(ii) In particular, is the learning factor likely to be constant over the three-year period? It is often experienced in practice that the learning effect plateaux off more quickly than the model forecasts.

(iii) Is it reasonable to have excluded the effects of inflation from the calculations?

(iv) Does RS plc wish to commit all its skilled labour to just one contract? Such a course of action is risky.

(v) Are there any alternative uses for the company's resources which would generate better profits?

(vi) Can additional skilled labour be bought in from outside?

10.4 AB Ltd

(a) We must calculate the net present value (NPV) of the flows arising from the proposed change in system.

The current system has sales of £250,000 in January, growing by $\frac{1}{2}$ % per month, with a cost of capital of $1\frac{1}{4}$ % per month, and January sales being collected at the end of March.

The cash receipt on 31 March	=	£250,000
The cash receipt on 30 April	=	£250,000 (1.005)
The cash receipt on 31 May	=	£250,000 $(1.005)^2$

The sum of the present values of the cash receipts as at 31 March

$$= \quad 250,000 + 250,000 \left(\frac{1.005}{1.0125}\right) + 250,000 \left(\frac{1.005}{1.0125}\right)^2 + \ldots$$

$$= \quad 250,000 \left[1 + \left(\frac{1.005}{1.0125}\right) + \left(\frac{1.005}{1.0125}\right)^2 + \ldots \right]$$

$$= \quad 250,000$$

$$= \quad 250,000 \times 135$$

$$= \quad £33.75m$$

Tutorial note: You should remember that the sum of a reducing geometric progression can be calculated using the standard formula:

$$1+\left(\frac{1+g}{1+r}\right)+\left(\frac{1+g}{1+r}\right)^2 + \ldots = \frac{1+r}{r-g}$$

The PV at 31 March is £33.75m, so we can say that the PV at time 0 (ie. at 1 January) is:

$$\frac{£33.75m}{(1.0125)^3} = £32,515,369$$

The proposed new system collects debts one month earlier, but involves a new reducing monthly cost.

$$\text{PV of revised cashflow} = \frac{£33.75m}{(1.0125)^2} = £32,921,811$$

PV of staff costs = a monthly payment of £2,000 starting at time 1, ie. at 31 January, so there is no payment at time 0.

$$\text{PV} = £2,000\left(\frac{1.0125}{0.0125+0.0025}\right) - £2,000 = £133,000$$

The NPV of the proposed new system is £32,788,811.

The net present value of the proposed system is greater than the net present value of the current system (by £32,788,811 less £32,515,369 = £273,442), so I advise that it is worthwhile to introduce the proposed in-house credit control system.

(b) (i) The bureau costs £5,000 per month.

AB Ltd's cost savings would be £4,000 per month.

So monthly outgoings would be increased by a net £1,000.

In perpetuity, this increase has a PV of $\frac{£1,000}{0.0125} = £80,000$

Maximum amount to be paid for the initial systems charge

= Net savings from new system
= PV of costs saved – PV of increased outgoings
= £133,000 (staff costs from part (a)) – £80,000
= £53,000

(ii) Other factors to be considered before a final decision is taken about the change in credit policy include the following.

Effect on customer relations – Customers may be unhappy being more rigorously chased for their debts and may seek alternative suppliers who grant longer credit periods.

Accuracy of estimates in the question – The decision may be sensitive to variations in the figures used, for example the $1^{1}/_{4}$ % per month cost of capital figure.

Possible actions by competitors – Competitors of AB Ltd may highlight the revised, less favourable, credit terms being offered and seek to undermine AB's goodwill in the market.

Back-up facilities – Offered by the bureau in case of their systems failure or seasonal peaks in sales.

Other methods of encouraging early payment – Such as offering settlement discounts if debtors pay promptly.

Period of time covered by a contract with the bureau and cancellation notice if either party wished to terminate the contract.

11 INFORMATION TECHNOLOGY AND SIMULATION

11.1 Data collection

(a) Typical problems and inadequacies encountered in data collection processes include the following.

(i) Inaccuracies in amounts measured, eg. weights, lengths, times.

(ii) Errors inherent in sampling exercises.

(iii) Human errors, for example giving lengths in inches rather than centimetres by mistake.

(iv) Delays while the data collected is being gathered together for input into a system.

(v) Lack of briefing to the employees collecting the data will mean that they have no idea of the purpose of what they are doing.

(vi) Cheating – for example, an employee may not be bothered to collect his data properly and simply invent a set of results.

(vii) Impossibility of the task – for example, deciding on the number of operational sticks of dynamite in stock. The only way to know the correct number is to destroy the entire stock held.

(b) The key objectives of effective data collection are as follows.

Quantity of information

The quantity collected should be appropriate for the planned use of the data. Too much information will overload the user and it will not be possible to identify the key matters arising. Insufficient information will mean that no proper conclusions can be drawn.

Accuracy of information

Again the required accuracy depends on the uses to which the data will be put. For example, the total figure for directors' remuneration disclosed in a set of financial accounts should be exactly correct as a matter of legal necessity. Other figures need only be given to the nearest thousand pounds, say, so that a true and fair view is given. There is no point giving spurious accuracy to a figure which will only mislead the user.

Timing of information

Generally, information will be more valuable with the least time having elapsed between the publishing of the information and the end of the period in which the data was collected. However, there may be a necessary trade-off between timeliness on the one hand, and expense and accuracy on the other.

(c)   The entire method of the data collection process should be designed to account for the decision-maker's information needs. There is no point in collecting data if no decision-maker needs to see information derived from the data. So the decision-maker's needs come first.

If the decision-maker is making short-term decisions, then time is of the essence. Where time is the critical factor, the subsidiary factors (such as quantity and accuracy of information) can only be fixed within the constraints of the critical factor.

If the decision-maker is making medium-term or longer-term decisions, a more balanced approach to setting up the data collection process may be possible, in which quantity, accuracy and timing of information can all be concentrated upon.

Modern developments in information technology, such as computer networks and database management systems, mean that the time spent processing data into information can be substantially reduced, with no loss of accuracy. However, there are costs associated with such technological tools and crucially it is still up to management, with the assistance of management accountants, to carry out a full interpretation of the information produced.

11.2   Simulation

(a)   Weekly demand requires simulation for input into the model and may be generated using random numbers ascribed to demand as follows.

Weekly demand	Frequency	Probability	Cumulative probability	Random number
500	10	3	3	00 – 02
525	15	5	8	03 – 07
550	30	10	18	08 – 17
575	50	17	35	18 – 34
600	55	19	54	35 – 53
625	60	20	74	54 – 73
650	40	14	88	74 – 87
675	20	7	95	88 – 94
700	10	3	98	95 – 97
725	5	2	100	98 – 99

A random number generator will then be used to determine which level of demand to input to the model.

Flowchart describing the model would be as follows.

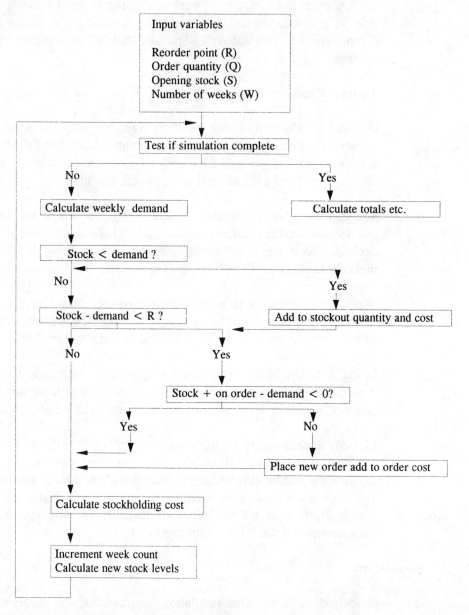

(b)   The summary shows that stockout costs far exceed stockholding costs. This indicates that the reorder level should be increased significantly having the effect of raising the average level of stock held, so reducing stockouts but increasing the carrying cost. Thought should also be given to increasing the order quantity of 2,000 units since average demand in lead time is given as 2,424 units (606 × 4).

A more realistic simulation could be achieved by inputting variable lead time.

11.3   DB plc

(a)   Buffer stock level = Reorder level – Expected demand in lead time

Reorder level = 150,000 units

Expected demand in lead time = 123,000 units (W)

∴ Implicit buffer stock level = 150,000 − 123,000 = 27,000 units

Working

Demand (units)	Lead time (days)	Demand in lead time (units)	Joint probability		Expected value
5,000	15	75,000	0.5 × 0.2 =	0.1	7,500
5,000	20	100,000	0.5 × 0.5 =	0.25	25,000
5,000	25	125,000	0.5 × 0.3 =	0.15	18,750
7,000	15	105,000	0.5 × 0.2 =	0.1	10,500
7,000	20	140,000	0.5 × 0.5 =	0.25	35,000
7,000	25	175,000	0.5 × 0.3 =	0.15	26,250
				1.00	123,000

(b) A stock-out occurs when demand in the lead time exceeds the 150,000 units in each order. The working in part (a) shows that this only happens when demand in the lead time is 175,000 units, a situation with a probability of 0.15.

(c) The company operates an EOQ system.

$$EOQ = \frac{2 \times 1,000 \times (6,000 \times 240)}{0.15}$$

$$= \frac{2,88 \times 10^9}{0.15}$$

$$= 1.92 \times 10^{10} = 138,564 \text{ units}$$

The number of replenishments per year is therefore:

$$\frac{6,000 \times 240}{138,564} = 10.39 \text{ times}$$

The annual stock-outs occur on the occasions that 175,000 units are demanded in the lead time. The expected stock-outs in one year are therefore:

$$0.15 \times 10.39 \times (175,000 - 150,000)$$

$$= 38,963 \text{ units}$$

(d) At a reorder level of 150,000 units, we expect to have stock-outs of 38,963 units pa. At a re-order level of 175,000 units, we expect to have nil stock-outs (since demand cannot exceed 175,000 units in a lead time).

The incremental cost of moving from 150,000 units to 175,000 can be estimated as 25,000 units × 15p/unit = £3,750.

The stock-out cost per unit at which it would be worthwhile raising the reorder level to 175,000 units is therefore:

$$\frac{£3,750}{38,963} = 9.6\text{p per unit}$$

(e)   Possible alternatives to an EOQ fixed reorder level system are:

(i)   periodic review system;
(ii)   just-in-time (JIT) system.

In a periodic review system, purchase orders are placed at fixed regular intervals of time (say monthly), and the quantity to be ordered on any occasion will be decided by reviewing the trend of demand for or usage of the item concerned. Variable reorder quantities are therefore ordered at fixed time intervals. The main problem arises when an unexpected increase in demand arises, in which case the stock of an item may be exhausted before the next regular ordering date.

In a just-in-time system, orders are placed with suppliers so that delivery occurs just as the stock is about to run out. Clearly such a system depends enormously on the speed and reliability of the delivery service from suppliers. The advantage is that unnecessary stocks are eliminated completely, so that stock holding costs are low, but the dependence on receiving good quality goods exactly when expected from suppliers can cause problems.

Mock examination

Time allowed: Three hours

Attempt *five* questions only:
the *three* questions in Section A and *two* from Section B

Answer the questions using:

- effective arrangement and presentation

- clarity of explanation

- logical argument

- clear and concise English

Questions

1   **Washbrook Ltd**

The operational research manager of Washbrook Ltd has recently formulated a linear programme, which covers the company's activities for the next three years. During that time it is expected that supplies of capital, storage space and raw material type MCC will be limited. The objective function of the linear programme involves maximisation of the discounted present value of ordinary dividends, subject to the following constraints:

(1)   that cash payments each year must not exceed cash receipts;

(2)   that storage space and raw material type MCC required each year must not exceed the quantities available for that year;

(3)   that no project may be undertaken more than once, although fractions of projects may be accepted;

(4)   that negative quantities of projects may not be undertaken nor may negative dividends be paid.

The solution to the linear programme produces the following dual prices:

Year	Cash per £ £	Storage space per ft^2 per annum £	Raw material MCC per unit £
1	3.20	22.15	15.05
2	2.40	0.00	12.60
3	1.85	10.70	10.40

Since the linear programme was formulated, the directors of Washbrook Ltd have learnt of the opportunity to undertake manufacture of a new product. If manufactured, the new product will have a commercial life of three years. It will require the use of existing machinery and storage space. The company will recruit the additional labour that will be required on three year contracts. The product will require 5,000 units of raw material type MCC in each of years 1 and 2, and 4,500 units in year 3. The market price of this raw material is expected to be £14.00 per unit during year 1, £15.40 per unit during year 2 and £16.95 per unit during year 3. The new product will utilise 3,000 ft^2 of storage space during each of years 1, 2 and 3.

The costing department of Washbrook Ltd has prepared the following profitability statement concerning the new product.

	Year 1 £	Year 2 £	Year 3 £
Variable costs (labour, materials, etc.)	200,000	225,000	205,000
Fixed costs (depreciation, rent, etc. allotted on the basis of labour hours)	20,000	21,700	18,600
Total costs	220,000	246,700	223,600
Total revenues	240,000	260,000	225,000
Net profit	20,000	13,300	1,400

All revenues and costs associated with the product will be received or paid during the year in which they arise. The present total market value of the ordinary shares of Washbrook Ltd is £55 million. The directors estimate that the minimum return required by ordinary shareholders from their investment in the company is 15% per annum.

Required

(a) Write brief notes criticising the profitability statement prepared by the costing department as a basis for assessing the desirability of the new product.　　(4 marks)

(b) Prepare calculations, with supporting explanations, showing whether manufacture of the new product is worthwhile.　　(9 marks)

(c) Explain the meaning of the dual prices calculated by the operational research manager, and comment on their usefulness and limitations.　　(9 marks)

Ignore taxation.　　**(Total 22 marks)**

2　Haydn Ltd

The management of Haydn Ltd is planning the launch of a new microcomputer, the SQ. The market for microcomputers is very competitive and the anticipated product life of the SQ is only three years. The marketing director of Haydn Ltd has produced the following table showing three different estimates of likely demand for the SQ during each year of its life.

Demand predictions	Probability	Year 1 Units	Year 2 Units	Year 3 Units
Most optimistic	0.2	32,000	16,000	12,000
Best guess	0.5	16,000	8,000	6,000
Most pessimistic	0.3	4,000	2,000	1,500

The above estimates assume a constant selling price of £500 over the three years. The variable production cost per unit of an SQ is £400.

The production director has indicated that the factory is in a position to produce 32,000, 16,000 or 4,000 units per annum, but, once decided, the chosen production level could not be increased until the start of the following year. The total cost of setting up the production line would consist of fixed costs of £1 million, and variable costs of £50 for each unit of production capacity. These costs would be paid at the start of the year's production.

A market research firm has offered, for a fee of £300,000, to carry out a detailed survey which would determine precisely the level of demand for the SQ. The management of Haydn Ltd wishes to know whether the market survey is likely to be worthwhile.

In order to assess whether the survey is worth undertaking, the directors of Haydn Ltd have asked that the following simplifying assumptions be made:

(1)   cashflows relating both to sales and variable production costs are to be deemed to arise at the end of the year in which they are incurred;

(2)   demand can be represented by only one of the three sets of possibilities envisaged by the marketing director;

(3)   the level of demand in the first year will determine the levels demanded in the second and third years;

(4)   the appropriate discount rate for the venture is 10% per annum; and

(5)   stock levels will remain unchanged.

Required

(a)   Determine the initial production capacity that Haydn Ltd should choose, and compute the resulting expected net present value of producing and selling at that level.

(12 marks)

(b)   Calculate whether the market survey should be commissioned, and comment on any reservations you might have relating to the use of expected values as an aid in decision-making.

(6 marks)

(c)   Discuss the advantages to the company of conducting a market survey of this kind.

(4 marks)

(Total 22 marks)

3   **A Project (M87)**

The managers of a company have analysed a project, and the coded activities have been listed below along with their durations and immediate predecessors.

Activity code	Immediate predecessor	Duration (days)
A	–	13
B	A	2
C	A	6
D	B	20
E	B	5
F	C	2
G	E, F	4
H	F	3
I	D	5
J	D	10
K	C	5
L	G, I	2
M	G, I, J	3
N	G, I, J, H, K	15
O	L, M, N	2

Required

(a)   Draw up and analyse the project planning diagram to show the duration of the project and the critical path.   (8 marks)

(b)   Present the results you have obtained in (a) above in the form of a bar chart or Gantt chart based on earliest start dates.   (8 marks)

(c)   Calculate when the project should begin and when it will finish, assuming the estimated hours are adhered to and using the calendar printed below. Note that the company operates on a five-day week basis and that G, H, I, J and K must be completed by Friday 26 June.   (4 marks)
(Total 20 marks)

Calendar

	April		*May*				*June*					*July*				
Monday	20 27		4	11	18	25	1	8	15	22	29	6	13	20	27	
Tuesday	21 28		5	12	19	26	2	9	16	23	30	7	14	21	28	
Wednesday	22 29		6	13	20	27	3	10	17	24		1	8	15	22	29
Thursday	23 30		7	14	21	28	4	11	18	25		2	9	16	23	30
Friday	24	1	8	15	22	29	5	12	19	26		3	10	17	24	31

Section B
Answer two questions – 17 marks each

4   **Budgetary control system (N89)**

The typical budgetary control system in practice does not encourage **goal congruence**, contains **budgetary slack**, ignores the **aspiration levels** of participants and attempts to control operations by **feedback**, when **feedforward** is likely to be more effective; in summary the typical budgetary control system is likely to have **dysfunctional effects**.

Required

(a)   Explain briefly each of the **six** terms in **bold**.   (6 marks)

(b)   Describe how the major dysfunctional effects of budgeting could be avoided.
(11 marks)
(Total 17 marks)

5 Company X (M90)

(a) The following budget was prepared for the overhead of Department X:

Budget for period

Fixed overhead	£5,600
Variable overhead	£10,400
Machine hours	1,600
Standard hours of production	1,600

After the period the *actual results* were:

Total overhead	£17,400
Machine hours	1,630
Standard hours produced	1,590

Required

Calculate the overhead variances for the period. (7 marks)

(b) The company is introducing a comprehensive computer system which will deal with all aspects of management accounting, including the calculation and display of variances. The systems analysts are quite familiar with the method of calculating the variances but are less sure how the budget and actual figures and the calculated variances could be shown graphically. This is intended to be a feature of the computer system and you have been requested to provide technical accounting assistance.

Required

Draw a graph showing the standard overhead recovery line, plotting hours against cost. Superimpose on this graph a sectionalised bar chart showing all variances.
(10 marks)
(Total 17 marks)

6 Efficiency and profitability (M91)

The efficiency and profitability of products and departments are frequently appraised using such factors as return on capital employed, profit and historical costs, yet these factors are not generally considered relevant to decision-making.

Required

(a) Reconcile the apparent contradiction in the above statement. (10 marks)
(b) Describe the characteristics of factors which are relevant to decision-making.
(7 marks)
(Total 17 marks)

Answers to mock examination

1   Washbrook Ltd

(a)   The following points should be made:

(i)   Fixed costs should be omitted from the statement as they are unaltered by acceptance of the project.

(ii)   The statement does not take into account the effect of accepting the project upon other activities of the company.

(iii)   As the labour is employed on a three year contract, its cost should be treated as as additional fixed cost (unless the labour could be utilized elsewhere when not working on this product).

(iv)   The statement should show the effect of changes in the level of demand for the new product.

(b)

	Year 1 £	Year 2 £	Year 3 £
Profit	20,000	13,300	1,400
Fixed costs	20,000	21,700	18,600
Cash inflow	40,000	35,000	20,000
Storage space required	3,000 ft²	3,000 ft²	3,000 ft²
Raw material MCC required	5,000 units	5,000 units	4,500 units

Increase in present value of future dividend stream

Year 1 $(40,000 \times 3.20) - (3,000 \times 22.15) - (5,000 \times 15.05)$ $=$ $-£13,700$

Year 2 $(35,000 \times 2.40) - (5,000 \times 12.60)$ $=$ $£21,000$

Year 3 $(20,000 \times 1.85) - (3,000 \times 10.70) - (4,500 \times 10.40)$ $=$ $-£41,900$

Gain $= -13,700 + 21,000 - 41,900 = -£34,600$

Present value of the additional cash generated.

$$= \frac{40,000}{1.15} + \frac{35,000}{1.15^2} + \frac{20,000}{1.15^3} = £74,398$$

Net gain $= 74,398 - 34,600 = +£39,798$

∴ Manufacture of the new product is not worthwhile.

(c)   The following points should be made:

(i)   In general the dual price of a scarce resource is the amount by which the value of the objective function changes if the constraint relating to the resource is increased or decreased by one unit.

(ii)   *Usefulness of dual prices*

1   Dual prices give the opportunity cost of scarce resources and thus indicate how much it is worth paying to obtain a marginal extra amount of a particular resource.

2   Calculation of dual prices highlights the critical resources, (ie. those which are totally used up in the optimal solution.)

3   If any resource has an extremely high dual price in a maximisation problem, it indicates that the firm should direct its efforts towards increasing the supply of that resource.

4   Dual prices help in sensitivity analysis where small changes in availability of resources are investigated. This is particularly useful where figures are only estimated and therefore subject to uncertainty.

5   The example given in part (b) of this question shows how dual prices can be useful in evaluating the effect of additional projects which affect the availability of the original resources.

(iii) *Limitations*

1   Although a dual price can indicate whether it is worthwhile changing the availability of a resource, it in no way helps in determining how to effect this change.

2   The dual price is only valid for marginal increases in scarce resources. Further analysis must be carried out to establish by how much a constraint may be relaxed before it ceases to be critical and hence has a dual price of zero.

3   The dual price is not a helpful measure if extra units of a scarce resource are unobtainable.

2   Haydn Ltd

Assumptions

(i)   In any year production can be matched to demand up to capacity limitation.

(ii)   The variable capacity cost is paid at time of installation or increase of capacity; capacity cannot be reduced (there would be no point in doing so since no cost would be saved).

(iii) Line 2 of paragraph 2 of the question means chosen *capacity* level could not be increased.

(iv)   The fixed installation costs of £1 million are only incurred at the initial set-up.

(a) **Decision tree**

Let A and B be decisions at time 0

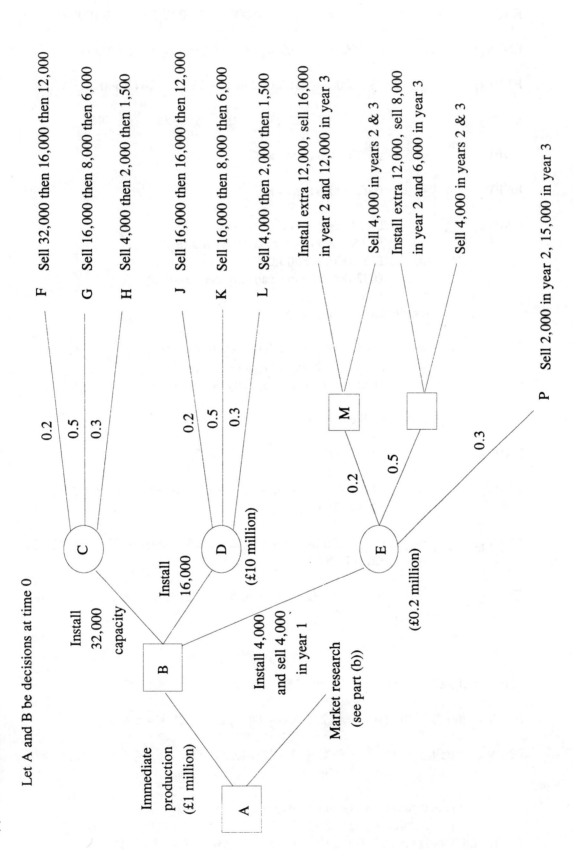

We can determine the decision at B by 'roll back' through the tree (see workings for PV calculations).

$ENPV_G$	=	Expected net present value at point G, etc.
$ENPV_F$	=	£2,912,000 + £1,328,000 + £900,000 = £5,140,000
$ENPV_G$	=	£1,456,000 + £664,000 + £450,000 = £2,570,000
$ENPV_H$	=	£364,000 + £166,000 + £112,500 = £642,500
$ENPV_J$	=	£1,456,000 + £1,328,000 + £900,000 = £3,684,000
$ENPV_K$	=	£2,570,000 (same as G)
$ENPV_L$	=	£642,500 (save as H)

$ENPV_M$	=	£1,328,000 + £900,000 – £546,000
	=	£1,682,000 (if extra capacity installed)
	or	£332,000 + £300,000
	=	£632,000 (if extra capacity not installed)

Install extra capacity at M

$ENPV_N$	=	£664,000 + £450,000 – £546,000
	=	£568,000 (if extra capacity installed)
	or	£632,000 (if extra capacity not installed)

Don't install capacity at N

$ENPV_P$	=	£166,000 + £112,500 – £278,500
$ENPV_C$	=	(0.2 × £5,140,000) + (0.5 × £2,570,000) + (0.3 × £642,500
	=	£2,505,750
$ENPV_D$	=	(0.2 × £3,684,000) + (0.5 × £2,570,000) + (0.3 × £642,500)
	=	£2,214,550
$ENPV_E$	=	(0.2 × £1,682,000) + (0.5 × £632,000) + (0.3 × £278,500)
	=	£735,950

So, at B:

ENPV of install 32,000 = £2,505,750 – £1,600,000 = £905,750

ENPV of install 16,000 = £2,214,550 – £800,000 = £1,414,550

ENPV of install 4,000 = £735,950 + £364,000 (year 1 sales) – £200,000
= £899,950

Thus initial production capacity should be set at 16,000 units.

The resulting net present value is £1,414,550 – £1,000,000 = £414,550

(b) The market research gives us an alternative decision at point A, as follows:

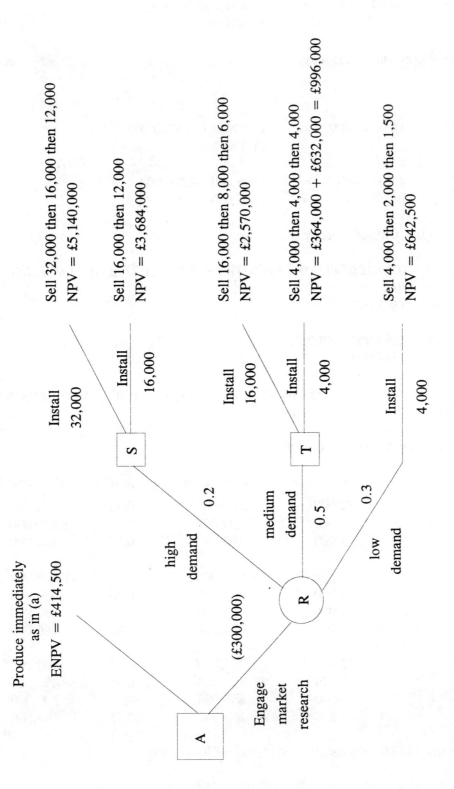

Produce immediately
as in (a)
ENPV = £414,500

Install 32,000 — Sell 32,000 then 16,000 then 12,000
NPV = £5,140,000

S — Install 16,000 — Sell 16,000 then 12,000
NPV = £3,684,000

high demand 0.2

(£300,000)

Engage market research

R

medium demand 0.5

Install 16,000 — Sell 16,000 then 8,000 then 6,000
NPV = £2,570,000

T — Install 4,000 — Sell 4,000 then 4,000 then 4,000
NPV = £364,000 + £632,000 = £996,000

low demand 0.3

Install 4,000 — Sell 4,000 then 2,000 then 1,500
NPV = £642,500

A

Pay £1 million
if ENPV$_R$ > £1 million

Note: As low demand branch offers expected future cashflows of less than £1,000,000 no capacity will be installed.

At S:

If install   32,000, NPV   =   £5,140,000 − £1,600,000
                                           =   £3,540,000

If install   16,000, NPV   =   £3,684,000 − £800,000
                                           =   £2,884,000

∴ Install 32,000 units of capacity.

At T:

If install   16,000, NPV   =   £2,570,000 − £800,000
                                           =   £1,770,000

If install   4,000, NPV   =   £996,000 − £200,000
                                           =   £796,000

∴ Install 16,000 units of capacity.

$$\text{ENPV}_R = 0.2 \times (£3,540,000 - 1,000,000) + 0.5 \times (£1,770,000 - 1,000,000) + (0.3 \times 0)$$
$$= £893,000$$

$$\text{ENPV}_A = £893,000 - £300,000$$
$$= £593,000$$

This exceeds the £494,550 from part (a) so we can say that, on the basis of expected NPVs, the market survey should be commissioned.

Workings: Present values of contributions

	Number sold	Contribution	PV @ 10%	PV of contribution
Year 1	32,000	3,200,000	0.91	2,912,000
	16,000	1,600,000	0.91	1,456,000
	4,000	400,000	0.91	364,000
Year 2	16,000	1,600,000	0.83	1,328,000
	8,000	800,000	0.83	664,000
	4,000	400,000	0.83	332,000
	2,000	200,000	0.83	166,000
Year 3	12,000	1,200,000	0.75	900,000
	6,000	600,000	0.75	450,000
	4,000	400,000	0.75	300,000
	1,500	150,000	0.75	112,500

Cost of extra 12,000 units capacity = 12,000 × £50 = £600,000

If installed at time 1, PV = £600,000 × 0.91 = £546,000

Limitations on the calculations of net present values

The use of probability forecasts of the outcome of a project enable the 'expected' net present value to be calculated. The word 'expected' is, however, something of a misnomer. The calculated figure is in fact an average of the possible outcomes weighted by their relative probabilities. As such, it is an essentially hypothetical figure – in fact one or other of the outcomes must occur, not some average.

This does not invalidate the concept of expected value. It does, however, give them an air of unreality which discourages their use.

There are other problems associated with expected values. One important factor is that they ignore the decision maker's attitude towards risks. Risk averse decision makers will often accept considerable reductions in expected value for only small decreases in risk.

Calculations of the expected net present values do not of themselves give any idea of the nature of the dispersion of possible outcomes around the expected value. Where uncertainty is present, the investor needs to know more than just what the expected return would be from the investment. The expected net present value does not tell us what the maximum possible loss which could be incurred is, or how rapidly the proceeds would fall with a decrease in business activity. Furthermore, it may be necessary to consider the relationship between the return on the current investment and the return on other investment already made – eg. would something happening to cause a low return from the other investments also cause a low return on the investment under consideration?

Finally, consider the validity of the probability distributions themselves. If an organisation has been through many similar situations in the past, it can tabulate the results of each previous similar situation to obtain an objective measure of the probability of each range of possible outcomes. If, however, the situation were changing – eg. the operation were becoming more efficient with each recurrence, then earlier outcomes would be of little use in predicting the likely output in other conditions. In practice, business decisions are very unlikely to be made in anything other than a changing environment and hence the strict definition of probability as estimated from a long run of similar activities is rarely, if ever, applicable. The use of expected net present values as a basis for investment decisions is almost certain to rest on the use of 'subjective' probabilities, as opposed to 'objective' probabilities derived from empirical research. This of itself is a major limitation of the technique.

(c)   In this situation, the advantages largely depend on the quality of the market research undertaken. No survey can ever precisely determine the level of demand for a product but any result that reduces uncertainty can be useful. The major advantages may be summarised as follows:

(i)   The reduction in uncertainty will ease the company's planning problems. Cash budgets, production schedules, manpower plans and capital requirements may all be projected with more accuracy and hence the firm can operate more efficiently.

(ii)   Although the risk reduction effect may not be of great consequence to shareholders in the context of a well-diversified portfolio, they can be of particular value to other interested parties. Management, employees, suppliers and customers would all welcome a reduction in the total risk of the firm assuming the costs of the research were not too high.

(iii)   A well researched proposal can often make it easier for the firm to raise new finance. Banks and other suppliers of finance are likely to be more impressed with a well thought out plan backed by an independent research company rather than simply relying on the firm's own estimates. This is particularly true in a highly competitive market such as microcomputers.

(iv) It is likely that any reputable market research survey will yield more information than just the size of the market. Information on why the market is of a certain size is also likely to result. This could allow Haydn Ltd to adjust its pricing, quality, promotion and distribution policies to increase the profitability of the project.

3 A Project

(a) The network (project planning diagram) is shown on the separate sheet.

Note that dummy activities are represented by dotted lines, and the critical path by the double line. In order to ensure the logical 'flow' of the diagram, all arrows should be drawn from left to right.

The critical path is ABDJNO and the duration of the project is therefore
$13 + 2 + 20 + 10 + 15 + 2 = 62$ days.

(b) The chart requested in the question is slightly unusual in that it asks for the activities to be shown at their earliest start dates, when in practice only activities on the critical path *have* to start at these dates; all other activities can be delayed by up to the difference between their earliest start dates and latest start dates without increasing the duration of the project, and a more useful chart would show this.

The earliest start dates are:

A	= 0	G	= 21	M	= 45
B	= 13	H	= 21	N	= 45
C	= 13	I	= 35	O	= 60
D	= 15	J	= 35		
E	= 15	K	= 19		
F	= 19	L	= 40		

The chart is shown on the separate sheet. The critical activities, ABDJNO are shown at the foot of the chart. The other activities are then shown alphabetically from bottom to top, although the order does not really matter as the question requests earliest start times.

(c) G, H, I, J, K must be completed by 26 June. All these activities have a latest finish time of 45, as can be seen from the network; since J is on the critical path, then day 45 must be 26 June; working back from this gives a project start time of 26 June less 45 days, ie. Monday 27 April.

The duration of the project is 62 days, ie. 17 days after 26 June which gives a project completion date of Tuesday 21 July.

Project planning diagram

X = Earliest event time
Y = Latest event time

= Critical path
ABDJNO = 62 days

Gantt or bar chart

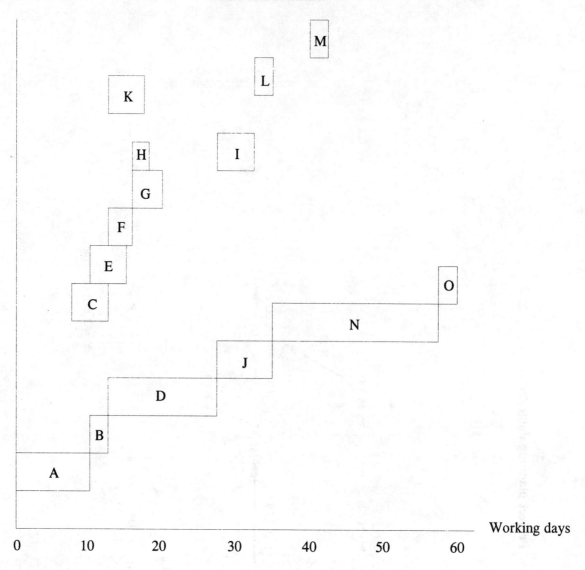

Working days

0   10   20   30   40   50   60

4   Budgetary control system

(a)   **Goal congruence** has been defined as 'the state that exists in a control system when it leads individuals and/or groups to take actions which are both in their self-interest and also in the best interest of the entity'.

Budgetary slack is introduced into a budget by a manager who is attempting to reduce the probability of adverse budget variances occurring. For example, if a manager believes that the cost of his required materials next year will actually be £100,000, he may budget for £120,000, thus introducing slack of £20,000. He then hopes that, even in the worst possible case, he will still be able to operate within budget next year.

The **aspiration level** of an employee is the level of performance that he personally hopes to attain. This is not necessarily the same as the performance level budgeted for him by his supervisors. Part of the task of management is to raise the aspiration levels of the workforce.

Feedback has been defined as 'Modification or control of a process or system by its results or effects, by measuring differences between desired and actual results.

Feedback is an element in a feedback system and forms the link between planning and control'. An example is a simple central heating system, where differences between planned and actual temperatures are used as signals to effect automatic control.

Feedforward is similar, being the modification or control of a process or system, by measuring differences between desired and forecast results. An example is the cashflow budget exercise carried out by a company, to ensure that the business can stay within the agreed overdraft limit for the period.

Dysfunctional effects arise where each sub-part of an organisation operates by seeking to achieve their own objectives, but through lack of goal congruence not all these individual objectives are consistent with the overall objectives of the organisation as a whole.

(b) The major dysfunctional effects of budgeting can be avoided if the following principles are borne in mind.

(i) **Participative budgeting**

Most organisations now recognise that effective budgeting demands participation by the people who are to be controlled, in the budget-setting process. Note however the problem identified by both Argyris and Hofstede that operations people are less well trained in the financial aspects of business than their supervisors, so they are reticent to participate fully in an area where they lack knowledge and experience. Instead of proper participation there will be 'pseudo-participation'.

(ii) **Leadership style**

A good attitude towards budgets will be fostered where there are regular departmental meetings and open access to senior management. Likert's work suggests that the best results come from a group oriented consultative style of management.

(iii) **Purpose of budgets**

Hopwood's research has highlighted the problems caused by the different and conflicting purposes of budgets. Budgets being used to motivate managers should be based on the aspirations of those managers, whereas a budget which is being used for decision making purposes should be based on more realistic, and hence lower, expectations of possible performance. In general, a 'profit conscious' style of evaluating managerial performance is most likely to involve the manager in controlling costs, a style in which each manager is evaluated on the basis of his ability to increase the general effectiveness of his unit's operations in relation to the long-term purposes of the organisation.

Summary

There is a large volume of literature written on avoiding the dysfunctional effects of budgeting. The only certain fact is that this is a most complex area. What is vital is that it is understood that no solutions will be applicable in all situations; each budget must be established in a way that is suitable and acceptable to the organisation for which it was designed.

---

5   Company X

(a)   Expenditure variance   =   Actual overhead − Budgeted overhead

$$= \; £17,400 - (£5,600 + £1,630 \times \frac{£10,400}{1,600})$$

$$= \; £17,400 - (£5,600 + £10,595)$$

$$= \; £1,205 \text{ Adverse}$$

        Volume variance   =   Budgeted overhead − Actual overhead absorbed

$$= \; (£5,600 + £10,595) - (1,630 \times \frac{£5,600 + £10,400}{1,6000})$$

$$= \; £16,195 - £16,300$$

$$= \; £105 \text{ Favourable}$$

        Efficiency variance   =   Actual overhead absorbed − Overhead for standard hours produced

$$= \; £16,300 - (1,630 \times \frac{£5,600 + £10,400}{1,6000})$$

$$= \; £16,300 - £15,900$$

$$= \; £400 \text{ Adverse}$$

(b)

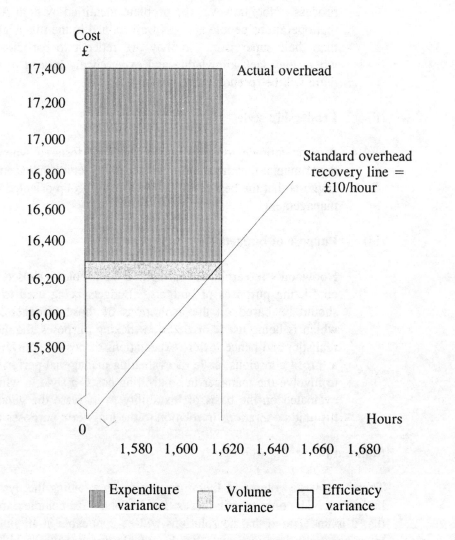

6   Efficiency and profitability

(a)   The statement is perfectly true in identifying the multiple objectives for which accounting information is prepared. Efficiency and profitability are essentially measures of *short-term* performance, for example comparing this period's return on capital employed with the comparable statistic in the previous period. Calculations are normally made directly from the published financial accounts of the enterprise which will traditionally be prepared according to the historical cost convention.

Decision-making is concerned with more *long-term* matters. Management should take decisions in the overriding objective of maximising shareholder wealth, which will normally be achieved by maximising the present values of cashflows arising from the decision. Historical costs of assets owned are sunk costs and are therefore irrelevant to a current decision to maximise shareholder value.

Efficiency and profitability measures can therefore be calculated using historical costs. Historical cost accounting is well understood by managers who will have faith in efficiency ratios say, calculated on this convention. Stocks can be valued according to SSAP 9 on a total absorption costing basis. However, decision-making will call for stocks to be valued at their opportunity costs to the business, since it is this value which is relevant to the decision as to their disposal.

We have therefore identified the root cause of the apparent contradiction in the statement in the question. In assessing efficiency and profitability, managers are interested in short-term factors which may reflect well on their competence as managers but will have little impact on the longer term. In decision-making, managers are interested in the long-term cashflows arising from their decision in an attempt to achieve the objective function of maximising shareholder wealth.

Practical ways of reconciling the apparent contradiction are as follows.

(i)   Move away from traditional historical cost accounting in the preparation of financial accounts. For years accountants have recognised the problems associated with historical cost accounts in a time of changing prices, but no consensus has emerged as an alternative. If financial accounts were routinely prepared according to the current cost convention, then the financial accounts would become more relevant for decision-making as well as stewardship reporting purposes.

(ii)   It would be still better if accounts could be reported on a cashflow basis, so that decision-making and reporting bases were in line with each other, but such an objective is impractical.

(iii)   Set longer-term performance targets. A company's management should be encouraged to set targets for profitability, etc. for several years ahead rather than treating performance measures as always a backwards looking exercise comparing current performance with prior period performance.

(b)   Factors which are relevant for decision-making should have the following characteristics.

(i)   **Cashflow** – Only items involving a flow of cash should be considered, so that non-cash items such as depreciation charges should be ignored.

(ii)   **Relevance** – Only items relevant to the decision under consideration should be considered.

(iii) **Long term** – All future cashflows arising which can be foreseen, however distantly into the future, should be taken into account.

(iv)   **Objective function** – The decision will be taken in the objective of optimising some objective function. The identity of this function must be kept in mind closely while relevant factors are identified.

(v)   **Incremental costs and revenues** – We are only interested in additional costs and revenues resulting from the decision taken.

Tutor's commentary

1   Part (a) of this question is a relatively simple decision-making exercise requiring the identification of relevant costs.

   Parts (b) and (c) provide a thorough examination of your knowledge of dual prices and how they can be used to evaluate new products. Note particularly the calculation in (b).

2   This question involves the use of traditional decision trees. The student requires a facility with numbers in order to get through the volume of calculations required. There is an element of ambiguity in respect of the second paragraph. In the exam room you should clearly state your assumptions if you consider that ambiguity exists. With regard to the written part of the answer, the well prepared student should be able to explain the drawbacks and limitations on the calculation of expected net present values including the use of subjective (as opposed to objective) probabilities.

   Part (c) requires an intelligent evaluation of the advantages of market research in a situation of this kind. A good student should be aware of the advantages of a well researched project which would be a distinct asset in any presentation to a bank or finance house.

3   Note that 80% of the marks on this question are for diagrams. Maximise those gained by making your network and Gantt chart clear, neat and properly labelled. Use a ruler! Whatever notation you use (for earliest/latest times etc) make sure you include a key.

   When drawing the chart in (b) it is useful to separate out the critical activities from the rest to emphasise the sequence of the activities that have to run immediately consecutively if the project is not to be delayed.

   Be sure to give adequate explanation for your answer to (c) to get full credit.

4   Part (a) should provide six easy marks relying on some basic Stage 2 knowledge and simple definitions. Part (b) on behavioural aspects should also be straightforward and several alternative points could have been made.

5   Overhead variances cause more problems than others but the information was presented in simple form. Note the vital step of calculating the flexed budget for comparison with actual. Part (b) is unusual and the graph needs careful thought to be meaningful.

6   Many points could be made here and planning of your answer would be important, as with any written question. Make sure that you have used short, sharp paragraphs and clear headings.

Extracts from 'Mathematical tables for students'

LOGARITHMS

	0	1	2	3	4	5	6	7	8	9	1	2	3	4	5	6	7	8	9
10	0000	0043	0086	0128	0170	0212	0253	0294	0334	0374	4	9	13	17	21	26	30	34	38
11	0414	0453	0492	0531	0569	0607	0645	0682	0719	0755	4	8	12	16	19	23	27	31	36
12	0792	0828	0864	0899	0934	0969	1004	1038	1072	1106	4	7	11	15	19	22	26	30	33
13	1139	1173	1206	1239	1271	1303	1335	1367	1399	1430	3	7	10	14	17	21	24	28	31
14	1461	1492	1523	1553	1584	1614	1644	1673	1703	1732	3	6	10	13	16	19	23	26	29
15	1761	1790	1818	1847	1875	1903	1931	1959	1987	2014	3	6	8	11	14	17	20	22	25
16	2041	2068	2095	2122	2148	2175	2201	2227	2253	2279	3	5	8	11	13	16	18	21	24
17	2304	2330	2355	2380	2405	2430	2455	2480	2504	2529	2	5	7	10	12	15	17	20	22
18	2553	2577	2601	2625	2648	2672	2695	2718	2742	2765	2	5	7	9	12	14	16	19	21
19	2788	2810	2833	2856	2878	2900	2923	2945	2967	2989	2	4	7	9	11	13	16	18	20
20	3010	3032	3054	3075	3096	3118	3139	3160	3181	3201	2	4	6	8	11	13	15	17	19
21	3222	3243	3263	3284	3304	3324	3345	3365	3385	3404	2	4	6	8	10	12	14	16	18
22	3424	3444	3464	3483	3502	3522	3541	3560	3579	3598	2	4	6	8	10	12	14	15	17
23	3617	3636	3655	3674	3692	3711	3729	3747	3766	3784	2	4	6	7	9	11	13	15	17
24	3802	3820	3838	3856	3874	3892	3909	3927	3945	3962	2	4	5	7	9	11	12	14	16
25	3979	3997	4014	4031	4048	4065	4082	4099	4116	4133	2	3	5	7	9	10	12	14	15
26	4150	4166	4183	4200	4216	4232	4249	4265	4281	4298	2	3	5	7	8	10	11	13	15
27	4314	4330	4346	4362	4378	4393	4409	4425	4440	4456	2	3	5	6	8	9	11	13	14
28	4472	4487	4502	4518	4533	4548	4564	4579	4594	4609	2	3	5	6	8	9	11	12	14
29	4624	4639	4654	4669	4683	4698	4713	4728	4742	4757	1	3	4	6	7	9	10	12	13
30	4771	4786	4800	4814	4829	4843	4857	4871	4886	4900	1	3	4	6	7	9	10	11	13
31	4914	4928	4942	4955	4969	4983	4997	5011	5024	5038	1	3	4	6	7	8	10	11	12
32	5051	5065	5079	5092	5105	5119	5132	5145	5159	5172	1	3	4	5	7	8	9	11	12
33	5185	5198	5211	5224	5237	5250	5263	5276	5289	5302	1	3	4	5	6	8	9	10	12
34	5315	5328	5340	5353	5366	5378	5391	5403	5416	5428	1	3	4	5	6	8	9	10	11
35	5441	5453	5465	5478	5490	5502	5514	5527	5539	5551	1	2	4	5	6	7	9	10	11
36	5563	5575	5587	5599	5611	5623	5635	5647	5658	5670	1	2	4	5	6	7	8	10	11
37	5682	5694	5705	5717	5729	5740	5752	5763	5775	5786	1	2	3	5	6	7	8	9	10
38	5798	5809	5821	5832	5843	5855	5866	5877	5888	5899	1	2	3	5	6	7	8	9	10
39	5911	5922	5933	5944	5955	5966	5977	5988	5999	6010	1	2	3	4	5	7	8	9	10
40	6021	6031	6042	6053	6064	6075	6085	6096	6107	6117	1	2	3	4	5	6	8	9	10
41	6128	6138	6149	6160	6170	6180	6191	6201	6212	6222	1	2	3	4	5	6	7	8	9
42	6232	6243	6253	6263	6274	6284	6294	6304	6314	6325	1	2	3	4	5	6	7	8	9
43	6335	6345	6355	6365	6375	6385	6395	6405	6415	6425	1	2	3	4	5	6	7	8	9
44	6435	6444	6454	6464	6474	6484	6493	6503	6513	6522	1	2	3	4	5	6	7	8	9
45	6532	6542	6551	6561	6571	6580	6590	6599	6609	6618	1	2	3	4	5	6	7	8	9
46	6628	6637	6646	6656	6665	6675	6684	6693	6702	6712	1	2	3	4	5	6	7	7	8
47	6721	6730	6739	6749	6758	6767	6776	6785	6794	6803	1	2	3	4	5	5	6	7	8
48	6812	6821	6830	6839	6848	6857	6866	6875	6884	6893	1	2	3	4	4	5	6	7	8
49	6902	6911	6920	6928	6937	6946	6955	6964	6972	6981	1	2	3	4	4	5	6	7	8

LOGARITHMS

	0	1	2	3	4	5	6	7	8	9	1	2	3	4	5	6	7	8	9
50	6990	6998	7007	7016	7024	7033	7042	7050	7059	7067	1	2	3	3	4	5	6	7	8
51	7076	7084	7093	7101	7110	7118	7126	7135	7143	7152	1	2	3	3	4	5	6	7	8
52	7160	7168	7177	7185	7193	7202	7210	7218	7226	7235	1	2	2	3	4	5	6	7	7
53	7243	7251	7259	7267	7275	7284	7292	7300	7308	7316	1	2	2	3	4	5	6	6	7
54	7324	7332	7340	7348	7356	7364	7372	7380	7388	7396	1	2	2	3	4	5	6	6	7
55	7404	7412	7419	7427	7435	7443	7451	7459	7466	7474	1	2	2	3	4	5	5	6	7
56	7482	7490	7497	7505	7513	7520	7528	7536	7543	7551	1	2	2	3	4	5	5	6	7
57	7559	7566	7574	7582	7589	7597	7604	7612	7619	7627	1	2	2	3	4	5	5	6	7
58	7634	7642	7649	7657	7664	7672	7679	7686	7694	7701	1	1	2	3	4	4	5	6	7
59	7709	7716	7723	7731	7738	7745	7752	7760	7767	7774	1	1	2	3	4	4	5	6	7
60	7782	7789	7796	7803	7810	7818	7825	7832	7839	7846	1	1	2	3	4	4	5	6	6
61	7853	7860	7868	7875	7882	7889	7896	7903	7910	7917	1	1	2	3	4	4	5	6	6
62	7924	7931	7938	7945	7952	7959	7966	7973	7980	7987	1	1	2	3	3	4	5	6	6
63	7993	8000	8007	8014	8021	8028	8035	8041	8048	8055	1	1	2	3	3	4	5	5	6
64	8062	8069	8075	8082	8089	8096	8102	8109	8116	8122	1	1	2	3	3	4	5	5	6
65	8129	8136	8142	8149	8156	8162	8169	8176	8182	8189	1	1	2	3	3	4	5	5	6
66	8195	8202	8209	8215	8222	8228	8235	8241	8248	8254	1	1	2	3	3	4	5	5	6
67	8261	8267	8274	8280	8287	8293	8299	8306	8312	8319	1	1	2	2	3	4	4	5	6
68	8325	8331	8338	8344	8351	8357	8363	8370	8376	8382	1	1	2	2	3	4	4	5	6
69	8388	8395	8401	8407	8414	8420	8426	8432	8439	8445	1	1	2	2	3	4	4	5	6
70	8451	8457	8463	8470	8476	8482	8488	8494	8500	8506	1	1	2	2	3	4	4	5	5
71	8513	8519	8525	8531	8537	8543	8549	8555	8561	8567	1	1	2	2	3	4	4	5	5
72	8573	8579	8585	8591	8597	8603	8609	8615	8621	8627	1	1	2	2	3	4	4	5	5
73	8633	8639	8645	8651	8657	8663	8669	8675	8681	8686	1	1	2	2	3	4	4	5	5
74	8692	8698	8704	8710	8716	8722	8727	8733	8739	8745	1	1	2	2	3	4	4	5	5
75	8751	8756	8762	8768	8774	8779	8785	8791	8797	8802	1	1	2	2	3	3	4	5	5
76	8808	8814	8820	8825	8831	8837	8842	8848	8854	8859	1	1	2	2	3	3	4	5	5
77	8865	8871	8876	8882	8887	8893	8899	8904	8910	8915	1	1	2	2	3	3	4	4	5
78	8921	8927	8932	8938	8943	8949	8954	8960	8965	8971	1	1	2	2	3	3	4	4	5
79	8976	8982	8987	8993	8998	9004	9009	9015	9020	9025	1	1	2	2	3	3	4	4	5
80	9031	9036	9042	9047	9053	9058	9063	9069	9074	9079	1	1	2	2	3	3	4	4	5
81	9085	9090	9096	9101	9106	9112	9117	9122	9128	9133	1	1	2	2	3	3	4	4	5
82	9138	9143	9149	9154	9159	9165	9170	9175	9180	9186	1	1	2	2	3	3	4	4	5
83	9191	9196	9201	9206	9212	9217	9222	9227	9232	9238	1	1	2	2	3	3	4	4	5
84	9243	9248	9253	9258	9263	9269	9274	9279	9284	9289	1	1	2	2	3	3	4	4	5
85	9294	9299	9304	9309	9315	9320	9325	9330	9335	9340	1	1	2	2	3	3	4	4	5
86	9345	9350	9355	9360	9365	9370	9375	9380	9385	9390	1	1	2	2	3	3	4	4	5
87	9395	9400	9405	9410	9415	9420	9425	9430	9435	9440	0	1	1	2	2	3	3	4	4
88	9445	9450	9455	9460	9465	9469	9474	9479	9484	9489	0	1	1	2	2	3	3	4	4
89	9494	9499	9504	9509	9513	9518	9523	9528	9533	9538	0	1	1	2	2	3	3	4	4
90	9542	9547	9552	9557	9562	9566	9571	9576	9581	9586	0	1	1	2	2	3	3	4	4
91	9590	9595	9600	9605	9609	9614	9619	9624	9628	9633	0	1	1	2	2	3	3	4	4
92	9638	9643	9647	9652	9657	9661	9666	9671	9675	9680	0	1	1	2	2	3	3	4	4
93	9685	9689	9694	9699	9703	9708	9713	9717	9722	9727	0	1	1	2	2	3	3	4	4
94	9731	9736	9741	9745	9750	9754	9759	9763	9768	9773	0	1	1	2	2	3	3	4	4
95	9777	9782	9786	9791	9795	9800	9805	9809	9814	9818	0	1	1	2	2	3	3	4	4
96	9823	9827	9832	9836	9841	9845	9850	9854	9859	9863	0	1	1	2	2	3	3	4	4
97	9868	9872	9877	9881	9886	9890	9894	9899	9903	9908	0	1	1	2	2	3	3	4	4
98	9912	9917	9921	9926	9930	9934	9939	9943	9948	9952	0	1	1	2	2	3	3	4	4
99	9956	9961	9965	9969	9974	9978	9983	9987	9991	9996	0	1	1	2	2	3	3	3	4

PERCENTAGE POINTS OF THE t-DISTRIBUTION

The values of t given in the body of the table have a probability α of being exceeded for v degrees of freedom.

α (1 tail)	0.10	0.05	0.025	0.01	0.005	0.001	0.0005
α (2 tail)	0.20	0.10	0.050	0.02	0.010	0.002	0.0010
v							
1	3.078	6.314	12.706	31.821	63.657	318.31	636.62
2	1.886	2.920	4.303	6.965	9.925	22.326	31.598
3	1.638	2.353	3.182	4.541	5.841	10.213	12.924
4	1.533	2.132	2.776	3.747	4.604	7.173	8.610
5	1.476	2.015	2.571	3.365	4.032	5.893	6.869
6	1.440	1.943	2.447	3.143	3.707	5.208	5.959
7	1.415	1.895	2.365	2.998	3.499	4.785	5.408
8	1.397	1.860	2.306	2.896	3.355	4.501	5.041
9	1.383	1.833	2.262	2.821	3.250	4.297	4.781
10	1.372	1.812	2.228	2.764	3.169	4.144	4.587
11	1.363	1.796	2.201	2.718	3.106	4.025	4.437
12	1.356	1.782	2.179	2.681	3.055	3.930	4.318
13	1.350	1.771	2.160	2.650	3.012	3.852	4.221
14	1.345	1.761	2.145	2.624	2.977	3.787	4.140
15	1.341	1.753	2.131	2.602	2.947	3.733	4.073
16	1.337	1.746	2.120	2.583	2.921	3.686	4.015
17	1.333	1.740	2.110	2.567	2.898	3.646	3.965
18	1.330	1.734	2.101	2.552	2.878	3.610	3.922
19	1.328	1.729	2.093	2.539	2.861	3.579	3.883
20	1.325	1.725	2.086	2.528	2.845	3.552	3.850
21	1.321	1.721	2.080	2.518	2.831	3.527	3.819
22	1.321	1.717	2.074	2.508	2.819	3.505	3.792
23	1.319	1.714	2.069	2.500	2.807	3.485	3.767
24	1.318	1.711	2.064	2.492	2.797	3.467	3.745
25	1.316	1.708	2.060	2.485	2.787	3.450	3.725
26	1.315	1.706	2.056	2.479	2.779	3.435	3.707
27	1.314	1.703	2.052	2.473	2.771	3.421	3.690
28	1.313	1.701	2.048	2.467	2.763	3.408	3.674
29	1.311	1.699	2.045	2.462	2.756	3.396	3.659
30	1.310	1.697	2.042	2.457	2.750	3.385	3.646
40	1.303	1.684	2.021	2.423	2.704	3.307	3.551
60	1.296	1.671	2.000	2.390	2.660	3.232	3.460
120	1.289	1.658	1.980	2.358	2.617	3.180	3.373
∞	1.282	1.645	1.960	2.326	2.576	3.090	3.291

AREA UNDER THE NORMAL CURVE

This table gives the area under the normal curve between the mean and a point x standard deviations above the mean. The corresponding area for deviations below the mean can be found by symmetry.

$(x-\mu)/\sigma$	0.00	0.01	0.02	0.03	0.04	0.05	0.06	0.07	0.08	0.09
0.0	.0000	.0040	.0080	.0120	.0159	.0199	.0239	.0279	.0319	.0359
0.1	.0398	.0438	.0478	.0517	.0557	.0596	.0636	.0675	.0714	.0753
0.2	.0793	.0832	.0871	.0910	.0948	.0987	.1026	.1064	.1103	.1141
0.3	.1179	.1217	.1255	.1293	.1331	.1368	.1406	.1443	.1480	.1517
0.4	.1554	.1591	.1628	.1664	.1700	.1736	.1772	.1808	.1844	.1879
0.5	.1915	.1950	.1985	.2019	.2054	.2088	.2123	.2157	.2190	.2224
0.6	.2257	.2291	.2324	.2357	.2389	.2422	.2454	.2486	.2518	.2549
0.7	.2580	.2611	.2642	.2673	.2704	.2734	.2764	.2794	.2823	.2852
0.8	.2881	.2910	.2939	.2967	.2995	.3023	.3051	.3078	.3106	.3133
0.9	.3159	.3186	.3212	.3238	.3264	.3289	.3315	.3340	.3365	.3389
1.0	.3413	.3438	.3461	.3485	.3508	.3531	.3554	.3577	.3599	.3621
1.1	.3643	.3665	.3686	.3708	.3729	.3749	.3770	.3790	.3810	.3830
1.2	.3849	.3869	.3888	.3907	.3925	.3944	.3962	.3980	.3997	.4015
1.3	.4032	.4049	.4066	.4082	.4099	.4115	.4131	.4147	.4162	.4177
1.4	.4192	.4207	.4222	.4236	.4251	.4265	.4279	.4292	.4306	.4319
1.5	.4332	.4345	.4357	.4370	.4382	.4394	.4406	.4418	.4430	.4441
1.6	.4452	.4463	.4474	.4485	.4495	.4505	.4515	.4525	.4535	.4545
1.7	.4554	.4564	.4573	.4582	.4591	.4599	.4608	.4616	.4625	.4633
1.8	.4641	.4649	.4656	.4664	.4671	.4678	.4686	.4693	.4699	.4706
1.9	.4713	.4719	.4726	.4732	.4738	.4744	.4750	.4756	.4762	.4767
2.0	.4772	.4778	.4783	.4788	.4793	.4798	.4803	.4808	.4812	.4817
2.1	.4821	.4826	.4830	.4834	.4838	.4842	.4846	.4850	.4854	.4857
2.2	.4861	.4865	.4868	.4871	.4875	.4878	.4881	.4884	.4887	.4890
2.3	.4893	.4896	.4898	.4901	.4904	.4906	.4909	.4911	.4913	.4916
2.4	.4918	.4920	.4922	.4925	.4927	.4929	.4931	.4932	.4934	.4936
2.5	.4938	.4940	.4941	.4943	.4945	.4946	.4948	.4949	.4951	.4952
2.6	.4953	.4955	.4956	.4957	.4959	.4960	.4961	.4962	.4963	.4964
2.7	.4965	.4966	.4967	.4968	.4969	.4970	.4971	.4972	.4973	.4974
2.8	.4974	.4975	.4976	.4977	.4977	.4978	.4979	.4980	.4980	.4981
2.9	.4981	.4982	.4983	.4983	.4984	.4984	.4985	.4985	.4986	.4986
3.0	.49865	.4987	.4987	.4988	.4988	.4989	.4989	.4989	.4990	.4990
3.1	.49903	.4991	.4991	.4991	.4992	.4992	.4992	.4992	.4993	.4993
3.2	.49931	.4993	.4994	.4994	.4994	.4994	.4994	.4995	.4995	.4995
3.3	.49952	.4995	.4995	.4996	.4996	.4996	.4996	.4996	.4996	.4997
3.4	.49966	.4997	.4997	.4997	.4997	.4997	.4997	.4997	.4997	.4998
3.5	.49977									

SIGNIFICANT VALUE OF THE CORRELATION COEFFICIENT

If the calculated value of r exceeds the table value of r_α, a significant correlation has been established at the α significance level.

d.f.	$r_{.1}$	$r_{.05}$	$r_{.02}$	$r_{.01}$	$r_{.001}$
1	·98769	·99692	·999507	·999877	·999988
2	·90000	·95000	·98000	·990000	·99900
3	·8054	·8783	·93433	·95873	·99116
4	·7293	·8114	·8822	·91720	·97406
5	·6694	·7545	·8329	·8745	·95074
6	·6215	·7067	·7887	·8343	·92493
7	·5822	·6664	·7498	·7877	·8982
8	·5494	·6319	·7155	·7646	·8721
9	·5214	·6021	·6851	·7348	·8471
10	·4973	·5760	·6581	·7079	·8233
11	·4762	·5529	·6339	·6835	·8010
12	·4575	·5324	·6120	·6614	·7800
13	·4409	·5139	·5923	·6411	·7603
14	·4259	·4973	·5742	·6226	·7420
15	·4124	·4821	·5577	·6055	·7246
16	·4000	·4683	·5425	·5897	·7084
17	·3887	·4555	·5285	·5751	·6932
18	·3783	·4438	·5155	·5614	·6787
19	·3687	·4329	·5034	·5487	·6652
20	·3598	·4227	·4921	·5368	·6524
25	·3233	·3809	·4451	·4869	·5974
30	·2960	·3494	·4093	·4487	·5541
35	·2746	·3246	·3810	·4182	·5189
40	·2573	·3044	·3578	·3932	·4896
45	·2428	·2875	·3384	·3721	·4648
50	·2306	·2732	·3218	·3541	·4433
60	·2108	·2500	·2948	·3248	·4078
70	·1954	·2319	·2737	·3017	·3799
80	·1829	·2172	·2566	·2830	·3568
90	·1726	·2050	·2422	·2673	·3375
100	·1638	·1948	·2301	·2540	·3211

d.f. = degrees of freedom

THE CHI-SQUARED DISTRIBUTION (χ^2)

Degrees of freedom	Probability level %					
	99	95	10	5	1	0·1
1	0·03157	0·00393	2·71	3·84	6·63	10·83
2	0·0201	0·103	4·61	5·99	9·21	13·81
3	0·115	0·352	6·25	7·81	11·34	16·27
4	0·297	0·711	7·78	9·49	13·28	18·47
5	0·554	1·15	9·24	11·07	15·09	20·52
6	0·872	1·64	10·64	12·59	16·81	22·46
7	1·24	2·17	12·02	14·07	18·48	24·32
8	1·65	2·73	13·36	15·51	20·09	26·12
9	2·09	3·33	14·68	16·92	21·67	27·88
10	2·56	3·94	15·99	18·31	23·21	29·59
11	3·05	4·57	17·28	19·68	24·73	31·26
12	3·57	5·23	18·55	21·03	26·22	32·91
13	4·11	5·89	19·81	22·36	27·69	34·53
14	4·66	6·57	21·06	23·68	29·14	36·12
15	5·23	7·26	22·31	25·00	30·58	37·70
16	5·81	7·96	23·54	26·30	32·00	39·25
17	6·41	8·67	24·77	27·59	33·41	40·79
18	7·01	9·39	25·99	28·87	34·81	42·31
19	7·63	10·12	27·20	30·14	36·19	43·82
20	8·26	10·85	28·41	31·41	37·67	46·31
21	8·90	11·59	29·62	32·67	38·93	46·80
22	9·54	12·34	30·81	33·92	40·29	48·27
23	10·20	13·09	32·01	35·17	41·64	49·73
24	10·86	13·85	33·20	36·42	42·98	51·18
25	11·52	14·61	34·38	37·65	44·31	52·62
26	12·20	15·38	35·56	38·89	45·64	54·06
27	12·88	16·15	36·74	40·11	46·96	55·48
28	13·56	16·93	37·92	41·34	48·28	56·89
29	14·26	17·71	39·09	42·56	49·59	58·30
30	14·95	18·49	40·26	43·77	50·89	59·70
40	22·16	26·51	51·81	55·76	63·69	73·40
50	29·71	34·76	63·17	67·50	76·15	86·66
60	37·48	43·19	74·40	79·08	88·38	99·61
70	45·44	51·74	85·53	90·53	100·4	112·3
80	53·54	60·39	96·58	101·9	112·3	124·8
90	61·75	69·13	107·6	113·1	124·1	137·2
100	70·08	77·93	118·5	124·3	135·8	149·4

The entry in the table is the value of χ^2 which would be exceeded with the given probability by random variations if the null hypothesis were true.

THE F-DISTRIBUTION (0·05 level)

Denominator \ Numerator	1	2	3	4	5	6	7	8	10	12	24	∞
1	161·4	199·5	216·7	224·6	230·2	234·0	236·8	238·9	241·9	243·9	249·0	254·3
2	18·5	19·0	19·2	19·2	19·3	19·3	19·4	19·4	19·4	19·4	19·5	19·5
3	10·13	9·55	9·28	9·12	9·01	8·94	8·89	8·85	8·79	8·74	8·64	8·53
4	7·71	6·94	6·59	6·39	6·26	6·16	6·09	6·04	5·96	5·91	5·77	5·63
5	6·61	5·79	5·41	5·19	5·05	4·95	4·88	4·82	4·74	4·68	4·53	4·36
6	5·99	5·14	4·76	4·53	4·39	4·28	4·21	4·15	4·06	4·00	3·84	3·67
7	5·59	4·74	4·35	4·12	3·97	3·87	3·79	3·73	3·64	3·57	3·41	3·23
8	5·32	4·46	4·07	3·84	3·69	3·58	3·50	3·44	3·35	3·28	3·12	2·93
9	5·12	4·26	3·86	3·63	3·48	3·37	3·29	3·23	3·14	3·07	2·90	2·71
10	4·96	4·10	3·71	3·48	3·33	3·22	3·14	3·07	2·98	2·91	2·74	2·54
11	4·84	3·98	3·59	3·36	3·20	3·09	3·01	2·95	2·85	2·79	2·61	2·40
12	4·75	3·89	3·49	3·26	3·11	3·00	2·91	2·85	2·75	2·69	2·51	2·30
13	4·67	3·81	3·41	3·18	3·03	2·92	2·83	2·77	2·67	2·60	2·42	2·21
14	4·60	3·74	3·34	3·11	2·98	2·85	2·76	2·70	2·60	2·53	2·35	2·13
15	4·54	3·68	3·29	3·06	2·90	2·79	2·71	2·64	2·54	2·48	2·29	2·07
16	4·49	3·63	3·24	3·01	2·85	2·74	2·66	2·59	2·49	2·42	2·24	2·01
17	4·45	3·59	3·20	2·96	2·81	2·70	2·61	2·55	2·45	2·38	2·19	1·96
18	4·41	3·55	3·16	2·93	2·77	2·66	2·58	2·51	2·41	2·34	2·15	1·92
19	4·38	3·52	3·13	2·90	2·74	2·63	2·54	2·48	2·38	2·31	2·11	1·88
20	4·35	3·49	3·10	2·87	2·71	2·60	2·51	2·45	2·35	2·28	2·08	1·84
21	4·32	3·47	3·07	2·84	2·68	2·57	2·49	2·42	2·32	2·25	2·05	1·81
22	4·30	3·44	3·05	2·82	2·66	2·55	2·46	2·40	2·30	2·23	2·03	1·78
23	4·28	3·42	3·03	2·80	2·64	2·53	2·44	2·37	2·27	2·20	2·00	1·76
24	4·26	3·40	3·01	2·78	2·62	2·51	2·42	2·36	2·25	2·18	1·98	1·73
25	4·24	3·39	2·99	2·76	2·60	2·49	2·40	2·34	2·24	2·16	1·96	1·71
26	4·23	3·37	2·98	2·74	2·59	2·47	2·39	2·32	2·22	2·15	1·95	1·69
27	4·21	3·35	2·96	2·73	2·57	2·46	2·37	2·31	2·20	2·13	1·93	1·67
28	4·20	3·34	2·95	2·71	2·56	2·45	2·36	2·29	2·19	2·12	1·91	1·65
29	4·18	3·33	2·93	2·70	2·55	2·43	2·35	2·28	2·18	2·10	1·90	1·64
30	4·17	3·32	2·92	2·69	2·53	2·42	2·33	2·27	2·16	2·09	1·89	1·62
32	4·15	3·29	2·90	2·67	2·51	2·40	2·31	2·24	2·14	2·07	1·86	1·59
34	4·13	3·28	2·88	2·65	2·49	2·38	2·29	2·23	2·12	2·05	1·84	1·57
36	4·11	3·26	2·87	2·63	2·48	2·36	2·28	2·21	2·11	2·03	1·82	1·55
38	4·10	3·24	2·85	2·62	2·46	2·35	2·26	2·19	2·09	2·02	1·81	1·53
40	4·08	3·23	2·84	2·61	2·45	2·34	2·25	2·18	2·08	2·00	1·79	1·51
60	4·00	3·15	2·76	2·53	2·37	2·25	2·17	2·10	1·99	1·92	1·70	1·39
120	3·92	3·07	2·68	2·45	2·29	2·18	2·09	2·02	1·91	1·83	1·61	1·25
∞	3·84	3·00	2·60	2·37	2·21	2·10	2·01	1·94	1·83	1·75	1·52	1·00

Values of F which would be exceeded with only 5% probability by random variations if the null hypothesis were true. They are valid for two-tailed tests.

THE F-DISTRIBUTION (0·01 level)

Denominator \ Numerator	1	2	3	4	5	6	7	8	10	12	24	∞
1	4052	5000	5403	5625	5764	5859	5928	5981	6056	6106	6235	6366
2	98·5	99·0	99·2	99·2	99·3	99·3	99·4	99·4	99·4	99·4	99·5	99·5
3	34·1	30·8	29·5	28·7	28·2	27·9	27·7	27·5	27·2	27·1	26·6	26·1
4	21·2	18·0	16·7	16·0	15·5	15·2	15·0	14·8	14·5	14·4	13·9	13·5
5	16·26	13·27	12·06	11·39	10·97	10·67	10·46	10·29	10·05	9·89	9·47	9·02
6	13·74	10·92	9·78	9·15	8·75	8·47	8·26	8·10	7·87	7·72	7·31	6·88
7	12·25	9·55	8·45	7·85	7·46	7·19	6·99	6·84	6·62	6·47	6·07	5·65
8	11·26	8·65	7·59	7·01	6·63	6·37	6·18	6·03	5·81	5·67	5·28	4·86
9	10·56	8·02	6·99	6·42	6·06	5·80	5·61	5·47	5·26	5·11	4·73	4·31
10	10·04	7·56	6·55	5·99	5·64	5·39	5·20	5·06	4·85	4·71	4·33	3·91
11	9·65	7·21	6·22	5·67	5·32	5·07	4·89	4·74	4·54	4·40	4·02	3·60
12	9·33	6·93	5·95	5·41	5·06	4·82	4·64	4·50	4·30	4·16	3·78	3·36
13	9·07	6·70	5·74	5·21	4·86	4·62	4·44	4·30	4·10	3·96	3·59	3·17
14	8·86	6·51	5·56	5·04	4·70	4·46	4·28	4·14	3·94	3·80	3·43	3·00
15	8·68	6·36	5·42	4·89	4·56	4·32	4·14	4·00	3·80	3·67	3·29	2·87
16	8·53	6·23	5·29	4·77	4·44	4·20	4·03	3·89	3·69	3·55	3·18	2·75
17	8·40	6·11	5·18	4·67	4·34	4·10	3·93	3·79	3·59	3·46	3·08	2·65
18	8·29	6·01	5·09	4·58	4·25	4·01	3·84	3·71	3·51	3·37	3·00	2·57
19	8·18	5·93	5·01	4·50	4·17	3·94	3·77	3·63	3·43	3·30	2·92	2·49
20	8·10	5·85	4·94	4·43	4·10	3·87	3·70	3·56	3·37	3·23	2·86	2·42
21	8·02	5·78	4·87	4·37	4·04	3·81	3·64	3·51	3·31	3·17	2·80	2·36
22	7·95	5·72	4·82	4·31	3·99	3·76	3·59	3·45	3·26	3·12	2·75	2·31
23	7·88	5·66	4·76	4·26	3·94	3·71	3·54	3·41	3·21	3·07	2·70	2·26
24	7·82	5·61	4·72	4·22	3·90	3·67	3·50	3·36	3·17	3·03	2·66	2·21
25	7·77	5·57	4·68	4·18	3·86	3·63	3·46	3·32	3·13	2·99	2·62	2·17
26	7·72	5·53	4·64	4·14	3·82	3·59	3·42	3·29	3·09	2·96	2·58	2·13
27	7·68	5·49	4·60	4·11	3·78	3·56	3·39	3·26	3·06	2·93	2·55	2·10
28	7·64	5·45	4·57	4·07	3·75	3·53	3·36	3·23	3·03	2·90	2·52	2·06
29	7·60	5·42	4·54	4·04	3·73	3·50	3·33	3·20	3·00	2·87	2·49	2·03
30	7·56	5·39	4·51	4·02	3·70	3·47	3·30	3·17	2·98	2·84	2·47	2·01
32	7·50	5·34	4·46	3·97	3·65	3·43	3·26	3·13	2·93	2·80	2·42	1·96
34	7·45	5·29	4·42	3·93	3·61	3·39	3·22	3·09	2·90	2·76	2·38	1·91
36	7·40	5·25	4·38	3·89	3·58	3·35	3·18	3·05	2·86	2·72	2·35	1·87
38	7·35	5·21	4·34	3·86	3·54	3·32	3·15	3·02	2·83	2·69	2·32	1·84
40	7·31	5·18	4·31	3·83	3·51	3·29	3·12	2·99	2·80	2·66	2·29	1·80
60	7·08	4·98	4·13	3·65	3·34	3·12	2·95	2·82	2·63	2·50	2·12	1·60
120	6·85	4·79	3·95	3·48	3·17	2·96	2·79	2·66	2·47	2·34	1·95	1·38
∞	6·63	4·61	3·78	3·32	3·02	2·80	2·64	2·51	2·32	2·18	1·79	1·00

Values of F which would be exceeded with only 1% probability by random variations if the null hypothesis were true. They are valid for two-tailed tests.

THE POISSON DISTRIBUTION

x	3·1	3·2	3·3	3·4	3·5	3·6	3·7	3·8	3·9	4·0
0	·0450	·0408	·0369	·0334	·0302	·0273	·0247	·0224	·0202	·0183
1	·1397	·1304	·1217	·1135	·1057	·0984	·0915	·0850	·0789	·0733
2	·2165	·2087	·2008	·1929	·1850	·1771	·1692	·1615	·1539	·1465
3	·2237	·2226	·2209	·2186	·2158	·2125	·2087	·2046	·2001	·1954
4	·1734	·1781	·1823	·1858	·1888	·1912	·1931	·1944	·1951	·1954
5	·1075	·1140	·1203	·1264	·1322	·1377	·1429	·1477	·1522	·1563
6	·0555	·0608	·0662	·0716	·0771	·0826	·0881	·0936	·0989	·1042
7	·0246	·0278	·0312	·0348	·0385	·0425	·0466	·0508	·0551	·0595
8	·0095	·0111	·0129	·0148	·0169	·0191	·0215	·0241	·0269	·0298
9	·0033	·0040	·0047	·0056	·0066	·0076	·0089	·0102	·0116	·0132
10	·0010	·0013	·0016	·0019	·0023	·0028	·0033	·0039	·0045	·0053
11	·0003	·0004	·0005	·0006	·0007	·0009	·0011	·0013	·0016	·0019
12	·0001	·0001	·0001	·0002	·0002	·0003	·0003	·0004	·0005	·0006
13	·0000	·0000	·0000	·0000	·0001	·0001	·0001	·0001	·0002	·0002
14	·0000	·0000	·0000	·0000	·0000	·0000	·0000	·0001	·0000	·0001

x	4·1	4·2	4·3	4·4	4·5	4·6	4·7	4·8	4·9	5·0
0	·0166	·0150	·0136	·0123	·0111	·0101	·0091	·0082	·0074	·0067
1	·0679	·0630	·0583	·0540	·0500	·0462	·0427	·0395	·0365	·0337
2	·1393	·1323	·1254	·1188	·1125	·1063	·1005	·0948	·0894	·0842
3	·1904	·1852	·1798	·1743	·1687	·1631	·1574	·1517	·1460	·1404
4	·1951	·1944	·1933	·1917	·1898	·1875	·1849	·1820	·1789	·1755
5	·1600	·1633	·1662	·1687	·1708	·1725	·1738	·1747	·1753	·1755
6	·1093	·1143	·1191	·1237	·1281	·1323	·1362	·1398	·1432	·1462
7	·0640	·0686	·0732	·0778	·0824	·0869	·0914	·0959	·1002	·1044
8	·0328	·0360	·0393	·0428	·0463	·0500	·0537	·0575	·0614	·0653
9	·0150	·0168	·0188	·0209	·0232	·0255	·0280	·0307	·0334	·0363
10	·0061	·0071	·0081	·0092	·0104	·0118	·0132	·0147	·0164	·0181
11	·0023	·0027	·0032	·0037	·0043	·0049	·0056	·0064	·0073	·0082
12	·0008	·0009	·0011	·0014	·0016	·0019	·0022	·0026	·0030	·0034
13	·0002	·0003	·0004	·0005	·0006	·0007	·0008	·0009	·0011	·0013
14	·0001	·0001	·0001	·0001	·0002	·0002	·0003	·0003	·0004	·0005
15	·0000	·0000	·0000	·0000	·0001	·0001	·0001	·0001	·0001	·0002

Entries in the table give the probabilities that an event will occur x times when the average number of occurrences is m.

THE POISSON DISTRIBUTION

x	0·1	0·2	0·3	0·4	0·5	0·6	0·7	0·8	0·9	1·0
0	·9048	·8187	·7408	·6703	·6065	·5488	·4966	·4493	·4066	·3679
1	·0905	·1637	·2222	·2681	·3033	·3293	·3476	·3595	·3659	·3679
2	·0045	·0164	·0333	·0536	·0758	·0988	·1217	·1438	·1647	·1839
3	·0002	·0011	·0033	·0072	·0126	·0198	·0284	·0383	·0494	·0613
4	·0000	·0001	·0002	·0007	·0016	·0030	·0050	·0077	·0111	·0153
5	·0000	·0000	·0000	·0000	·0002	·0004	·0007	·0012	·0020	·0031
6	·0000	·0000	·0000	·0000	·0000	·0000	·0001	·0002	·0003	·0005
7	·0000	·0000	·0000	·0000	·0000	·0000	·0000	·0000	·0000	·0001

x	1·1	1·2	1·3	1·4	1·5	1·6	1·7	1·8	1·9	2·0
0	·3329	·3012	·2725	·2466	·2231	·2019	·1827	·1653	·1496	·1353
1	·3662	·3614	·3543	·3452	·3347	·3230	·3106	·2975	·2842	·2707
2	·2014	·2169	·2303	·2417	·2510	·2584	·2640	·2678	·2700	·2707
3	·0738	·0867	·0998	·1128	·1255	·1378	·1496	·1607	·1710	·1804
4	·0203	·0260	·0324	·0395	·0471	·0551	·0636	·0723	·0812	·0902
5	·0045	·0062	·0084	·0111	·0141	·0176	·0216	·0260	·0309	·0361
6	·0008	·0012	·0018	·0028	·0035	·0047	·0061	·0078	·0098	·0120
7	·0001	·0002	·0003	·0005	·0008	·0011	·0015	·0020	·0027	·0034
8	·0000	·0000	·0001	·0001	·0001	·0002	·0003	·0005	·0006	·0009
9	·0000	·0000	·0000	·0000	·0000	·0000	·0001	·0001	·0001	·0002

x	2·1	2·2	2·3	2·4	2·5	2·6	2·7	2·8	2·9	3·0
0	·1225	·1108	·1003	·0907	·0821	·0743	·0672	·0608	·0550	·0498
1	·2572	·2438	·2306	·2177	·2052	·1931	·1815	·1703	·1596	·1494
2	·2700	·2681	·2652	·2613	·2565	·2510	·2450	·2384	·2314	·2240
3	·1890	·1966	·2033	·2090	·2138	·2176	·2205	·2225	·2237	·2240
4	·0992	·1082	·1169	·1254	·1336	·1414	·1488	·1557	·1622	·1680
5	·0417	·0476	·0538	·0602	·0668	·0735	·0804	·0872	·0940	·1008
6	·0146	·0174	·0206	·0241	·0278	·0319	·0362	·0407	·0455	·0504
7	·0044	·0055	·0068	·0083	·0099	·0118	·0139	·0163	·0188	·0216
8	·0011	·0015	·0019	·0025	·0031	·0038	·0047	·0057	·0068	·0081
9	·0003	·0004	·0005	·0007	·0009	·0011	·0014	·0018	·0022	·0027
10	·0001	·0001	·0001	·0002	·0002	·0003	·0004	·0005	·0006	·0008
11	·0000	·0000	·0000	·0000	·0000	·0001	·0001	·0001	·0002	·0002
12	·0000	·0000	·0000	·0000	·0000	·0000	·0000	·0000	·0000	·0001

Entries in the table give the probabilities that an event will occur x times when the average number of occurrences is m.

THE POISSON DISTRIBUTION

x	7·1	7·2	7·3	7·4	7·5	7·6	7·7	7·8	7·9	8·0
0	·0008	·0007	·0007	·0006	·0006	·0005	·0005	·0004	·0004	·0003
1	·0059	·0064	·0049	·0045	·0041	·0038	·0035	·0032	·0029	·0027
2	·0208	·0194	·0180	·0167	·0166	·0145	·0134	·0125	·0116	·0107
3	·0492	·0464	·0438	·0413	·0389	·0366	·0345	·0324	·0305	·0286
4	·0874	·0838	·0799	·0764	·0729	·0696	·0663	·0632	·0602	·0573
5	·1241	·1204	·1167	·1130	·1094	·1057	·1021	·0986	·0951	·0916
6	·1468	·1445	·1420	·1394	·1367	·1339	·1311	·1282	·1252	·1221
7	·1489	·1486	·1481	·1474	·1465	·1454	·1442	·1428	·1413	·1396
8	·1321	·1337	·1351	·1363	·1373	·1382	·1388	·1392	·1395	·1396
9	·1042	·1070	·1096	·1121	·1144	·1167	·1187	·1207	·1224	·1241
10	·0740	·0770	·0800	·0829	·0858	·0887	·0914	·0941	·0967	·0993
11	·0478	·0504	·0531	·0558	·0585	·0613	·0640	·0667	·0695	·0722
12	·0283	·0303	·0323	·0344	·0366	·0388	·0411	·0434	·0457	·0481
13	·0154	·0168	·0181	·0198	·0211	·0227	·0243	·0260	·0278	·0296
14	·0078	·0086	·0095	·0104	·0113	·0123	·0134	·0145	·0157	·0169
15	·0037	·0041	·0046	·0051	·0057	·0062	·0069	·0075	·0083	·0090
16	·0016	·0019	·0021	·0024	·0026	·0030	·0033	·0037	·0041	·0045
17	·0007	·0008	·0009	·0010	·0012	·0013	·0015	·0017	·0019	·0021
18	·0003	·0003	·0004	·0004	·0005	·0006	·0006	·0007	·0008	·0009
19	·0001	·0001	·0001	·0002	·0002	·0002	·0003	·0003	·0003	·0004
20	·0000	·0000	·0001	·0001	·0001	·0001	·0001	·0001	·0001	·0002
21	·0000	·0000	·0000	·0000	·0000	·0001	·0001	·0001	·0001	·0001

x	8·1	8·2	8·3	8·4	8·5	8·6	8·7	8·8	8·9	9·0
0	·0003	·0003	·0002	·0002	·0002	·0002	·0002	·0002	·0001	·0001
1	·0025	·0023	·0021	·0019	·0017	·0016	·0014	·0013	·0012	·0011
2	·0100	·0092	·0086	·0079	·0074	·0068	·0063	·0058	·0054	·0050
3	·0269	·0252	·0237	·0222	·0208	·0195	·0183	·0171	·0160	·0150
4	·0544	·0517	·0491	·0466	·0443	·0420	·0398	·0377	·0357	·0337
5	·0882	·0849	·0816	·0784	·0752	·0722	·0692	·0663	·0635	·0607
6	·1191	·1160	·1128	·1097	·1066	·1034	·1003	·0972	·0941	·0911
7	·1378	·1358	·1338	·1317	·1294	·1271	·1247	·1222	·1197	·1171
8	·1395	·1392	·1388	·1382	·1375	·1368	·1356	·1344	·1332	·1318
9	·1256	·1269	·1280	·1290	·1299	·1306	·1311	·1315	·1317	·1318
10	·1017	·1040	·1063	·1084	·1104	·1123	·1140	·1157	·1172	·1188
11	·0749	·0776	·0802	·0828	·0853	·0878	·0902	·0925	·0948	·0970

Entries in the table give the probabilities that an event will occur x times when the average number of occurrences is *m*.

THE POISSON DISTRIBUTION

x	5·1	5·2	5·3	5·4	5·5	5·6	5·7	5·8	5·9	6·0
0	·0061	·0055	·0050	·0045	·0041	·0037	·0033	·0030	·0027	·0025
1	·0311	·0287	·0265	·0244	·0225	·0207	·0191	·0178	·0162	·0149
2	·0793	·0746	·0701	·0659	·0618	·0580	·0544	·0509	·0477	·0446
3	·1348	·1293	·1239	·1185	·1133	·1082	·1033	·0985	·0938	·0892
4	·1719	·1681	·1641	·1600	·1558	·1515	·1472	·1428	·1383	·1339
5	·1753	·1748	·1740	·1728	·1714	·1697	·1678	·1656	·1632	·1606
6	·1490	·1515	·1537	·1555	·1571	·1584	·1594	·1601	·1605	·1606
7	·1086	·1125	·1163	·1200	·1234	·1267	·1298	·1326	·1353	·1377
8	·0692	·0731	·0771	·0810	·0849	·0887	·0925	·0962	·0998	·1033
9	·0392	·0423	·0454	·0486	·0519	·0552	·0586	·0620	·0654	·0688
10	·0200	·0220	·0241	·0262	·0285	·0309	·0334	·0359	·0386	·0413
11	·0093	·0104	·0116	·0129	·0143	·0157	·0173	·0190	·0207	·0225
12	·0039	·0045	·0051	·0058	·0065	·0073	·0082	·0092	·0102	·0113
13	·0015	·0018	·0021	·0024	·0028	·0032	·0036	·0041	·0046	·0052
14	·0006	·0007	·0008	·0009	·0011	·0013	·0015	·0017	·0019	·0022
15	·0002	·0002	·0003	·0003	·0004	·0005	·0006	·0007	·0008	·0009
16	·0001	·0001	·0001	·0001	·0001	·0002	·0002	·0002	·0003	·0003
17	·0000	·0000	·0000	·0000	·0000	·0001	·0001	·0001	·0001	·0001

x	6·1	6·2	6·3	6·4	6·5	6·6	6·7	6·8	6·9	7·0
0	·0022	·0020	·0018	·0017	·0015	·0014	·0012	·0011	·0010	·0009
1	·0137	·0126	·0116	·0106	·0098	·0090	·0082	·0076	·0070	·0064
2	·0417	·0390	·0364	·0340	·0318	·0296	·0276	·0258	·0240	·0223
3	·0848	·0806	·0765	·0726	·0688	·0652	·0617	·0584	·0552	·0521
4	·1294	·1249	·1205	·1160	·1118	·1078	·1034	·0992	·0952	·0912
5	·1579	·1549	·1519	·1487	·1454	·1420	·1385	·1349	·1314	·1277
6	·1605	·1601	·1595	·1586	·1575	·1562	·1546	·1529	·1511	·1490
7	·1399	·1418	·1435	·1450	·1462	·1472	·1480	·1486	·1489	·1490
8	·1066	·1099	·1130	·1160	·1188	·1215	·1240	·1263	·1284	·1304
9	·0723	·0757	·0791	·0825	·0858	·0891	·0923	·0954	·0985	·1014
10	·0441	·0469	·0498	·0528	·0558	·0588	·0618	·0649	·0679	·0710
11	·0245	·0265	·0285	·0307	·0330	·0353	·0377	·0401	·0426	·0452
12	·0124	·0137	·0150	·0164	·0179	·0194	·0210	·0227	·0245	·0264
13	·0058	·0065	·0073	·0081	·0089	·0098	·0108	·0119	·0130	·0142
14	·0025	·0029	·0033	·0037	·0041	·0046	·0052	·0058	·0064	·0071
15	·0010	·0012	·0014	·0016	·0018	·0020	·0023	·0026	·0029	·0033
16	·0004	·0005	·0005	·0006	·0007	·0008	·0010	·0011	·0013	·0014
17	·0001	·0002	·0002	·0002	·0003	·0003	·0004	·0004	·0005	·0006
18	·0000	·0001	·0001	·0001	·0001	·0001	·0001	·0002	·0002	·0002
19	·0000	·0000	·0000	·0000	·0000	·0000	·0000	·0001	·0001	·0001

Entries in the table give the probabilities that an event will occur x times when the average number of occurrences is *m*.

THE POISSON DISTRIBUTION

x	11	12	13	14	15	16	17	18	19	20
0	.0000	.0000	.0000	.0000	.0000	.0000	.0000	.0000	.0000	.0000
1	.0002	.0001	.0000	.0000	.0000	.0000	.0000	.0000	.0000	.0000
2	.0010	.0004	.0002	.0001	.0000	.0000	.0000	.0000	.0000	.0000
3	.0037	.0018	.0008	.0004	.0002	.0001	.0000	.0000	.0000	.0000
4	.0102	.0053	.0027	.0013	.0006	.0003	.0001	.0001	.0000	.0000
5	.0224	.0127	.0070	.0037	.0019	.0010	.0005	.0002	.0001	.0001
6	.0411	.0255	.0152	.0087	.0048	.0026	.0014	.0007	.0004	.0002
7	.0646	.0437	.0281	.0174	.0104	.0060	.0034	.0018	.0010	.0005
8	.0888	.0655	.0457	.0304	.0194	.0120	.0072	.0042	.0024	.0013
9	.1085	.0874	.0661	.0473	.0324	.0213	.0135	.0083	.0050	.0029
10	.1194	.1048	.0859	.0663	.0486	.0341	.0230	.0150	.0095	.0058
11	.1194	.1144	.1015	.0844	.0663	.0496	.0355	.0245	.0164	.0106
12	.1094	.1144	.1099	.0984	.0829	.0661	.0504	.0368	.0259	.0176
13	.0926	.1056	.1099	.1060	.0956	.0814	.0658	.0509	.0378	.0271
14	.0728	.0905	.1021	.1060	.1024	.0930	.0800	.0655	.0514	.0387
15	.0534	.0724	.0885	.0989	.1024	.0992	.0908	.0786	.0650	.0516
16	.0367	.0543	.0719	.0866	.0960	.0992	.0963	.0884	.0772	.0646
17	.0237	.0383	.0550	.0713	.0847	.0934	.0963	.0938	.0863	.0760
18	.0145	.0256	.0397	.0554	.0706	.0830	.0909	.0938	.0911	.0844
19	.0084	.0161	.0272	.0409	.0557	.0899	.0814	.0887	.0911	.0888
20	.0046	.0097	.0177	.0286	.0418	.0559	.0692	.0798	.0866	.0888
21	.0024	.0055	.0109	.0191	.0299	.0426	.0560	.0684	.0783	.0846
22	.0012	.0030	.0065	.0121	.0204	.0310	.0433	.0560	.0676	.0769
23	.0008	.0016	.0037	.0074	.0133	.0218	.0320	.0438	.0559	.0669
24	.0003	.0008	.0020	.0043	.0083	.0144	.0226	.0328	.0442	.0557
25	.0001	.0004	.0010	.0024	.0050	.0092	.0154	.0237	.0338	.0446
26	.0000	.0002	.0005	.0013	.0029	.0057	.0101	.0164	.0248	.0343
27	.0000	.0001	.0002	.0007	.0016	.0034	.0063	.0109	.0173	.0254
28	.0000	.0000	.0001	.0003	.0009	.0019	.0038	.0070	.0117	.0181
29	.0000	.0000	.0001	.0002	.0004	.0011	.0023	.0044	.0077	.0126
30	.0000	.0000	.0000	.0001	.0002	.0008	.0013	.0026	.0049	.0083
31	.0000	.0000	.0000	.0000	.0001	.0003	.0007	.0015	.0030	.0054
32	.0000	.0000	.0000	.0000	.0001	.0001	.0004	.0009	.0018	.0034
33	.0000	.0000	.0000	.0000	.0000	.0001	.0002	.0005	.0010	.0020
34	.0000	.0000	.0000	.0000	.0000	.0001	.0001	.0002	.0008	.0012
35	.0000	.0000	.0000	.0000	.0000	.0000	.0000	.0001	.0003	.0007
36	.0000	.0000	.0000	.0000	.0000	.0000	.0000	.0001	.0002	.0004
37	.0000	.0000	.0000	.0000	.0000	.0000	.0000	.0000	.0001	.0002
38	.0000	.0000	.0000	.0000	.0000	.0000	.0000	.0000	.0000	.0001
39	.0000	.0000	.0000	.0000	.0000	.0000	.0000	.0000	.0000	.0001

Entries in the table give the probabilities that an event will occur x times when the average number of occurrences is *m*.

THE POISSON DISTRIBUTION

x	8·1	8·2	8·3	8·4	8·5	8·6	8·7	8·8	8·9	9
12	.0505	.0530	.0555	.0579	.0604	.0629	.0654	.0679	.0703	.0728
13	.0315	.0334	.0354	.0374	.0395	.0416	.0438	.0459	.0481	.0504
14	.0182	.0196	.0210	.0225	.0240	.0256	.0272	.0289	.0306	.0324
15	.0098	.0107	.0116	.0126	.0136	.0147	.0158	.0169	.0182	.0194
16	.0050	.0055	.0060	.0066	.0072	.0079	.0086	.0093	.0101	.0109
17	.0024	.0026	.0029	.0033	.0036	.0040	.0044	.0048	.0053	.0058
18	.0011	.0012	.0014	.0015	.0017	.0019	.0021	.0024	.0026	.0029
19	.0005	.0005	.0006	.0007	.0008	.0009	.0010	.0011	.0012	.0014
20	.0002	.0002	.0002	.0003	.0003	.0004	.0004	.0005	.0005	.0006
21	.0001	.0001	.0001	.0001	.0001	.0002	.0002	.0002	.0002	.0003
22	.0000	.0000	.0000	.0000	.0001	.0001	.0001	.0001	.0001	.0001

x	9·1	9·2	9·3	9·4	9·5	9·6	9·7	9·8	9·9	10
0	.0001	.0001	.0001	.0001	.0001	.0001	.0001	.0001	.0001	.0000
1	.0010	.0009	.0009	.0008	.0007	.0007	.0006	.0005	.0005	.0005
2	.0046	.0043	.0040	.0037	.0034	.0031	.0029	.0027	.0025	.0023
3	.0140	.0131	.0123	.0115	.0107	.0100	.0093	.0087	.0081	.0076
4	.0319	.0302	.0285	.0269	.0254	.0240	.0226	.0213	.0201	.0189
5	.0581	.0555	.0530	.0506	.0483	.0460	.0439	.0418	.0398	.0378
6	.0881	.0851	.0822	.0793	.0764	.0736	.0709	.0682	.0656	.0631
7	.1145	.1118	.1091	.1064	.1037	.1010	.0982	.0955	.0928	.0901
8	.1302	.1286	.1269	.1251	.1232	.1212	.1191	.1170	.1148	.1126
9	.1317	.1315	.1311	.1306	.1300	.1293	.1284	.1274	.1263	.1251
10	.1198	.1210	.1219	.1228	.1235	.1241	.1245	.1249	.1250	.1251
11	.0991	.1012	.1031	.1049	.1067	.1083	.1098	.1112	.1125	.1137
12	.0752	.0776	.0799	.0822	.0844	.0868	.0888	.0908	.0928	.0948
13	.0526	.0549	.0572	.0594	.0617	.0640	.0662	.0685	.0707	.0729
14	.0342	.0361	.0380	.0399	.0419	.0439	.0459	.0479	.0500	.0521
15	.0208	.0221	.0235	.0250	.0265	.0281	.0297	.0313	.0330	.0347
16	.0118	.0127	.0137	.0147	.0157	.0168	.0180	.0192	.0204	.0217
17	.0063	.0069	.0075	.0081	.0088	.0095	.0103	.0111	.0119	.0128
18	.0032	.0035	.0039	.0042	.0046	.0051	.0055	.0060	.0065	.0071
19	.0015	.0017	.0019	.0021	.0023	.0026	.0028	.0031	.0034	.0037
20	.0007	.0008	.0009	.0010	.0011	.0012	.0014	.0015	.0017	.0019
21	.0003	.0003	.0004	.0004	.0005	.0006	.0006	.0007	.0008	.0009
22	.0001	.0001	.0002	.0002	.0002	.0002	.0003	.0003	.0004	.0004
23	.0001	.0001	.0001	.0001	.0001	.0001	.0001	.0001	.0002	.0002
24	.0000	.0000	.0000	.0000	.0000	.0000	.0000	.0001	.0001	.0001

Entries in the table give the probabilities that an event will occur x times when the average number of occurrences is *m*.

PRESENT VALUE OF £1

The table shows the value today of £1 to be received or paid after a given number of years
$$V_{n,r} = (1+r)^{-n}$$

At rate r / After n years	1%	2%	3%	4%	5%	6%	7%	8%	9%	10%	11%	12%
1	.99	.98	.97	.96	.95	.94	.93	.93	.92	.91	.90	.89
2	.98	.96	.94	.92	.91	.89	.87	.86	.84	.83	.81	.80
3	.97	.94	.92	.89	.86	.84	.82	.78	.77	.75	.73	.71
4	.96	.92	.89	.85	.82	.79	.76	.74	.71	.68	.66	.64
5	.95	.91	.86	.82	.78	.75	.71	.68	.65	.62	.59	.57
6	.94	.89	.84	.79	.75	.70	.67	.63	.60	.56	.53	.51
7	.93	.87	.81	.76	.71	.67	.62	.58	.55	.51	.48	.46
8	.92	.85	.79	.73	.68	.63	.58	.54	.50	.47	.43	.40
9	.91	.84	.77	.70	.64	.59	.54	.50	.46	.42	.39	.36
10	.91	.82	.74	.68	.61	.56	.51	.46	.42	.39	.35	.32
11	.90	.80	.72	.65	.58	.53	.48	.43	.39	.35	.32	.29
12	.89	.79	.70	.62	.56	.50	.44	.40	.36	.32	.29	.28
13	.88	.77	.68	.60	.53	.47	.41	.37	.33	.29	.26	.23
14	.87	.76	.66	.58	.51	.44	.39	.34	.30	.26	.23	.20
15	.86	.74	.64	.56	.48	.42	.36	.32	.27	.24	.21	.18

At rate r / After n years	13%	14%	15%	16%	17%	18%	19%	20%	30%	40%	50%
1	.88	.88	.87	.86	.85	.85	.84	.83	.77	.71	.67
2	.78	.77	.76	.74	.73	.72	.71	.69	.59	.51	.44
3	.69	.67	.66	.64	.62	.61	.59	.58	.46	.36	.30
4	.61	.59	.57	.55	.53	.52	.50	.48	.35	.26	.20
5	.54	.52	.50	.48	.46	.44	.42	.40	.27	.19	.13
6	.48	.46	.43	.41	.39	.37	.35	.33	.21	.13	.09
7	.43	.40	.38	.35	.33	.31	.30	.28	.16	.09	.06
8	.38	.35	.33	.31	.28	.27	.25	.23	.12	.07	.04
9	.33	.31	.28	.26	.24	.23	.21	.19	.09	.05	.03
10	.29	.27	.25	.23	.21	.19	.18	.16	.07	.03	.02
11	.26	.24	.21	.20	.18	.16	.15	.13	.06	.02	.01
12	.23	.21	.19	.17	.16	.14	.12	.11	.04	.02	.008
13	.20	.18	.16	.15	.13	.12	.10	.09	.03	.013	.005
14	.18	.16	.14	.13	.11	.10	.09	.08	.03	.009	.003
15	.16	.14	.12	.11	.09	.08	.07	.06	.02	.006	.002

BINOMIAL COEFFICIENTS

r:	0	1	2	3	4	5	6	7	8	9	10
n=1	1	1									
2	1	2	1								
3	1	3	3	1							
4	1	4	6	4	1						
5	1	5	10	10	5	1					
6	1	6	15	20	15	6	1				
7	1	7	21	35	35	21	7	1			
8	1	8	28	56	70	56	28	8	1		
9	1	9	36	84	126	126	84	36	9	1	
10	1	10	45	120	210	252	210	120	45	10	1
11	1	11	55	165	330	462	462	330	165	55	11
12	1	12	66	220	495	792	924	792	495	220	66
13	1	13	78	286	715	1287	1716	1716	1287	715	286
14	1	14	91	364	1001	2002	3003	3432	3003	2002	1001
15	1	15	105	455	1365	3003	5005	6435	6435	5005	3003
16	1	16	120	560	1820	4368	8008	11440	12870	11440	8008
17	1	17	136	680	2380	6188	12376	19448	24310	24310	19448
18	1	18	153	816	3060	8568	18564	31824	43758	48620	43758
19	1	19	171	969	3876	11628	27132	50388	75582	92378	92378
20	1	20	190	1140	4845	15504	38760	77520	125970	167960	184756

Example: $(a+b)^4 = a^4 + 4a^3b + 6a^2b^2 + 4ab^3 + b^4$

RANDOM NUMBERS

```
03 47 43 73 86   36 96 47 36 61   46 98 63 71 62   33 26 16 80 45   60 11 14 10 95
97 74 24 67 62   42 81 14 57 20   42 53 32 37 32   27 07 36 07 51   24 51 79 89 73
16 76 62 27 66   56 50 26 71 07   32 90 79 78 53   13 55 38 58 59   88 97 54 14 10
12 56 85 99 26   96 96 68 27 31   05 03 72 93 15   57 12 10 14 21   88 26 49 81 76
55 59 56 35 64   38 54 82 46 22   31 62 43 09 90   06 18 44 32 53   23 83 01 30 30

16 22 77 94 39   49 54 43 54 82   17 37 93 23 78   87 35 20 96 43   84 26 34 91 64
84 42 17 53 31   57 24 55 06 88   77 04 74 47 67   21 76 33 50 25   83 92 12 06 76
63 01 63 78 59   16 95 55 67 19   98 10 50 71 75   12 86 73 58 07   44 39 52 38 79
33 21 12 34 29   78 64 56 07 82   52 42 07 44 38   15 51 00 13 42   99 66 02 79 54
57 60 86 32 44   09 47 27 96 54   49 17 46 09 62   90 52 84 77 27   08 02 73 43 28

18 18 07 92 46   44 17 16 58 09   79 83 86 19 62   06 76 50 03 10   55 23 64 05 05
26 62 38 97 75   84 16 07 44 99   83 11 46 32 24   20 14 85 88 45   10 93 72 88 71
23 42 40 64 74   82 97 77 77 81   07 45 32 14 08   32 98 94 07 72   93 85 79 10 75
52 36 28 19 95   50 92 26 11 97   00 56 76 31 38   80 22 02 53 53   86 60 42 04 53
37 85 94 35 12   83 39 50 08 30   42 34 07 96 88   54 42 06 87 98   35 85 29 48 39

70 29 17 12 13   40 33 20 38 26   13 89 51 03 74   17 76 37 13 04   07 74 21 19 30
56 62 18 37 35   96 83 50 87 75   97 12 25 93 47   70 33 24 03 54   97 77 46 44 80
99 49 57 22 77   88 42 95 45 72   16 64 36 16 00   04 43 18 66 79   94 77 24 21 90
16 08 15 04 72   33 27 14 34 09   45 59 34 68 49   12 72 07 34 45   99 27 72 95 14
31 16 93 32 43   50 27 89 87 19   20 15 37 00 49   52 85 66 60 44   38 68 88 11 80

68 34 30 13 70   55 74 30 77 40   44 22 78 84 26   04 33 46 09 52   68 07 97 06 57
74 57 25 65 76   59 29 97 68 60   71 91 38 67 54   13 58 18 24 76   15 54 55 95 52
27 42 37 86 53   48 55 90 65 72   96 57 69 36 10   96 46 92 42 45   97 60 49 04 91
00 39 68 29 61   66 37 32 20 30   77 84 57 03 29   10 45 65 04 26   11 04 96 67 24
29 94 98 94 24   68 49 69 10 82   53 75 91 93 30   34 25 20 57 27   40 48 73 51 92

16 90 82 66 59   83 62 64 11 12   67 19 00 71 74   60 47 21 29 68   02 02 37 03 31
11 27 94 75 06   06 09 19 74 66   02 94 37 34 02   76 70 90 30 86   38 45 94 30 38
35 24 10 16 20   33 32 51 26 38   79 78 45 04 91   16 92 53 56 16   02 75 50 95 98
38 23 16 86 38   42 38 97 01 50   87 75 66 81 41   40 01 74 91 62   48 51 84 08 32
31 96 25 91 47   96 44 33 49 13   34 86 82 53 91   00 52 43 48 85   27 55 26 89 62

66 67 40 67 14   64 05 71 95 86   11 05 65 09 68   76 83 20 37 90   57 16 00 11 66
14 90 84 45 11   75 73 88 05 90   52 27 41 14 86   22 98 12 22 08   07 52 74 95 80
68 05 51 18 00   33 96 02 75 19   07 60 62 93 55   59 33 82 43 90   49 37 38 44 59
20 46 78 73 90   97 51 40 14 02   04 02 33 31 08   39 54 16 49 36   47 95 93 13 30
64 19 58 97 79   15 06 15 93 20   01 90 10 75 06   40 78 78 89 62   02 67 74 17 33

05 26 93 70 60   22 35 85 15 13   92 03 51 59 77   59 56 78 06 83   52 91 05 70 74
07 97 10 88 23   09 98 42 99 64   61 71 62 99 15   06 51 29 16 93   58 05 77 09 51
68 71 86 85 85   54 87 66 47 54   73 32 08 11 12   44 95 92 63 16   29 56 24 29 48
26 99 61 65 53   58 37 78 80 70   42 10 50 67 42   32 17 55 85 74   94 44 67 16 94
14 65 52 68 75   87 59 36 22 41   26 78 63 06 55   13 08 27 01 50   15 29 39 39 43

17 53 77 58 71   71 41 61 50 72   12 41 94 96 26   44 95 27 36 99   02 96 74 30 83
90 26 59 21 19   23 52 23 33 12   96 93 02 18 39   07 02 18 36 07   25 99 32 70 23
41 23 52 55 99   31 04 49 69 96   10 47 48 45 88   13 41 43 89 20   97 17 14 49 17
60 20 50 81 69   31 99 73 68 68   35 81 33 03 76   24 30 12 48 60   18 99 10 72 34
91 25 38 05 90   94 58 28 41 36   45 37 59 03 09   90 35 57 29 12   82 62 54 65 60

34 50 57 74 37   98 80 33 00 91   09 77 93 19 82   74 94 80 04 04   45 07 31 66 49
85 22 04 39 43   73 81 53 94 79   33 62 46 86 28   08 31 54 46 31   53 94 13 38 47
09 79 13 77 48   73 82 97 22 21   05 03 27 24 83   72 89 44 05 60   35 80 39 94 88
88 75 80 18 14   22 95 75 42 49   39 32 82 22 49   02 48 07 70 37   16 04 61 67 87
90 96 23 70 00   39 00 03 06 90   55 85 78 38 36   94 37 30 69 32   90 89 00 76 33
```

CUMULATIVE PRESENT VALUE OF £1

The table shows the Present Value of £1 per annum, Receivable or Payable at the end of each year for N Years

Net Rate of Interest Assumed

Years	1%	2%	3%	4%	5%	6%	7%	8%	9%	10%	11%	12%
1	.99	.98	.97	.96	.95	.94	.94	.93	.92	.91	.90	.89
2	1.97	1.94	1.91	1.89	1.86	1.83	1.81	1.78	1.76	1.74	1.71	1.69
3	2.94	2.88	2.83	2.78	2.72	2.67	2.62	2.58	2.53	2.49	2.44	2.40
4	3.90	3.81	3.72	3.63	3.55	3.47	3.39	3.31	3.24	3.17	3.10	3.04
5	4.85	4.71	4.58	4.45	4.33	4.21	4.10	3.99	3.89	3.79	3.70	3.61
6	5.80	5.60	5.42	5.24	5.08	4.92	4.77	4.62	4.49	4.36	4.23	4.11
7	6.73	6.47	6.23	6.00	5.79	5.58	5.39	5.21	5.03	4.87	4.71	4.56
8	7.65	7.33	7.02	6.73	6.46	6.21	5.97	5.75	5.54	5.34	5.15	4.97
9	8.57	8.16	7.79	7.44	7.11	6.80	6.52	6.25	6.00	5.76	5.54	5.33
10	9.47	8.98	8.53	8.11	7.72	7.36	7.02	6.71	6.42	6.15	5.89	5.65
11	10.37	9.79	9.25	8.76	8.31	7.89	7.50	7.14	6.81	6.50	6.21	5.94
12	11.26	10.58	9.95	9.39	8.86	8.38	7.94	7.54	7.16	6.81	6.49	6.19
13	12.13	11.35	10.64	9.99	9.39	8.85	8.36	7.90	7.49	7.10	6.80	6.42
14	13.00	12.11	11.30	10.56	9.90	9.30	8.75	8.24	7.79	7.37	6.98	6.63
15	13.87	12.85	11.94	11.12	10.38	9.71	9.11	8.56	8.06	7.61	7.19	6.81

Net Rate of Interest Assumed

Years	13%	14%	15%	16%	17%	18%	19%	20%	30%	40%	50%
1	.89	.88	.87	.86	.85	.85	.84	.83	.77	.71	.67
2	1.67	1.65	1.63	1.61	1.59	1.57	1.55	1.53	1.36	1.22	1.11
3	2.36	2.32	2.28	2.25	2.21	2.17	2.14	2.11	1.81	1.59	1.41
4	2.97	2.91	2.86	2.80	2.74	2.69	2.64	2.59	2.17	1.85	1.61
5	3.52	3.43	3.35	3.27	3.20	3.13	3.06	2.99	2.44	2.04	1.74
6	4.00	3.89	3.78	3.69	3.59	3.50	3.41	3.33	2.64	2.17	1.82
7	4.42	4.29	4.16	4.04	3.92	3.81	3.71	3.61	2.80	2.26	1.88
8	4.80	4.64	4.49	4.34	4.21	4.08	3.95	3.84	2.93	2.33	1.92
9	5.13	4.95	4.77	4.61	4.45	4.30	4.16	4.03	3.02	2.38	1.95
10	5.43	5.22	5.02	4.83	4.66	4.49	4.34	4.19	3.09	2.41	1.97
11	5.69	5.45	5.23	5.03	4.83	4.66	4.49	4.33	3.15	2.44	1.98
12	5.92	5.66	5.42	5.20	4.99	4.79	4.61	4.44	3.19	2.46	1.99
13	6.12	5.84	5.58	5.34	5.12	4.91	4.71	4.53	3.22	2.47	1.99
14	6.30	6.00	5.72	5.47	5.23	5.01	4.80	4.61	3.25	2.48	1.99
15	6.46	6.14	5.85	5.58	5.32	5.09	4.88	4.68	3.27	2.48	2.00

FORMULAE AND SYMBOLS

General section

± plus or minus; positive or negative

≠ not equal

≈ or ≐ approximately equal

> greater than

< less than

$a>b>c$, $c<b<a$ value of middle term lies between outer values

≯ not greater than

≥ greater than or equal to

∴ therefore

∵ because

∞ infinity

π ratio of circumference of plane circle to its diameter; 3·14159...

e exponential constant; base of natural (Napierian) logarithms; 2·71828...

$\log_e N$: Natural logarithm of N. Note that if $e^x=N$, $\log_e N=x$

$\log N$ $\log_{10} N$ common (Briggsian) logarithm of N. Note that if $10^x=N$, $\log N=x$

$e^x = 1 + \dfrac{x}{1!} + \dfrac{x^2}{2!} + \ldots$

xy $x.y$ product of x and y; x multiplied by y

dy/dx $f'(x)$ differential coefficient of $y=f(x)$; 1st derivative

d^2y/dx^2 $f''(x)$ 2nd derivative

x/y $x\div y$ $x:y$ x divided by y; ratio of x to y

x^n x to power n; the product $xx\ldots$to n factors; nth power of x

$\sqrt{x}$ $x^{\frac{1}{2}}$ square root of x

$\sqrt[n]{x}$ $x^{\frac{1}{n}}$ nth root of x

x^{-n} reciprocal of nth power of x

$|x|$ absolute value of x (sign ignored)

$x\sim y$ difference between x and y (sign ignored)

$\Sigma(x)$ summed values of variable x

$\sum\limits_{i=1}^{n} x_i$ summed values of variable x over range x_1 to x_n inclusive

$x!$ factorial x; the product $1.2.3\ldots x$

$y=f(x)$ y is a function of x

$P(n,r)$ $_nP_r$ number of permutations of r things from n

$C(n,r)$ $_nC_r$, ^nC_x number of combinations of r things from n

101_2 subscript $_2$ indicates binary number system

534_n subscript $_n$ indicates number system based on n

$\int f(x)dx$ Indefinite integral of f(x)

$\int_a^b f(x)dx$ definite integral of f(x) between limits $x=a$, $x=b$

Sets and Probability

$A=B$ set A equals set B

ε is an element of

⊂ inclusion: $A\subset B$ means set A is included in set B

∩ (cap) conjunction, intersection; $A\cap B$ defines all elements included in both A and B

∪ (cup) union; $A\cup B$ defines all elements in B, no element being counted twice

A′ A negation; the set of all elements not in A

$n(A)$ number of elements in set A

U universe of discourse, sample space; note that for any set $A+A'=U=1$

$\phi(\ )$ null or empty set

$p(A)$ probability of event A

$p(A/B)$ probability of event A, given B

General Rules

$P(A\cup B)=P(A)+P(B)-P(A\cap B)$

$P(A\cap B)=P(A).P(B/A)=P(B).P(A/B)$

Statistics and Quantitative methods

μ mean (of a population);

$\bar{x}$ mean value of variable x (sample)

$Q_1\ldots Q_n$ first...nth quantile

cum x cumulative total of variable x

d.f. degrees of freedom

χ^2 chi-squared

F F ratio

t Student's t-statistic

n number in the sample

N population size

s standard deviation (sample)

s^2 variance (sample)

σ standard deviation of a population;

σ^2 variance (population)

% coefficient of variation

r coefficient of correlation

r^2(or R^2) coefficient of determination

$E(x)$ expectation of x =probability x pay off

$p(X=x_1)$ probability that X equals x_1

Binomial Distribution

$Pr(x)= {}^nC_x.p^x.q^{n-x}$

$^nC_x = \dfrac{n!}{(n-x)!x!}$

Mean=n.p

Standard deviation=$\sqrt{n.p.q}$

Normal Distribution

$Z = \dfrac{x-\mu}{\sigma}$

Poisson Distribution

$Pr(x)= \dfrac{e^{-m}.m^x}{x!}$

where e=exponential constant

m=mean rate of occurrence

=variance

Arithmetic Mean

$\bar{x} = \dfrac{\Sigma x}{n}$ or $\bar{x} = \dfrac{\Sigma fx}{\Sigma f}$

Standard Deviation

$$SD = \sqrt{\frac{\Sigma(x - \bar{x})^2}{n-1}}$$

$SD^2 = $ variance

Statistical inference

Estimated Standard Errors —

Sample mean: $\dfrac{s}{\sqrt{n}}$

Sample proportion: $\sqrt{\dfrac{pq}{n}}$

$\overline{x_1} - \overline{x_2}: \quad \sqrt{\dfrac{S_1^2}{n_1} + \dfrac{S_2^2}{n_2}}$

Chi squared (χ^2)

$$\chi^2 = \Sigma \frac{(O - E)^2}{E}$$

Regression Analysis

The linear regression equation of Y on X is given by:

$Y = a + bX$ *or*

$Y - \bar{Y} = b(X - \bar{X})$, where

$$b = \frac{\text{Covariance } (XY)}{\text{Variance } (X)} = \frac{n\Sigma XY - (\Sigma X)(\Sigma Y)}{n\Sigma X^2 - (\Sigma X)^2}$$

and $a = \bar{Y} - b\bar{X}$,

or $\Sigma Y = na + b\Sigma X$
$\quad \Sigma XY = a\Sigma X + b\Sigma X^2$
$\quad$ Exponential $Y = ab^x$
$\quad$ Geometric $Y = aX^b$

Coefficient of Correlation (r)

$$r = \frac{\text{Covariance } (XY)}{\sqrt{\text{VAR}(X).\text{VAR}(Y)}} = \frac{\Sigma XY - n\bar{X}.\bar{Y}}{n(\sigma X)(\sigma Y)}$$

$$= \frac{n\Sigma XY - (\Sigma X)(\Sigma Y)}{\sqrt{\{n\Sigma X^2 - (\Sigma X)^2\}\{n\Sigma Y^2 - (\Sigma Y)^2\}}}$$

Queueing Theory — Simple Queues

Average time spent in *system* (i.e. both queueing and in the service point)

$$\frac{1}{\mu - \lambda} = \frac{1}{1 - \rho} \times \frac{1}{\mu}$$

Average number in the *system* (both queueing and in the service point)

$$\frac{\lambda}{\mu - \lambda} = \frac{\rho}{1 - \rho}$$

Average time spent in the queue

$$\frac{\rho}{\mu - \lambda} = \frac{\lambda}{\mu(\mu - \lambda)} = \frac{1}{\mu}\left(\frac{\rho}{1 - \rho}\right)$$

Average numbers in the queue

$$\frac{\rho\lambda}{\mu - \lambda}$$

Inventory Control

EOQ basic model $\sqrt{\dfrac{2CoD}{Ch}}$

EBQ (gradual replenishment)

$$\sqrt{\frac{2CoD}{Ch(1 - \frac{D}{R})}}$$